THE IRISH
IN AUSTRALIA

Rogues and Reformers,
First Fleet to Federation

THE IRISH IN AUSTRALIA

Rogues and Reformers, First Fleet to Federation

To Kenny,
with best wishes
Jarlath
18 March 2004

JARLATH RONAYNE

VIKING
an imprint of
PENGUIN BOOKS

Viking

Published by the Penguin Group
Penguin Books Australia Ltd
250 Camberwell Road, Camberwell, Victoria 3124, Australia
Penguin Books Ltd
80 Strand, London WC2R 0RL, England
Penguin Putnam Inc.
375 Hudson Street, New York, New York 10014, USA
Penguin Books, a division of Pearson Canada
10 Alcorn Avenue, Toronto, Ontario, Canada M4V 3B2
Penguin Books (NZ) Ltd
Cnr Rosedale and Airborne Roads, Albany, Auckland, New Zealand
Penguin Books (South Africa) (Pty) Ltd
24 Sturdee Avenue, Rosebank, Johannesburg 2196, South Africa
Penguin Books India (P) Ltd
11, Community Centre, Panchsheel Park, New Delhi 110 017, India

First published by Trinity College Dublin Press 2002
This revised edition published by Penguin Books Australia Ltd 2003

10 9 8 7 6 5 4 3 2 1

Cover design by Louise Leffler, Penguin Design Studio
Cover: The First Parliamentary Election, Bendigo, 1855
(Theodore King) Collection – Bendigo Art Gallery
Photography for illustrations 22, 26–8 and 43 by Robert Pointon
Typeset in 11/13.5pt Goudy by Axiom Typesetting and Graphic Services Pty Ltd,
Abbotsford, Victoria 3067, Australia
Printed by Paragon Rossprint Printing Company, Ringwood, Victoria 3134, Australia.

National Library of Australia
Cataloguing-in-Publication data:

Ronayne, Jarlath, 1938– .
The Irish in Australia: rogues and reformers: First fleet to federation.

New ed.
Bibliography.
Includes index.
ISBN 0 670 04105 X.

1. Trinity College (Dublin, Ireland) – Influence. 2. Irish – Australia – History.
3. Law – Australia – History. 4. Australia – Politics and government – To 1900.
5. Australia – History. I. Ronayne, Jarlath, 1938– First fleet to federation. II. Title.

994

www.penguin.com.au

To the memory of my brother JJ (1931-2000),
who had a quiet and caring interest in this project

Contents

List of Illustrations

List of Charts

Preface

In 1892 there were grand celebrations in Dublin to mark the three hundredth anniversary of the foundation of Trinity College. Representatives from universities around the world converged on the city to take part in the festivities, which extended over four days in July, and to marvel at three centuries of achievement. There were representatives from Sydney but none from Melbourne. Instead, a congratulatory address signed by the chief justice of Victoria and forty six other graduates of Trinity resident in Victoria was sent to the chancellor of the University which 'remembered with pride how large a share men trained in Trinity College, Dublin, had in the making of this colony'.

None of the forty-seven signatories to the congratulatory address, or the Trinity authorities, could have guessed at the real extent of the links between Trinity College, Dublin, and Australia. These links were not only forged by the graduates of the College in all of the colonies, but they extended back to the very founders and early provosts through descendants who went to Australia.

The first recorded Trinity-educated man to set foot in Australia was a surgeon's mate on HMS *Sirius*, flagship of the First Fleet, which arrived at Botany Bay in January 1788 to establish a penal colony. In 1901, the Trinity-educated lieutenant-governor of New South Wales signalled the end of the colonial period when he administered the oath of office to the first governor-general of the Commonwealth of Australia. In the period between these two events, men educated at Trinity set out for the Australian colonies and reached positions of power and influence in governance, the law, higher education and other walks of life, out of all proportion to their numbers relative to other groups. Some of the most influential were Catholics who had taken advantage of reforms in Ireland, which had removed obstacles to attendance at university; but most were Protestant Irish who had their religion, at least, in common with the English majority in the early colonial period.

Those who achieved eminence in their professions were generally men of high ability and principle, who were at the forefront of virtually every movement for liberal and democratic reform in the colonial period. They were active in public affairs, bringing culture and learning to the colonies, where populations in the early period consisted mainly of convicts, military personnel, and many poorly educated people.

The contribution of these well-educated Irish people to the building of a great nation has received little attention. They are a neglected group, possibly because of their backgrounds, which differed from that of the vast majority of the Irish people who went to Australia during the nineteenth century. In the story of the Eureka Stockade Rebellion of 1854 and the subsequent trials, for example, the key roles of Irish administrators and lawyers are overshadowed by a concentration on the parallels with events in Ireland six years before. The Ned Kelly trial more than twenty-five years later was also a very Irish affair on both sides of the Bench. The Trinity-educated trial judge and Ned's defence counsel, the son of a Trinity-educated judge, hold responsibility for the outcome and the creation of an Australian folk hero, who is cast in a role that echoes the struggle between the landlords and the landless in Ireland. Yet that same trial judge was for many years standing counsel for the Aborigines, providing them with representation before a system of law that they did not understand. And it was an Irish attorney-general who was the first to successfully prosecute whites for the murder of Aborigines. Furthermore, when the governor of New South Wales cried out for honest lawyers to be sent to the colonies instead of the 'rogues and vagabonds' who were constantly being appointed, it was Irish people like he who brought professionalism, effectiveness and dignity to the early colonial Bar.

There were contradictions, of course, as would be expected in any large group of people even from similar background. Some led a campaign against the power of the 'exclusives' in Sydney, while others were part of the Irish cousinage in Melbourne, a closely-knit group who were descended from people prominent in the affairs of Trinity. Some fought for land reform while others protected the interests of the landowners. Some wrote the colonial constitutions and codified the rule of law while others adhered to an honour code that permitted duelling and horsewhipping.

All of this adds an intrinsic interest to the group of colonists who occupied the stage for a considerable period of time in the history of Australia and with whom this book is concerned. Most of this group came to Victoria and to New South Wales and, although they made their presence felt in all the colonies, it was the two most heavily populated that provided most of the opportunities for them to affect the legal, political and educational landscape.

The book is selective in three ways. First, the concentration is on those educated at Trinity College, or who had close links with the College through family or other kinds of connections. It is selective, too, in the fields of endeavour taken up by these colonial administrators and practitioners, concentrating on law, politics and higher education, for it is in these areas that they achieved their greatest eminence. Third, the sheer extent of the contributions of these men over more than a century has necessitated excising much that is valuable and fascinating regarding the individual players.

In order to allow the general reader to place the contributions of these Trinity-educated men in context, there is some detail of the developments that took place in the colonies in governance, politics and the law before they arrived; and to give impressions of the College which educated these people, and which until recent times was quite small, a review of the foundation and the very modern outlook of the sixteenth century founders is also provided.

I believe that the story of this historically neglected group of Irish colonists needs to be given greater prominence; and I hope that there will be further exploration of a phenomenon that appears to be unique in the history of the emigration of a highly educated group of people.

Jarlath Ronayne
Melbourne, 2002

Acknowledgements

I should like to express my appreciation to Creighton Burns, foundation Chancellor of Victoria University, who, on my appointment as Vice-Chancellor, pointed out to me that I was not the first Trinity man to be the foundation head of an Australian university; thus stimulating my interest in the influence of Trinity men in colonial Australia.

I am grateful to Ernest Nicholson, Provost of Oriel College, Oxford, and to the governing body, for providing me with the facilities and scholarly support during my period as visiting fellow, when I was able to carry out much of my research for this book. My warm appreciation to Tom Mitchell, Provost of Trinity College, Dublin, who offered the assistance of the College in any way I needed, and to Lynn Mitchell for her continual encouragement. At Trinity, too, I should wish to thank Marcella Senior of the Secretary's Department, Jane Maxwell from the Manuscripts Department, and the University Librarian, Bill Simpson, whose welcoming ways made the scale of the project seem somehow less daunting. My special thanks are to Michael Ronayne, for his invaluable and constant support.

In Australia, I am grateful to Professor Ron Adams, Deputy Director of the Europe-Australia Institute of Victoria University, who gave invaluable editorial advice and assistance, and also to Niky Poposki of the Institute, who provided ongoing assistance with the sourcing of documents. My gratitude, too, to Bernie Hogan, who weaved his usual typesetting and artwork magic with his calm efficiency and total dedication to the task. And finally, I wish to express my deepest appreciation to my wife, Margaret, whose support for the project was critical, and whose production and editorial expertise was essential, in bringing the work forward for publication.

HMS Sirius *by maritime artist Frank Allen, 1987.*

CHAPTER 1

Bound for Botany Bay

> I like Botany Bay, but it is in grave danger of becoming respectable. It had a thrillingly bad reputation, but increased hygiene, much paint and hot and cold water brought Botany Bay, the outlaw colony, closer to the rest of the College.
>
> **Brendan Kennelly (1991)**

Terra Australis

In 1594, the Dutch cartographer Plancius published a map of the world that showed an enormous shapeless landmass in the southern hemisphere extending from the Pole almost to the Equator. He designated it as *Terra Australis*. It bore no relationship either in size or location to the real continent of Australia, and Plancius was not the first to show such an imaginary southern land. However, he was probably the first to drop from the name the *Nondum Cognita* – not known at all – of previous cartographers, signifying a greater degree of confidence in its existence.

In 1594 too, and not too far away from Amsterdam, Ireland's first university opened its doors. Founded two years before by a charter of England's Queen Elizabeth I, Trinity College, Dublin, 'the mother of an University', was destined to become one of the world's great centres of scholarship and learning with a record of achievement that is truly extraordinary when one appreciates its small size until relatively recent times. The University started out with a provost, three fellows, three scholars and a number of matriculated fee-paying students, or pensioners. At its tercentenary in 1892 it still had only about a thousand students on its books. In those three hundred years, though, it was to produce some of the world's finest classical and ecclesiastical scholars, literary figures, scientists, engineers, statesmen and patriots.

It seems as if Trinity College was destined from its very foundation to be linked to the continent that, in 1592, was beginning to emerge from romance to reality. In the seventeenth century the intrepid Dutch explorers gave the name 'New Holland' to the continent that by then, because of their efforts, was certainly no longer *incognita*; but even so, the weavers of tales gave it an air of mystery that attaches to any exotic region that is not fully explored. The reports of the English pirate, William Dampier, on his exploits in the stolen *Cygnet* off the coast of western New Holland induced the English admiralty, in 1699, to put the *Roebuck* at his disposal for legitimate exploration. Though Dampier's reports this time were not encouraging, his description of the region inspired that great son of Trinity, Jonathan Swift, in *Gulliver's Travels*, to locate the island home of the intelligent horse-like *Huoyhnhnyms* and doltish and filthy humanoid *yahoos* off the coast of south-west New Holland. The first voyage that the fictional Gulliver makes is in 1699 on board the *Antelope*, a clear reference to Dampier's second voyage in the *Roebuck* in that same year; Swift proposes Gulliver as a cousin of Dampier and refers to Dampier's *A Voyage Round the World* in the prefatory 'Letter to Sympson'.

When, in March 1770, Captain James Cook sailed HMS *Endeavour* westward from New Zealand towards New Holland and made landfall on the unexplored east coast, he named the magnificent harbour in which he anchored 'Botany Bay'. The name was suggested to him by Joseph Banks, the botanist on board *Endeavour*, to commemorate the variety of botanic species that were to be found around the bay. To generations of Trinity students the name Botany Bay conjures up memories of the rather austere residential square built between 1787 and 1816 and named by the inhabitants after the penal colony in far away New South Wales. As Brendan Kennelly's reminiscence shows, the name fitted not only the prison-like aspect of Botany Bay but also the wild characteristics of its inhabitants, removed as they were from the gaze of the University authorities in Front Square, and being in the unfashionable area behind 'Rotten Row' and the Dining Hall.

The first step was made to colonise New Holland when Captain Arthur Phillip, RN, set out from Plymouth in May 1787 on board HMS *Sirius,* the flagship of the First Fleet. Phillip, selected to be the first governor of the colony of New South Wales, later transferred to the faster HMS *Supply* in order to arrive well before the rest of the fleet. But John Hunter, the Captain of *Sirius*, was a better seaman than the captain of *Supply* and arrived at Botany Bay on 19 January 1788, only forty hours behind Phillip. The surgeon's mate on board *Sirius* was Thomas Jamison, who graduated from Trinity in 1768.

Phillip had decided against establishing the colony at Botany Bay by the time *Sirius* arrived. He took Hunter and others on an exploratory trip further north and had the joy of finding one of the most spectacular harbours in the world, one in which a 'thousand sail of the line might ride in perfect security'. Of the various coves in the harbour, preference was given to one which had the finest spring of water and in which ships could anchor so close to the shore that 'at a very small expense quays may be constructed at which the largest vessels may unload'. Governor Phillip called the site Sydney Cove in honour of Lord Sydney, the secretary of state for the colonies.

On 26 January 1788, now commemorated as 'Australia Day', Phillip unfurled the British flag at Sydney Cove and work commenced to establish a penal colony. On 7 February 1788, Lieutenant David Collins, the deputy judge advocate, formally established the colony and proclaimed Phillip as governor. The colony barely survived for the first four years, being dependent on supplies from England and with starvation regularly staring the inhabitants in the face. But Phillip never doubted the viability of his colony or its future prosperity. At the end of one despatch in which he recorded loss of livestock, conflict with the Aborigines and an earthquake, he was still able to say that he had no doubt that 'this country would prove to be the most valuable acquisition Great Britain ever made'. And even in the midst of their privation the people of the little colony could still put on an entertainment. On the evening of the King's birthday, 4 June 1789, a comedy was performed by a company of the convicts. It was George Farquhar's *The Recruiting Officer*. So the first play performed in Australia was written by a Trinity man, albeit one who had been expelled in 1695 for making a profane jest on being set to write an exercise upon the miracle of walking on water. His *Beaux' Stratagem* and *The Recruiting Officer* are performed to this day.

As far as we know, Thomas Jamison was the first Trinity man to set foot in Australia and he subsequently became principal surgeon of the colony of New South Wales. The next recorded Trinity man to arrive in Sydney set out from Cork on the *Minerva* under very different circumstances. Henry Fulton graduated in 1792 and was ordained into the ministry of the Church of Ireland. He was implicated in the 1798 Rebellion, convicted of seditious practices in 1799, and transported for life. Governor John Hunter, Phillip's successor, and former captain of *Sirius,* did not quite know what to do with prisoners like Fulton, 'bred up to the genteel life', and shortly after his arrival he was given a free pardon and sent as assistant chaplain to the notorious Norfolk Island penal settlement. Fourteen years later, back in Sydney, Fulton established the colony's first private school for the education of young gentlemen in classics, modern languages and 'such parts of mathematics both in theory and practice as may suit the taste of the scholar'.

Fulton was not the only Trinity-educated clergyman to be transported. William Bailey, for a time a resident tutor in Trinity, was sentenced in 1843 to transportation for life for uttering a forged promissory note for £2,875 in favour of his sister. When pardoned, he, too, opened a private school and taught in several girls' schools until his past misdemeanour was published in the *Sydney Morning Herald* and he was dismissed. A further term of six months imprisonment for performing an illegal marriage ceremony ended his career.

Fulton graduated in 1792, the year that Trinity should have been celebrating the two hundredth anniversary of its foundation. There was no celebration, however, perhaps because of the turmoil sweeping Europe at the time. The committee appointed in 1892 to produce, *inter alia*, an historical record volume for the tercentenary, reflected on what might have been the response to a celebration in 1792: 'Had Edmund Burke been invited to such a festival he surely would have replied: "Is this a time to make ceremonial speeches and receive complimentary addresses?", 'And what', the committee asked, 'would be the bicentenary without Edmund Burke!' There had been a celebration in 1692 but, as the committee admitted, the University could not point to many eminent alumni after only one hundred years: Berkeley was but a boy; Swift was unknown as an author; Congreve was writing his first comedy; Farquhar was about to enter university; and patriot Robert Emmett was yet to achieve immortality.

The tercentenary was different. Representatives from around the world, including Australia, converged on Dublin in July 1892 to take part in a great festival to commemorate three centuries of achievement. The record of the proceedings gives prominence to the commemorative activities in Australia: 'In Australia, a most influential committee was appointed and arrangements were made and admirably carried out for a celebration of the Tercentenary in Melbourne concurrently with its celebration at home'. In addition, a grand illuminated address was sent to Trinity by the University of Melbourne; Sir Henry Wrixon, later vice-chancellor of Melbourne University, sent a telegram on behalf of the 'Alumni of old Trinity'; Trinity-educated Peter Faucett, judge and member of the university senate attended the Dublin celebrations on behalf of the University of Sydney; and George Higinbotham, the chief justice of Victoria, and forty six other Victorian Trinity alumni sent a congratulatory address.

The prominence given to Australia in the records of the tercentenary reflected the special relationship between Trinity and Australia over the previous hundred years or so. But the committee that presided over the production of the record volume could hardly have guessed at the extent of the links. After Jamison and Fulton, many more Trinity-educated men, or men and women closely associated with the College in one way or another, began to arrive in New South Wales and the other colonies as they were established. The greatest influx took place before 1856, the year in which all the colonies except Western Australia were granted a significant degree of independence through what was known as 'responsible' government. After the 1860s, migration to Australia by Trinity men began to slow, though the influence of those already in the colonies remained profound. By the end of the nineteenth century the migration had all but ceased. Over the entire colonial period Trinity men and their families migrated or were sent as government officials to Australia and they reached the highest levels in law, politics and education. Their achievements are not as well known as they should be, however, and the possible reasons for this are explored in this brief retelling of their remarkable story.

The Irish Ascendancy

Many of those educated in Trinity who went to Australia were Anglo-Irish and some belonged to the 'ascendancy', the term still used to describe these Irish and their descendants long after their political and social ascendancy has passed. The term 'ascendancy' is succinctly defined by Roy Foster in his *Modern Ireland 1600–1972*. The term was introduced at the end of the eighteenth century and it describes a people who were in the ascendant in Ireland during the eighteenth and nineteenth centuries. Membership, according to Foster, was not restricted to descendants of families who had acquired 'nobility' through the acquisition of land or military service. It revolved around Anglicanism and the ascendancy members could be drawn from the descendants of the Norman invaders, the 'old English', the Cromwellian settlers, or even the ancient Gaelic chiefs.

They comprised an elite who monopolised law, politics and society and whose aspirations focused on the Irish House of Commons. The heyday of the ascendancy was the last decade of the eighteenth century. Henry Grattan, statesman and Trinity graduate, hailed the creation of an Irish nation in 1782, when the Irish Parliament achieved what turned out to be short-lived independence from Westminster. 'Ireland is now a nation', he said, but it was a nation controlled by a minority.

Trinity College was quintessentially an ascendancy foundation, Anglican since the time of its third chancellor, Archbishop Laud, who in 1633 with Thomas Wentworth revised its statutes to give it a stricter episcopalian focus, thus ending the old religious tolerance. The College reflected in the composition of its student body the various levels that existed within the ascendancy. Not all were the sons of nobility or landed gentry and the most illustrious were certainly not. In attempting to define the intellectual ethos of the ascendancy, Roy Foster calls on Swift, Berkeley, Burke, Goldsmith, Congreve and Sheridan. The aristocracy produced none of these yet they are representative of the 'ascendancy mind' by their use of wit, satire, rhetoric and verbal dexterity that even now characterises an Irish style. Swift, who by no means identified himself as Irish, and was disappointed early in his career not to have found preferment in England, nonetheless was sympathetic to the Gaelic Irish, and blamed the condition of the people on the 'poverty and slavery' they suffered at the hands of the English.

The settlers identifying themselves as Irish and representing the Kingdom of Ireland came after Swift's time; but some, even then, were at pains to emphasise their English heritage. Robert Boyle (1627–91), one of Ireland's most illustrious early scientists and son of the 'great' Earl of Cork, was sent for his education to the continent because his father did not want him to be 'infected with the leaven of Ireland'. The Duke of Wellington, from a post-Cromwellian settler family, is another notable example of the attitudes held by some of these settlers towards the Irish people. Born Wesley, later gentrified to Wellesley, the 'Iron Duke' is reported to have said about his birth in Ireland: 'Because one is born in a stable does not make one a horse'. Most did not think that way, however, and certainly not those who went to Australia; they regarded themselves as Irish.

The Decision to Go

The migration of Anglo-Irish to Australia began in earnest in the early nineteenth century. To set out on a dangerous sea voyage to a penal colony on the other side of the world was a courageous decision for these educated middle and upper class people. The question arises as to why they decided to leave Ireland, since emigration had not hitherto reached that far up the social scale. Much of the answer lies in Ireland itself, which was changing economically and politically. The long period of the ascendancy was beginning to draw to a close. Whereas the landlords had acceded to the *Act of Union of Great Britain and*

Ireland, passed in 1800, the lesser gentry and the lawyers, doctors and professionals were less enthusiastic from the beginning about union with Britain. There were positive trends in Westminster favouring repeal of the laws against Catholics and dissenters, laws that were described by Edmund Burke as 'the worst and most wicked laws that ever proceeded from the perverted ingenuity of man'. The *Relief Act* of 1793 lifted restrictions on Catholics entering university; and the *Catholic Emancipation Act* of 1829 allowed Catholics to vote, to have a voice in the parliament and to take up official appointments and positions previously reserved for members of the established church. The Church of Ireland lost further its favoured position later on, when Catholics were relieved of the requirements to pay tithes to it, thus seriously eroding the ability of the church to be one of the options of the sons of the landed gentry. And these sons and daughters were surviving in great numbers due to the general decline in infant mortality in the first half of the nineteenth century.

The catastrophe of the Great Famine of 1845–48 not only saw the overall population of Ireland fall by death and emigration from over eight million to six, with a steady decline thereafter, but it seriously affected the economic viability of landed estates, so that emigration now reached up into the middle classes. It is said that one-third of the landlords emerged from the Famine ruined, and in 1849 the parliament passed the *Encumbered Estates Act* to allow for the sale of ruined estates. Great numbers of estates passed into new hands – a mixed blessing for the peasantry, as these new 'improving' landlords often cleared out tenants to make their estates more profitable. The evictions provoked retaliation and the land question dominated Irish politics for the rest of the century.

The Gaelic revival of the nineteenth century emphasised the distinctions between the people of Ireland. To be true Irish was to be Gaelic and Catholic; the Anglo-Irish were Protestant and separate. This came as a shock to those who still considered that they represented the Irish. Roy Foster recalls one of the powerful Beresfords lamenting that when he was a boy 'the Irish people' meant the Protestants; and later still Stephen Gwynn, brother of Trinity's Provost Gwynn, said: 'I was brought up to think of myself as Irish without question or qualification, but the new nationalism prefers to describe me and the like of me as Anglo-Irish'. The identification of themselves as Irish by the Protestant figures who came to Australia is very evident and Sir Frederick Darley, chief justice of New South Wales, only wanted to be known as 'an old Irish gentleman' in his retirement, reflecting still the pride he had in representing his country.

It could be said that the Anglo-Irish in Ireland failed to adapt to the new political circumstances and, indeed, failed to take a lead in changing the economic profile in Ireland, at a time when Britain was entering the industrial age. This behaviour is in sharp contrast to the leadership shown in their Australian colonial careers, where they were in the forefront in promoting religious tolerance, secular education, universal suffrage, land reform, and democratic institutions. They had seen the loss of government to Westminster, but in going to the colonies they thought they would acquire a share in the further development of an empire. Arguing for 'responsible government' in colonial Australia, a form of government that they had lost in Ireland, did not constitute for most of them any kind of declaration of independence. They advocated religious tolerance because they had experienced the uncertainty, enmity, injustice and destructive reaction that religious intolerance had wrought at home. They saw education as the means of inculcating a commitment to religious freedom in the young and argued for free non-denominational state schools. John Winthrop Hackett, Trinity-educated first chancellor of the University of Western Australia, expanded this view to include tertiary education when the first senate of the university voted to reject fees.

These men were highly educated and highly ambitious individuals who travelled half way around the world to make their fortunes. But many also regarded themselves as agents of culture and civilisation and entered enthusiastically into public life. They were gentlemen by training and inclination and their loyalty was to the idea of a civilised liberal empire and to the notion of progress. Far from wishing to recreate the conditions of privilege they had left behind, they were anxious to ensure that the same mistakes were not made again.

The Australian colonies appeared to these educated Irishmen to be truly a land of opportunity. They had a chance to be in at the beginning, to acquire land for a fraction of the amount they would have to pay in the United States or Canada; to obtain government positions before these were monopolised by other groups; and to live in the best areas, not in ghettoes, as had happened in the United States, where, by the nineteenth century, the Irish were regarded as outsiders, and excluded for a time from the best jobs and districts. Being amongst the first in the colonies and having much in common with the majority, those who did not have a government post to come to were soon accommodated by their contacts. They came in family groups and built up networks, and the capital and the skills they possessed were assets to a new country whose free settlers were overwhelmingly poor and uneducated.

Some came because they had no choice but to go where their navy, army or civil service took them. Overseas posting was not unusual among these Irishmen. The fate of second and subsequent sons of the landed gentry was often a commission in the army or navy, a posting in the East India Company, or a church living. Irish governors and chief justices arrived in the colonies having served in other far-flung reaches of the empire. Many of the families had a military tradition and it was not unexpected that the sons would serve in foreign parts at some time in their careers. With the end of the Peninsular War in 1815 opportunities in the army declined and officers facing retirement on half pay would make their way to the colonies. Colonisation, too, was seen as heroic work.

Appointment to a lucrative government post, usually by influence and patronage, was an inducement for many. Legal appointments were particularly attractive in view of the scarcity of work for lawyers in Ireland and Britain. The often-quoted statement by Victoria's chief justice, William Stawell, as recorded by Lady Stawell in My Recollections, sums up the plight in the 1840s of the Irish lawyer: 'When I saw forty hats on the Munster Circuit with enough work for twenty I thought it was time to go'. The first law officers in a number of the Australian colonies were Trinity-educated and in Victoria the tradition of Irish dominance at the Bar and on the Bench is remarked upon to this day. Members of the Irish Bar who went to Australia without a position in mind could be confident that work would soon be to hand. They usually had friends or relations there who were able to welcome them, introduce them to good society, and make the right connections for them to be able to attract clients or to secure a government position. A relatively small number took advantage of the availability of free land, thus achieving the status of landowner, something that had been denied them because of the circumstances at home. In the case of these new landowners, they were generally able to lay their hands on enough capital to make the necessary investment in stock and equipment, and to add to their land grants or holdings. Through letters and journeys home on leave, and sometimes even published articles and books, the successful colonists spread the word about their experiences in Australia, which in turn encouraged further migration to the colonies.

A Neglected Set of Colonists

When the leaders of the Eureka Stockade Rebellion, widely regarded as one of the defining events in Australia's history, were tried for high treason in 1855, the trial was a very Irish affair. The judge for most of the trials was Redmond Barry; the two prosecutors were William Stawell and Robert Molesworth; and one of the leaders of the defence team was Richard Davies Ireland, assisted by

Joseph Henry Dunne. All of these were educated at Trinity; and seven of the thirteen defendants were Irish. The leader of the rebellion, Peter Lalor, is said to be a graduate of Trinity, though evidence of that is fragile.

Similarly, when the bushranger and folk hero Ned Kelly, son of Tipperary-born John and Ellen Kelly, was tried for murder twenty-six years after Eureka, the trial judge was again Barry. The prosecutors Chomley and Smythe were Anglo-Irish barristers and the defence counsel, first Hickman Molesworth and then Samuel Bindon, were the sons of Trinity-educated judges.

For historian Patrick O'Farrell, this shows that in the Australia of 1850–1880 if there were Irish at the disadvantaged base of the pyramid there were also Irish at the pinnacle. To O'Farrell, it is because these Irish at the top have been so much a part of the colonising process that historians have taken them for granted; they have not associated them with being Irish since they shared with the majority a common ancestry and religion. Historians have supposed that these Trinity-educated Irish were merely part of the English majority with their achievements subsumed under those of the middle class well-to-do immigrants who would be expected, in any case, to take leadership roles in the colonising process.

So the Anglo-Irish, when dealt with at all by modern historians, are identified with the English majority and not as a particular branch of Ireland's family. The busts, portraits and statues commemorating their achievements rarely depict them as Irish and the populace could be forgiven for not knowing that these particular Irish people contributed so much to Australia's legal, political, cultural and educational development. And it is understandable if few in Ireland or Britain would be aware of the presence and achievements of an extraordinarily influential group of Irishmen at the top of the colonial establishment in nineteenth century Australia.

It may be asked why the role and influence of the Anglo-Irish in Australia has been overlooked by historians; why their contribution to the development of Australian institutions has been neglected in the story of the building of the Australian nation. The reason generally put forward is that many were already anglicised when they arrived, and, if not, they assimilated very quickly thereafter because of their identification with the Protestant English majority. This is not a convincing explanation. The Trinity-educated Irish had attitudes of mind and social and cultural values that set them apart from the English and Scottish immigrants, and some of the most distinguished were Trinity-educated Catholics. These, too, are generally ignored. They all may have merged into the Australian landscape by now, but from the 1830s until the end of the century few contemporaries had any doubts about the Irishness of the men, generally educated in Trinity College, who dominated the professions of law, politics and education during this time.

It has sometimes been suggested, quite convincingly, that enough of the old English Catholics had survived in seventeenth century Ireland to hand on to later 'settlers' distinctive Irish ways and traditions, making the newcomers more Irish than the Irish themselves. The Anglo-Irish, long before they began to set forth to the colonies, considered themselves Irish, spoke English with a distinct Irish accent and possessed the loquacious wit and other idiosyncracies that remain characteristic of Irish people around the world. That being so, the assimilationist argument loses much force.

The neglect of the contributions of this general class of people has been recognised by Paul de Serville, who has written authoritatively on the gentlemen of the Port Phillip District in general; and a small number of others, notably J.J.Auchmuty, F.B.Smith, Gordon Forth and Patrick O'Farrell, have reflected on the fate of the Anglo-Irish in the history of Australia. Smith, who has particular interest in the role of the Anglo-Irish in the universities, observed that men like Hackett, Barlow and Lyle, 'begetters of many of the arrangements that are best in Australian life', do not feature in books on great Australians, or the Irish in Australia. He regards P.S.Cleary's *Australia's Debt to Irish Nation-Builders* as the most generous in this regard. Published in 1933, this is the most comprehensive record to date of the contributions of the Anglo-Irish to Australia's development, though Cleary might not have meant it to be so. It is not really so generous except in some rather specific cases, like Redmond Barry – 'a great judge and a fine citizen'. Cleary's treatment of Trinity is quite unsympathetic: for example, he refers to the Eureka Stockade rebel leader Lalor as 'one of the few Irishmen who passed unscathed through the atmosphere of Trinity College'.

Much more generous is O'Farrell's monumental *The Irish in Australia*. He regards the Anglo-Irish as a neglected but crucial factor in the colonising process, there from the very beginning but most in evidence between 1850 and 1880. The thrust of O'Farrell's book is, however, the history of the Gaelic Irish who, he says, 'throughout the nineteenth century took out a monopoly on the concept and image of Irishness, obscuring the true complexity of the multiple and various contributions of the Irish to national life and character'.

Neglect of the gentlemen immigrants is explained by de Serville as a manifestation of the Australian obsession with the myth of the 'fair go' and romantic attachment to the concept of the 'battler' who, from humble beginnings, conquers all adversity, to win fame and fortune. Allied to this is the strong sense of 'tall-poppyism', a characteristic feature of the Australian psyche directed against those who are deemed to perceive themselves to be superior, are thought to have airs and graces, or are otherwise in need of being brought down to size. Though many of the educated Irish were liberal and enlightened, which derived substantially from their time at Trinity, others were imbued with the feelings of superiority that allowed them to look down upon many of the English and Scots 'gentry', who they considered socially inferior. They were talented, confident, well travelled and sophisticated, leading the way in establishing cultural institutions and in pressing for reforms in a penal and pastoral environment, while still espousing old world attitudes, traditions and values. They were not always in tune with the more egalitarian immigrants who had none of their sense of social superiority or reverence for those who had it.

In a country seized of these sentiments about opportunity, class, wealth and privilege, the gentry would not be seen to be appropriate people to hold up as the nation-builders; they would, as de Serville says, 'be seen as undemocratic and even un-Australian'. He states his position most eloquently when he says that 'the gentlemen have been ignored by the scholars or when noticed it is in that uneasy manner which overtakes many Australians confronted by evidence of inequality.' His Port Phillip gentlemen of the 1830s were mainly English and Scottish, rather than Anglo-Irish. They lived by, and tried to impose on society, an honour code based upon social position and good breeding, not on merit and the ordinary rule of law. They tried to recreate in the colony elements of the class structure that existed at home. They were obsessed with lineage showing links to the aristocracy and landed gentry. Courts of honour dispensed justice and satisfaction was sought through a challenge to a duel, or by a horse-whipping, which would be duly recorded in their own haven for the elite, the Melbourne Club. In a new colony with no police force or legal and judicial apparatus, the code of honour may have served a useful purpose. As the colony developed, in the absence of a class system based on social position and the absence of a tradition of social control based upon heredity and position, the code became irrelevant and the gentry left the stage, except for the Trinity men, who, as de Serville accepts, were the most aristocratic and educated of them all.

With their education from Trinity, which, in O'Farrell's words, was 'then the premier of British universities, liberal and innovative', these Irishmen were well placed to occupy positions of power and influence in the post-goldrush era of 'responsible' government. It is for the long period of their influence that these sons of the landed gentry and the professional classes in Ireland should be remembered. This sets them apart from the Scottish and English gentlemen whose period of dominance was relatively short. Yet these Trinity-educated 'gentlemen' remain overlooked. Serle, historian of early Victoria, where the Trinity men were most numerous, writes of 'the younger sprigs of the nobility and gentry, Oxford or Cambridge-educated, professional men of every description [who] landed in Victoria in shoals'; but he confines the Trinity men mainly to footnotes while acknowledging that 'graduates of Trinity College, Dublin, were to make a remarkable contribution to Victorian history'. For Margaret Kiddle, who has written a definitive history of the Western District of Victoria, where the Trinity-educated or connected formed a large and successful pastoral enclave, it is Oxford and Cambridge that provided the educated young men who colonised Victoria, even though she is sceptical of some of the squatters' claims to 'Oxbridge' status.

It is sometimes proposed that the relatively small numbers of Anglo-Irish migrants may have contributed to their neglect in the history of Australia. It is true that the numbers reaching Australia were relatively small and that, if attention were to be focussed on the Irish, it would inevitably be on the greater numbers of Gaelic Irish who emigrated after the Great Famine. The Anglo-Irish were never more than about four or five per cent of the nineteenth-century non-indigenous Australian population, and about ten per cent of the Irish population in Australia overall. But the educated Trinity men quickly assumed leadership positions in the law, politics, clerical and other professions. The few who took up pastoral leases or became squatters on 'vacant' land in the Western District of Victoria were successful, the Pratt Winters in Victoria and Talbots in Tasmania being outstanding examples. In general, however, the Trinity men entered the professions and prospered. The numbers of highly successful and influential Trinity-educated men was out of all proportion to their percentage in the population. They occupied positions at the highest levels, and many espoused political ideas and social policies that were at variance with the conservative orthodoxy and which would inevitably raise their profiles, not as hybrid English but as Irishmen. They were generally not the type to merge into the background or to disguise their Irishness by affecting the manners and mores of the English dominant class, as has been supposed. It has even been suggested that not to lose their 'Irishness' could have been detrimental to their prospects in the colony, subjecting them to discriminatory behaviour by the ruling class. Though some discrimination did occur, as we shall see, claims of substantial discrimination are not compelling. Rather, the evidence is that those who reached high office did not hide their Irish background. This was so evident that the conservative Melbourne newspaper the *Argus*, reporting on Victoria's first parliament under the Act that gave responsible government, complained that 'in addition to the Irish speaker of the Legislative Assembly [lower house] we have an Irish colonial secretary, an Irish attorney-general, an Irish solicitor-general, an Irish surveyor-general, an Irish commissioner of police, an Irish president of the roads board and an Irish commissioner of water supply'. Most of these were educated at Trinity or had family connections with the College.

Sir Charles Gavan Duffy, the 1848 revolutionary-turned-statesman and premier of Victoria, believed that there was some tendency of the Irish to dispense with the characteristics that identified them in order to do well, and he regretted this: 'To strangers at a distance,' he said, 'who read of the Murphys, Barrys, MacMahons and Fitzgeralds in high places, Australia seemed the paradise of the Celt – but they were Celts whose fathers had broken with the traditions and creed of the island'. Butler Cole Aspinall, brilliant lawyer and Victorian politician, himself half-Irish, disagreed, and waspishly responded that it was a standing joke that every public position is given to Hibernians whether it be a postman's job or a judgeship and 'only while Mr Stawell [then attorney-general] holds office they should add Orange theology to the indispensable brogue'. And as Galbally notes in her definitive biography of Judge Redmond Barry, his aunt living in Malvern warned him about being 'far too Irish'; but he declined to alter his ways.

There would have been some professionals who adopted the manners and mores of the English, just as there would be some colonial landlords who adopted the pose of the country squire. These were the exceptions, the types who would be ambivalent about their Irish birth and gravitate towards the English part of their heritage because they saw advantage in it. Although the Anglo-Irish had much in common with the English middle class, overall the successful ones did not appear to regard themselves as anything other than Irish.

Trinity's Tercentenary

The very success of the Trinity men virtually ensured that their achievements would be identified with those of the majority, not as those of a distinct group. By the end of the century they were assimilated into the majority and were not being replenished from Ireland. Their dominance, especially in Victoria, was a colonial phenomenon. Their numbers were, in the end, too small to give rise to the identifying clubs, societies and institutions that keep alive the history and traditions of a particular group. In reflecting on the influence of the Anglo-Irish on the development of Australia, only one identifier is still used, though now rarely – that of the 'Irish cousinage', representing a closely knit group, mostly

Trinity-educated, who in going to Victoria displayed all the characteristics of chain migration. A small number would set out first, report in letters home on the prospects in the colony, and thereby encourage others to follow.

As previously mentioned, during the tercentenary celebrations of Trinity College in July 1892, Lord Rosse, the chancellor of the University, announced that an address and congratulatory telegram had been received from graduates and alumni of Trinity College resident in Victoria, Australia. In the congratulatory address George Higinbotham, the chief justice, and forty-six other alumni and graduates of Trinity wrote:

> 'As citizens of Victoria we remember with pride how large a share men who have been trained in Trinity College, Dublin, have had in the making of this Colony. The public careers of Sir William Foster Stawell, Sir Redmond Barry, Sir Robert Molesworth, Mr. Peter Lalor, and Dr. William Edward Hearn, to speak only of those who are no longer living, form no small part of the history of our adopted country'.

The address in full, together with the list of alumni and graduates, are at Appendix I, and the careers of some of those on the list will be featured in the chapter on Trinity men in Victoria. At this point, I would draw attention only to one to illustrate the scope of the connections between Trinity and Australia.

In 1883, Peter Labertouche, the twenty-fourth alumnus on Higinbotham's list, who graduated from Trinity in 1847, became secretary of the Victorian Railways. Not very much is known about Labertouche except that his daughter Ethel married Augustus Loftus, aide-de-camp to his father Lord Augustus Loftus, governor of New South Wales from 1879–1885. Lord Loftus was a direct descendant of Adam Loftus, first provost of Trinity College, Dublin.

PARLIAMENT AND LIBRARY SQUARES.

Figure 1. Parliament and Library Squares, Trinity College, Dublin, 1892.

CHAPTER 2

The Mother of a University

... so notable and excellent a purpose as this will prove to the benefit of the whole country whereby knowledge, learning and civility may be increased to the banishing of barbarism, tumults and disordered living.

Sir William Fitzwilliam (1592)

Foundation

The College of the Holy and Undivided Trinity of Queen Elizabeth near Dublin, also referred to in its charter as Trinity College, was founded in 1592, and is the only college of the University of Dublin. It is generally thought that there was an intention to found other colleges of the University in the manner of Cambridge and Oxford but, for various reasons, this never happened. Trinity College and the University of Dublin are now synonymous.

Trinity was not the first institution of higher learning to be founded in Dublin. In 1311 Pope Clement granted a *Papal Bull*, the necessary authority at the time for the establishment of a *studium generale*, and in 1320 such a body, centred on St Patrick's Cathedral, was founded. Though lectures took place and 'degrees' awarded, the institution failed.

Ireland, the island of saints and scholars in the Middle Ages, was, by the mid-1500s, one of the very few European countries without a university. In the mid-sixteenth century proposals for the foundation of a university in Dublin came forward. By then the country was coming under the complete control of the English, and powerful elements were convinced of the need for an institution of higher learning for 'the training up of reformed clergy, administrators, and lawyers and for the encouragement of learning in the arts and sciences'. It was also considered essential that the gentry be relieved of the necessity to send their sons to England, Scotland or Europe for their university education. This was seen as an undesirable adventure for them, particularly in regard to Europe, not only because of the perilous journeys they had to undertake but also because of the 'dangerous' religious and political influences to which they would be exposed.

In 1547, the Archbishop of Dublin proposed to Edward VI that a 'fair and large college' be founded on the site of St Patrick's Cathedral. The cathedral, recently disestablished by Henry VIII, was in a state of ruin, and the Archbishop proposed that its buildings and endowment be used to found and support a university. With Catholic Queen Mary's accession in 1553, however, the cathedral was re-established and the plan was put aside, only to be revived in 1563 by Sir William Cecil, later Lord Burghley, Queen Elizabeth's chief secretary of state. Cecil's proposal received the support of Adam Loftus, Archbishop of Armagh. Further support was elicited in 1581 from Sir Francis Walsingham, the Queen's principal secretary of state, but nothing happened until 1584 when Lord Deputy Perrot, the Queen's representative in Ireland, proposed again that St Patrick's Cathedral be used to support the establishment of two colleges. He clearly had in mind the Oxford and Cambridge model of a university.

Though the original proposal for the use of St Patrick's had the support of Adam Loftus, now, having since been translated to the See of Dublin as Archbishop and Dean of St Patrick's, he was vehemently opposed. His public position was that the city's interests would be best served by siting the university elsewhere; the St Patrick's site was, after all, quite small – only five acres. It is suspected, however, that the real reason for Loftus's opposition was that he was anxious to protect the interest he and his family had in the cathedral's livings.

Despite his opposition to the St Patrick's proposal, Loftus was still convinced of the need for a university, and he, together with Sir William Fitzwilliam, the new Lord Deputy; Henry Ussher, the Archdeacon of Dublin; and Dr Luke Challoner, the Prebendary of St Patrick's Cathedral, succeeded where others had failed. In a well-orchestrated campaign, these four men set out to persuade the Corporation of Dublin to grant the forty-acre site of a four hundred year old suppressed Augustinian priory for the erection of a college.

The site was about a quarter of a mile from the walled city, and the buildings were derelict. In July 1590 Loftus addressed the city's Corporation stressing the economic and social benefits of siting a university in the city. 'I pray you consider', he said, 'that the erecting of a college will not only be a means of cultivating civility and of enriching this city but your children by their birth in this place will, as it were, fall opportunely into the lap of the Muses and you need not send them abroad for the acquiring of foreign accomplishments, having a well endowed university at your door'.

Many of the city councillors were Catholic so that Loftus was appealing to them, not for the establishment of a Protestant institution, but for a university for all of Ireland. This was made abundantly clear, too, by Lord Deputy Fitzwilliam. The Corporation of Dublin was convinced and it ordered that 'the site of All Hallowes and the parks thereof be wholly given for the erection of a college there'.

The site having been secured, Lord Deputy Fitzwilliam was asked to petition the Queen for a charter and this he did. Henry Ussher was sent to London in November 1591 and he obtained from Queen Elizabeth a warrant which indicated her willingness 'to license a College whereby knowledge and civility might be increased by the instruction of our people in our kingdom of Ireland whereof many have usually heretofore used to travel to France Italy and Spain to get learning in such foreign universities whereby they have become infected with Popery and other ill qualities and so become bad subjects'.

The practice of the gentry of sending their sons to the continent had been drawn to Elizabeth's attention before, when Jesus College, Oxford, intended mainly for Welsh students, was founded in her name in 1571. She was told then of the growing desire for a university in Dublin by the principal gentry who were sending their sons to the continental colleges, 'where she is rather hated than honoured'.

Fitzwilliam's emissary, Henry Ussher, was educated in Cambridge, Oxford and Paris. The Usshers were one of the oldest, most respected and most distinguished families in Ireland. It was Henry's uncle, James Ussher, Lord Mayor of Dublin, who had petitioned Sir William Cecil for a university in 1571 and who took the matter up again with Sir Francis Walsingham in 1581. Henry was Archdeacon of Dublin and would soon become Archbishop of Armagh. His credentials were impeccable in presenting the case for a university to the Queen's advisors.

Luke Challoner, Prebendary of St Patrick's Cathedral, was also well connected. Educated at Cambridge, his father was a prominent property owner in Dublin and his uncle was chief secretary of state for Ireland. Challoner

Figure 2. Adam Loftus, Provost of Trinity College 1592–94.

rented a large farm from Adam Loftus from which he later supplied the College with provisions in its early years, when it was poor and unendowed. Challoner must be regarded as a prime founder since he undertook much of the business of running Trinity in its first years. He was described by Cecil as 'a careful and painful instrument for the building of the College', undertaking the hazardous trip to England several times after Trinity's foundation to solicit funds and books.

Adam Loftus, educated at Cambridge, was descended from a wealthy Yorkshire family, and he went to Ireland in 1560 as chaplain to the Earl of Sussex, the then Lord Deputy. Loftus subsequently became Archbishop of Armagh and then Dean of St Patrick's Cathedral and Archbishop of Dublin, posts that he held concurrently. He was Keeper of the Great Seal, a Lord Justice and finally Lord High Commissioner of Ireland. Described as 'a politic priest, educated beyond his age, unscrupulous and rapacious of high office', Loftus was one of the most powerful men in Ireland. Sir John Perrot, Sir William Fitzwilliam's predecessor as Lord Deputy, was recalled to London and imprisoned in the Tower following arguments with Loftus and others over matters that included the exploitation of Church lands for their private benefit. Loftus's nephew Sir Adam Loftus also rose to high office, eventually becoming Lord Chief Justice as a result of the influence of his powerful uncle. What is of interest here is that Sir Adam was related to the Wentworth family, one of whose branches gave rise to the powerful Australian Wentworths. This connection will be explored later.

The Charter

When Ussher took the Queen's warrant back to Dublin a charter was written, which was ready for her assent by March 1592. The charter declared that there should be one college, 'the mother of an University' called *the College of the Holy and Undivided Trinity near Dublin founded by Elizabeth*, for the education, training and instruction of youths and students in the arts and faculties. Adam Loftus was named as the first provost, Challoner and Ussher as fellows and Lord Burghley, also the chancellor of the University of Cambridge, was appointed as the first chancellor. Trinity was given the same degree of independence as had previously been granted to the colleges of Oxford and Cambridge, creating a 'body corporate and politic, for ever, incorporated and formed by the name of provost, fellows and scholars', who were enjoined to 'make, constitute and confirm laws, statutes and ordinances for the pious and faithful government of their College; and that they were to establish among themselves whatever well-constituted laws they may perceive in either of our Universities of Cambridge or Oxford provided they shall consider them proper and suitable'.

The designation 'mother of an University' has caused debate over the centuries, but the eminent historian of Trinity, J.V.Luce, who points out that the phrase appeared in Ussher's petition to the Queen, considers that the phrase may have been designed by the drafting team in Dublin to give the appearance of a modest proposal and thus obtain approval. What Loftus and his co-founders wanted was an institution that would have the facilities and independence of a Cambridge college, and this is what they obtained. No other college was founded. Trinity remained unique, 'the mother of an University', with a chancellor, provost, fellows and degree-granting powers.

The first stone was laid on 13 March 1592, and this was only possible through the efforts of the founders to raise the money to demolish the dilapidated priory and to construct the first College building. Although the Queen claimed responsibility for the foundation of the College in the charter, she contributed no money whatsoever towards its construction. So, Lord Deputy Fitzwilliam, referring to the foundation of a 'College of an University, near Dublin', sent a letter to the most powerful and wealthy men of Ireland seeking any contribution, 'whether in money, some portion of lands, or any other chattels ... to the putting forward of so notable and excellent a purpose as this will prove to the benefit of the whole country, whereby knowledge, learning and civility may be increased to the banishing of barbarism, tumults and disordered living'. Fitzwilliam stressed the fact that the College was to be for the whole country and also, importantly, that by their contribution the gentry would assist the disadvantaged, so that 'children ... that be poor ... may have their learning and education given them with much more ease and lesser charges, than in other universities they can obtain it'.

Many responded to this well organised fund-raising effort. Fitzwilliam himself contributed £200 and Loftus £100. In all, £2047 was raised and this was used to construct and fit out a building. When Walter Travers arrived from Cambridge in 1594 to take over from Loftus as the second provost, he was able to report to Burghley on the impressive progress in constructing the three-story red brick Elizabethan quadrangle, which formed the nucleus of the College. So, without actually having to put her hand in her pocket, so to speak, Queen Elizabeth managed to claim the title of founder in the charter of Trinity College as she had done in the case of Jesus College, Oxford.

Development

Trinity opened its doors to ten students in January 1594, with accommodation for two hundred and thirty fellows, scholars and pensioners planned for the first quadrangle of buildings. Between 1594 and 1609, eighty-nine students were admitted and by the 1620s up to sixteen students a year entered. Students were admitted in their early teens, generally aged fourteen to sixteen, and completed the Bachelor of Arts degree in four years. For four hundred years the undergraduate classes have been divided into two Freshman and two Sophister years.

The first grant of estates was made in 1597 from confiscated lands, but the turbulence of the period meant that little by way of rent was available and Trinity was very poor. It received ad hoc grants until 1687 when an annual grant of £300, exclusive of rents, was given by the Crown. Although Loftus's term as first provost extended only for two years, his appointment was an important one because his prestige, and that of Burghley, the first chancellor, played an important role in convincing the gentry that Trinity could be trusted with their teenage sons. After the poverty-stricken first years, the College was given substantial endowments by James I and it began to attract the sons of the aristocracy and the well to do. There were no religious tests for admission or graduation, but the purpose of the College was clearly seen as sectarian, as is evident in the petitions that were made for the establishment of a Catholic university in Ireland. In the late 1590s Catholics in exile petitioned the Pope for a university, pointing to the building of a college near Dublin in which 'Irish youth shall be taught heresy by English teachers'; and in 1598 one of the great Irish chiefs, Hugh O'Neill, proposed that there be created a university upon the Crown rents of Ireland, 'wherein all sciences shall be taught according to the manner of the Catholic Roman Church'. In the 1600s the Spanish Catholic college at Salamanca complained of its loss of students due to the 'crafty' English installing 'heretical masters to teach their pestiferous doctrines and uproot the desire of Catholics to cross the sea'.

The 'old English' Catholics tended to support the continental colleges despite Trinity's foundation, and Thomas Plunkett, whose kinsman John Hubert Plunkett rose to high office in New South Wales two hundred years later, is recorded as having donated £1000 to Douai, the French Catholic college, half the entire amount raised by Fitzwilliam for Trinity. However, as we have seen, James I supported the College by grants and lands, and when he established the Court of Wards in 1617 he ordered that the minors of noble families in Ireland should be maintained and educated at Trinity College, Dublin. These sons of the nobility wore special gowns, enjoyed certain privileges including course abridgement, and had precedence over senior fellows. They paid for the privilege in good Trinity tradition: their fees were twice those of the fellow commoners, the sons of the gentry; and four times that of the pensioners, the ordinary students, normally from the middle merchant and professional classes.

Although the College at its foundation had no religious tests, the counter-reformation encouraged the Lord Deputy, Thomas Wentworth, and Archbishop Laud, appointed chancellor in 1633, to revise the statutes in such a way as to discriminate against Catholics. For fellowships, scholarships and the award of degrees, Catholics would have to swear religious oaths and take part in ceremonies that would be abhorrent to them. Such constraints lasted until 1793 when the *Reform Bill* removed the tests for admission and for holding most offices. All religious tests were removed by the *Fawcett's Act* of 1879, but then the Catholic Church imposed a ban on attendance at Trinity by Catholics, which lasted until 1970.

In establishing its curriculum Trinity looked to Cambridge, which supplied all its provosts except two for the first hundred years. As students entered between fourteen and sixteen years of age, they were less prepared for university study than their counterparts in England, and instruction was more by way of lecture than by disputation as was common in the first two years at Cambridge. In the centuries after its foundation Trinity generally prospered and was always prominent in Irish affairs, but was never quite secure. By 1892 it had 1100 students, small by comparison with Oxford and Cambridge, but with a record of distinction in its fellows and its graduates that was quite remarkable.

In the seventeenth century it produced the previously mentioned James Ussher, Archbishop of Armagh and an intellectual who has been compared with Erasmus. His name was among the first to be entered in the College books in 1594 and he became professor of theological controversies in 1608. John Stearne (1624–69), fellow of the College and professor of physic, laid the foundations for Trinity's great medical tradition and established the Royal College of Physicians in Ireland. William Molyneux (1656–98), mathematician, astronomer, and friend of John Locke, issued the first English translation of Descartes' *Meditations* in 1680. He established the Dublin Philosophical Society, similar in its aims to the Royal Society of London, and published the first book on optics in English. Towards the end of the seventeenth century and into the eighteenth century, an extraordinary group of talented students entered the College, whose subsequent careers brought international renown not only to themselves but to Trinity as well. I mention only a few to illustrate just a small part of the literary legacy.

Jonathan Swift (1667–1745), Dean of St Patrick's Cathedral, entered in 1682 and graduated 'by special grace' four years later. As noted previously, he is best remembered as the author of *Gulliver's Travels*, a satire on human behaviour which, in a sanitised version, is one of the most popular children's stories of all time. The fourth part, previously mentioned, intended to portray two extremes of human behaviour, cold rationality and raw bestiality, and it is often construed as an example of Swift's misanthropy. Gulliver returns home quite unbalanced in his outlook and prefers the intellectual company of his horse to that of his family. The satire was published anonymously in 1726 and is only one example of Swift's extraordinary satirical and prose output.

William Congreve (1670–1729), dramatist and friend of Swift and Dryden, entered Trinity in 1686. He went to the Bar in England but never practised. Instead, he achieved fame as one of the most successful playwrights in early eighteenth century London. *The Way of the World* is one of the best examples of English comedy of manners; and *The Mourning Bride* has provided us with the immortal lines, 'Music has charms to soothe the savage breast', 'married in haste we may regret at leisure', and 'Heaven has no rage like love to hatred turned, nor hell a fury like a woman scorned'.

George Farquhar (1677–1707) entered Trinity in 1694 as a sizar, a student

*Figure 3. Edmund Burke, statesman and kinsman of Sir Richard Bourke,
Governor of New South Wales, 1831–38.*

from a poor background who paid nominal fees and who was able to supplement his income by undertaking tasks in the College. Farquhar is best remembered for Restoration comedy, especially *The Recruiting Officer* (1706) and *The Beaux' Stratagem* (1707). His line, 'crimes, like virtues, are their own rewards', in *The Inconstant* is usually misquoted. He extended the range of Restoration comedy by removing it from the fashionable drawing rooms into a more realistic outside world. In so doing he set a trend followed by others, including Oliver Goldsmith.

Oliver Goldsmith (1728–74), poet and dramatist, entered Trinity as a sizar in 1744. He is renowned for *The Vicar of Wakefield, She Stoops to Conquer* and *The Deserted Village*. His statue by Foley stands with that of his contemporary, Edmund Burke, outside the front gates of Trinity.

Edmund Burke (1729–97), the great statesman, orator and writer, founded the oldest university debating club in the world while a student at Trinity.

Known as Burke's Club, it is now the College Historical Society and it continues a fine tradition of debate. Burke was the kinsman of Sir Richard Bourke, governor of New South Wales, who spent his vacations while at Oxford in Burke's family home. Burke was also guardian to John Therry, father of Sir Roger Therry, judge of the Supreme Court of New South Wales. Burke entered Trinity in 1744 and became a 'scholar' by examination in 1746. Thus, he was a member of the corporation of the College, had free rooms, an allowance and was able to vote for the Dublin University member of parliament. Burke, who made a reputation as an outstanding orator after entering parliament, is ranked as one of the foremost political thinkers, whose brilliant speeches and writings extend to eight volumes. In his most famous work, *Reflections on the Revolution in France*, he attacks revolutionary movements based on even the most noble humanitarian grounds and laments that, with the destruction of the French monarchy, 'the age of chivalry is gone'. Burke, together with Swift and George Berkeley, are the founders of the great Trinity-based Anglo-Irish literary and philosophical tradition that has extended right to the present day.

And far from being a haven for the humanities, Trinity, in the eighteenth century, also produced some of the world's finest mathematicians, scientists and engineers, some of whom I shall have cause to mention when we observe Trinity men in Victoria.

CHAPTER 3

Founders, Provosts and Australia

I find myself in the society of a strange people ... the most intent upon their own ends that I ever met with.

Thomas Wentworth (1633)

Loftus, Wentworth and Fitzwilliam

Although the links between the Australian colonies and Trinity, through those who were educated at the College, developed spectacularly during the nineteenth century, it is also possible to find other links that reach back to the founders and several provosts of the College through descendants who went to Australia as migrants or on colonial service. With respect to the founders, it is of passing interest that Peter Ussher, a direct descendant of Henry Ussher, went to Port Phillip District in 1838 and then, forsaking his Anglican upbringing, became a Wesleyan minister in Adelaide. Of more general significance are the extraordinary relationships between the families of founding provost Adam Loftus, the then Lord Deputy Sir William Fitzwilliam, and the Wentworth family.

Thomas Wentworth, the first Earl of Strafford, was Lord Deputy of Ireland from 1633 until his recall to England in 1645. When he first arrived in Dublin he wrote that he had found himself 'in the society of a strange people ... of men the most intent upon their own ends that I ever met with'. He identified one of these strange people as Sir Adam Loftus, nephew of the founding

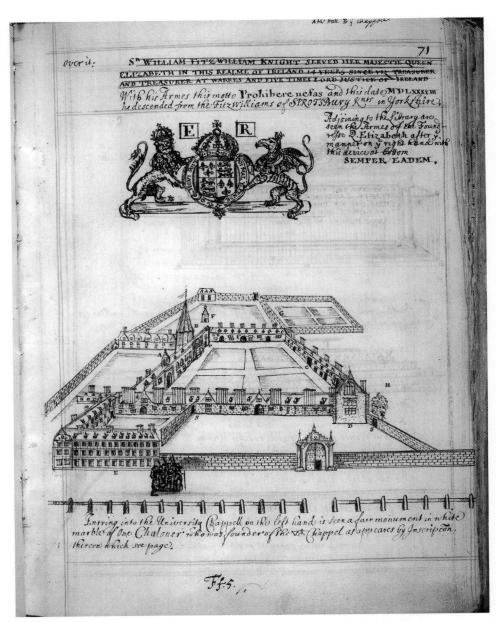

Figure 4. Thomas Dineley's sketch of Trinity College in 1681,
with a related description of Sir William Fitzwilliam.

provost of Trinity. Sir Adam Loftus (1568–1643) was related to Thomas Wentworth by marriage of his son Robert into the Wentworth family (see Chart 1, pp.34–35), but he fell foul of his powerful relative when he was unable, or unwilling, to provide an agreed marriage settlement. Wentworth imprisoned him in Dublin Castle, without trial, from 1637–9, and this was used later by the English Parliament as an example of Wentworth's arbitrary punitive actions. It formed the eighth article at Wentworth's impeachment, and Loftus had the satisfaction of seeing him convicted of treason and executed. The wily Sir Adam, observing that the Wentworth estates had not been forfeited to the Crown following Thomas Wentworth's execution, swiftly claimed that his granddaughter was betrothed to William, Wentworth's heir, who had entered Trinity in 1637 at the age of eleven. Loftus sent the young woman to Yorkshire to stake her claim but William had already left for Denmark.

In 1622, Sir Adam had been created Marquis of Ely and the title devolved later to direct descendants of his uncle, Provost Adam Loftus. Lord Augustus Loftus, fourth son of a descendant Marquis of Ely, was sent to New South Wales in 1879 as governor. Lord Loftus had entered the diplomatic service at the age of twenty, eventually becoming Ambassador to Berlin and St Petersburg. His appointment to New South Wales was the result of his desire for less arduous duties and a more genial climate. The only reminder of Loftus's governorship is the naming after him of a Sydney suburb and a street in central Sydney. His governance, which extended for seven years, left little mark on the colony. His son married the daughter of Peter Labertouche who, it will be recalled, was a signatory to the congratulatory letter that Victorian alumni sent to Trinity in 1892. As we shall see, another member of the Loftus family, Madeleine Emma Loftus, married Sir Alexander Onslow, chief justice of Western Australia.

It is the Loftus-Wentworth-Fitzwilliam connection, however, that is the most extraordinary in terms of the links between founders of Trinity and Australia. The importance of Sir William Fitzwilliam, Lord Deputy of Ireland, in the foundation of Trinity is rarely emphasised, yet he played a key role in obtaining Queen Elizabeth's assent to the granting of a charter to the new college. He gave the authority to Henry Ussher to travel to London to petition the Queen, and when the charter was granted he used his office as Lord Deputy to seek financial support from the gentry for the 'furthering of so good a purpose' as the founding of a university. He is of interest because of his connection with an Australian branch of the great Wentworth–Fitzwilliam family.

In 1744 Louisa Watson Wentworth, great granddaughter of Thomas Wentworth, married the first Earl Fitzwilliam, Sir William's direct descendant, and their son, the second Earl, inherited the vast Rockingham estates. The Fitzwilliam-Wentworths thereby became one of England and Ireland's great landed families. It is of some interest that the second Earl Fitzwilliam followed Sir William Fitzwilliam's footsteps as Lord Deputy of Ireland, though only from 4 January until 24 February 1795. As a result of his presenting a proposal for Catholic emancipation that was impossibly premature, followed by his dismissal of leading conservatives in the administration, the British government recalled him. Subsequently, Henry Grattan made an inflammatory speech in the Irish House of Commons denouncing the recall, to tumultuous cheering of Trinity students. As a result, the Speaker, John Foster, who presents a further link to Australia to be explored later, expelled the students from the Chamber and they were barred from attending debates in the House from that time. Trinity admitted the Earl to the degree of LL.D in 1795.

The connection between the Loftus, Fitzwilliam and Wentworth of Woodhouse families is shown in Chart 1, pp.34–35. Even more fascinating links appear with the introduction of the Australian branch of the Wentworth family.

The Wentworths of Sydney

John Ritchie, biographer of the Wentworths of Sydney, notes that all great families have their poor relations, and the Fitzwilliam-Wentworths were no exception. The name Wentworth is one of the most illustrious in New South Wales and is honoured in many ways in that state. The Wentworths of Sydney are descended from a 'collateral' branch of the Wentworths of Woodhouse, Yorkshire, but each branch derives from the same thirteenth century landowner, William Wentworth of Woodhouse. D'Arcy Wentworth (1640–1710) travelled to Ireland as steward to his kinsman, the Earl of Roscommon, in the seventeenth century, and by 1692 he had obtained his own leasehold property at Fyanstown, County Meath. Despite good connections made through marriage with the Anglo-Irish gentry, the family fortunes declined to the extent that D'Arcy's great grandson, also D'Arcy, was an innkeeper, proud of his aristocratic relations, the Fitzwilliams, but not counted amongst the gentry. This D'Arcy and his wife, Martha, had eight children, one of whom was the great grandmother of Trinity man, James J. Auchmuty, foundation Vice-Chancellor of the University of Newcastle, in New South Wales. Also amongst D'Arcy and Martha's eight children was a son, also D'Arcy, who migrated first to London and then to Sydney with the Second Fleet in 1789.

Burke's *Colonial Gentry* does not mention D'Arcy Wentworth's period in London in the two years before his departure for Sydney, and with good reason.

It had been intended that D'Arcy might find work as a doctor in the army or navy, or in the colonies, but he fell into bad company. In 1787, whilst being apprenticed to a surgeon, he was indicted three times on charges of highway robbery, then a capital offence. On the first occasion he was able to call upon the family's good name and standing, supported by his kinsman, the previously mentioned second Earl Fitzwilliam, and was acquitted. He was arrested again later in the same year and was again acquitted. The third time he was put on trial his acquittal came with an announcement that he would be leaving for Botany Bay on the *Neptune* as ship's surgeon. During D'Arcy's court appearances Earl Fitzwilliam, who kitted him out and paid for his passage to the colonies, provided him with defence counsel. The hostile press, which had taken an interest in D'Arcy's adventures in court, called him and others who had escaped the noose that day 'the lucky dogs'. When D'Arcy arrived at Norfolk Island in 1790 after a brief stop in Sydney, he was appointed as assistant surgeon to the penal settlement. He also acknowledged as his son a child born to Catherine Crowley, who had been convicted at Stafford Assizes for 'feloniously stealing wearing apparel' and was also aboard the *Neptune*. The child was named William Charles Wentworth.

D'Arcy was soon superintendent of convicts, quite a turnaround in his fortunes, and he held this position until his translation to Sydney, where he became one of the assistant surgeons of the colony, succeeding Thomas Jamison as principal surgeon of the Civil Medical Department in 1809. Appointment as justice of the peace, chief police magistrate and chief of police followed. He eventually became one of the wealthiest men in the colony.

D'Arcy corresponded regularly with Earl Fitzwilliam, who had arranged for an agent to deal with his affairs both before he set out for Australia and subsequently, when William Charles was sent to school in Greenwich. It was thought that while there William might obtain a place in the military academy at Woolwich. This did not eventuate and young Wentworth returned to Sydney to farm one of his father's properties on the Nepean River. In 1813 he joined an expedition with Blaxland and Lawson, in which they were the first to successfully cross the Blue Mountains.

Despite his general popularity, especially amongst the convicts, D'Arcy mixed very little in society, probably because of the stigma attaching to him from his indictments in England and his relationship with William's mother, whom he did not marry. William greatly resented the 'exclusives' who slighted his father on account of his past, and waged a campaign against them later in his career. He wrote of the exclusives that they 'would monopolise all positions of power, dignity and emolument and raise an eternal barrier of separation

Figure 5. Lord Augustus Loftus, Governor of New South Wales, 1879–85.

between their offspring and the offspring of the unfortunate convict'. William returned to London in 1816, entered Middle Temple and was called to the Bar. He decided to 'keep' a few terms at Peterhouse, Cambridge, but did not graduate. He returned to Sydney in 1826 to stay, and set up the *Australian* newspaper with Robert Wardell, a Cambridge-educated lawyer who had edited the *Statesman*. The paper provided an outlet for Wentworth's attacks upon the exclusives, according to him the 'the yellow snakes' of the colony.

In 1843, Wentworth entered the Legislative Council of New South Wales and his pioneering work in education began. In 1848 he played a leading part in establishing the first real system of primary education in New South Wales. Until then the religious orders had provided less than universal primary education. As we shall see, in 1849–50 he followed this initiative, alongside Trinity-educated Henry Grattan Douglass, with shared leadership of the movement to establish the first university in the British colonies. Thus the foundation of Ireland's first university in 1592 is linked to the foundation of Australia's first by a connection that is both extraordinary and direct.

From Loftus to Winter

To return to early Trinity College, Dublin – Loftus remained as provost for two years, with Lord Burghley as his chancellor. In 1594 he manoeuvred William Travers, a fellow of Trinity College, Cambridge, into the position of provost, as his replacement. Travers stayed until 1598, when Burghley died. The next chancellor was Robert Dudley, Earl of Essex, who was executed two years after his appointment, and then Burghley's son, the Earl of Salisbury, held office as chancellor until 1633, bringing great stability and prestige to the office. Archbishop Laud, already chancellor of Cambridge University, succeeded Salisbury, and in 1645 he suffered the same fate as Essex.

After the departure of Travers during the troubled times of the late sixteenth century, the provostship remained vacant for two years. Then three consecutive appointments of Cambridge men followed and, in 1629, Robert Ussher, cousin of James Ussher, became the first Trinity-educated provost. Considered too soft by Wentworth, who became Lord Deputy in 1633, Robert was 'persuaded' by Wentworth to step down to take the Bishopric of Meath. Trinity's independence was now being compromised by Wentworth, the price it had to pay for the support it was by now receiving from the Crown. William Chappell from Emmanuel College, Cambridge, replaced Ussher and then, in 1640, Richard Washington from Oxford took over, but he lasted only fifteen months, returning to England at the outbreak of the 1641 Rebellion, never to return.

In the next ten years the fortunes of the College declined to a point where it might have closed. There was to be no provost for four years, the Dublin government appointing Faithful Teate as pro-provost in 1641. Teate, brother of composer Nahum Teate, best known for his Christmas Carol *When Shepherds Watch Their Flocks By Night*, shared the administration of the College with Dudley Loftus, great grandson of the founder, and about whom a senior colleague said, 'Never have I seen such learning in the keeping of a fool'. Teate, an excessive puritan, was removed in 1643 and Anthony Martin, also educated at Emmanuel College, Cambridge, was appointed provost in 1645. Importantly, as we shall see, Henry Jones was made vice-chancellor of the University at about the same time. Jones was scoutmaster-general during the period of parliamentary rule following the death of Charles I; and his brother Michael was a major-general in Cromwell's army and parliamentary governor of Dublin.

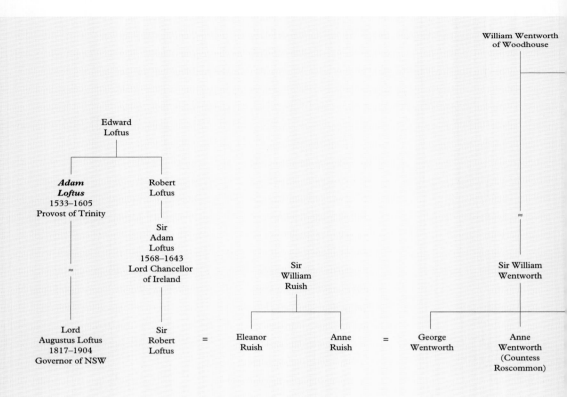

Italics denote attendance at Trinity College, Dublin.

Chart 1. The Loftus–Wentworth–Fitzwilliam Links.

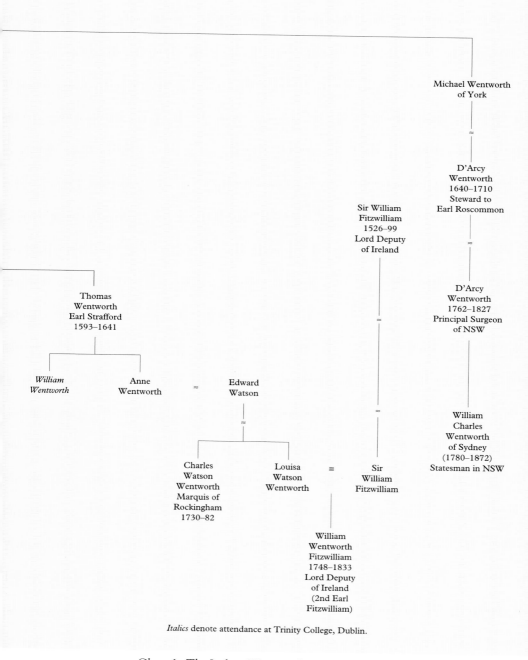

Michael Wentworth
of York

≈

D'Arcy
Wentworth
1640–1710
Steward to
Earl Roscommon

≈

D'Arcy
Wentworth
1762–1827
Principal Surgeon
of NSW

William
Charles
Wentworth
of Sydney
(1780–1872)
Statesman in NSW

Sir William
Fitzwilliam
1526–99
Lord Deputy
of Ireland

≈

≈

Sir
William
Fitzwilliam

Thomas
Wentworth
Earl Strafford
1593–1641

*William
Wentworth*

Anne
Wentworth

≈

Edward
Watson

≈

Charles
Watson
Wentworth
Marquis of
Rockingham
1730–82

Louisa
Watson
Wentworth

=

William
Wentworth
Fitzwilliam
1748–1833
Lord Deputy
of Ireland
(2nd Earl
Fitzwilliam)

Italics denote attendance at Trinity College, Dublin.

Chart 1. The Loftus–Wentworth–Fitzwilliam Links.

Provost Winter

In 1650 Provost Martin died of the plague then sweeping through Dublin and, under an Act of the Commonwealth Parliament 'for the better advancement of the Gospel and Learning', Samuel Winter was appointed provost in 1651. Winter, educated at Emmanuel College, Cambridge, continued a tradition of Cambridge or Oxford-educated provosts that was now to last until the end of the seventeenth century. Samuel Winter had come over from England as chaplain to the parliamentary commissioners and travelled around the country with them, preaching as he went. His sermons were well attended by the poor, to whom he distributed large quantities of bread at the conclusion of the sermon.

When he took over the College it was in a parlous state. Discipline was almost non-existent, fellows were not fulfilling the functions of their office, and there had been no graduations for some time. Winter set about restoring discipline and improving the College's finances. He went about the country performing marriages and baptisms, endowed scholarships, paid for books from his own pocket, and collected long overdue rents. At this time, in a highly political move, the Lord Protector, Oliver Cromwell, installed his son, Henry Cromwell, as chancellor, even though royalist Lord Ormonde was still officially in post. Ormonde, however, had left the country for his own safety. Winter continued to enforce discipline, and in the best puritan tradition he insisted on the importance of sound knowledge of the scriptures in the curriculum. Under Winter's stewardship the crisis in the College was at an end and a sense of order and sobriety returned. Winter recalled distinguished fellows from England and added to the fellowship by appointing staff such as Myles Symner, a major in Cromwell's army, who was a strong supporter of the new learning of Francis Bacon. Symner's role was to train students and soldiers in the technique of land survey, a most practical purpose for a man like Symner, who 'abhored all those ventosities, froth and idle speculation of the [Aristotelian] schoolmen'.

During Winter's provostship the first steps were taken to establish what would become one of the great medical schools of Europe. In 1651 Winter appointed Dr John Stearne (1623–69) to a fellowship, and in 1656 dedicated Trinity Hall, a student residence west of the College, for his use. This enabled Stearne to found a fraternity of physicians, which received a charter as the Royal College of Physicians in 1667. He undertook to treat the provost and senior fellows of Trinity without fee in return for the use of the Hall and held the positions of professor of medicine, Hebrew and law, as well as being the registrar of Trinity.

Figure 6. Samuel Winter, Provost of Trinity, 1651–60.

Ussher's Library and the Book of Kells

James Ussher, nephew of the founder and professor of theological controversies in Trinity, had 'a kind of laudable covetousness' for books and never thought a good book, either printed or manuscript, too dear. He travelled to England with Luke Challoner to buy books for the College on a number of occasions. His own collection, which he carefully gathered over many years, escaped destruction in the 1641 Rebellion and was sent to England, only to be seized by the English Parliament and ordered to be sold. The King of Denmark and Cardinal Mazarin were interested in buying the magnificent collection, but Oliver Cromwell, for reasons that will become clear, refused to allow the collection to be exported. John Selden, a parliamentarian, academic and friend of Ussher, acquired the collection and restored it to its owner.

Figure 7. Benjamin Pratt, Provost of Trinity, 1710–17.

It was probably Ussher's intention to bequeath the collection to Trinity, but, as most of his property had been destroyed in the rebellion of 1641, he left it to his only daughter, who was in straitened circumstances. When Ussher died in 1656, although he was a committed royalist, Cromwell ordered a public funeral and that he be buried in Westminster Abbey. His library was purchased by contributions from the army in Ireland and the Irish Exchequer, and for a particular reason. As we have seen, Oliver Cromwell had appointed his son Henry as chancellor of the University in 1654 and Lord Deputy of Ireland in 1657, so that Henry was undoubtedly a good friend and protector of Trinity. It is also clear that the strong relationship between Provost Winter and the Cromwellian regime saved the College from the ruinous confiscations of land that took place in Ireland after Oliver Cromwell's campaigns of 1650–51. Fundamental to Henry's support, however, was the pursuit of a particularly personal objective, the establishment of a second college in the University of

Dublin. The Ussher Library was to form the nucleus of a library for 'Cromwell' College.

When the monarchy was restored Winter was dismissed, Henry Cromwell was recalled to England and Ormonde resumed his chancellorship. The Cromwell College proposal lapsed and the King was persuaded by the Irish House of Commons to donate the Ussher collection to Trinity.

It was thought that the *Book of Kells*, Ireland's precious ninth–century illuminated set of the four Gospels, as well as the almost equally beautiful books of *Durrow* and *Dimma*, formed a part of the Ussher collection. It is now recognised that this is not the case. The *Book of Kells*, for centuries held in the Monastery of Kells in County Meath, was sent to Dublin in 1653 for safekeeping. Little seems to be known of the whereabouts of the Book in the period 1653–60, but in 1661 it was donated to the Trinity Library by Henry Jones, who was, as we have noted, the vice-chancellor of the University during Winter's provostship, and subsequently Bishop of Meath. Although it is now certain that Jones made a gift of the *Book of Kells* to Trinity after Provost Winter's departure, it is very likely that the ground may have been prepared during Winter's tenure of office.

It is ironic that, having been sent to Dublin for safe keeping, the precious manuscript might have gone up in flames in 1689, a mere thirty-six years later, when the College was occupied by James II's army and the Library was threatened with destruction. The provost of Trinity, Michael Moore, installed by James II, saved the Library and the College. He is remembered, and his action commemorated, by a plaque in the College chapel. The troops who threatened the College with destruction were led by Richard Talbot, Earl of Tyrconnell, whose descendants became landowners in Van Diemen's Land.

Provost Winter returned to England after his dismissal but some of his family remained in Ireland at the family estates in Agher, County Meath, and some of their descendants later set out for Van Diemen's Land too. These were the Pratt Winters, a family that combined by marriage those of Provosts Winter and Pratt.

The Pratt Winters

Benjamin Pratt (1669–1721), Provost of Trinity from 1710 until 1717, was descended from a Captain Richard Pratt of Leicestershire, who had invested money in Cromwell's Irish campaign. When the war was over, Pratt received lands in Garradice, County Meath, adjacent to the Winter estates at Agher. His two sons, Joseph and Benjamin, were sent to Trinity to be under the care of

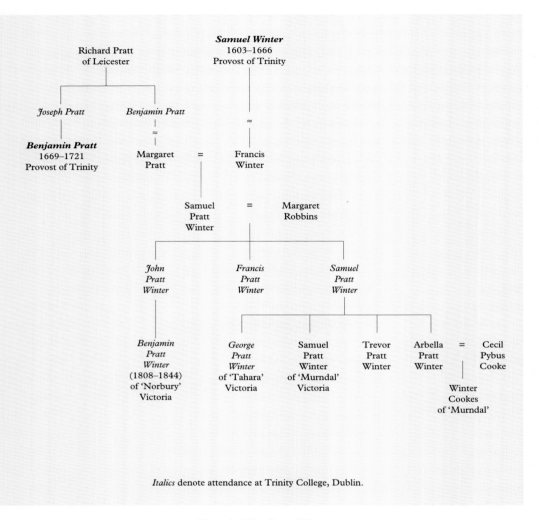

Italics denote attendance at Trinity College, Dublin.

Chart 2. The Pratt Winters.

Provost Winter. Joseph's son Benjamin was also sent to Trinity and he became a fellow in 1693. Benjamin's granddaughter married into the Winter family and this alliance gave rise to the Pratt Winters.

By the end of the eighteenth century the provostship of Trinity was regarded as 'one of the great employments of Ireland' and the Queen had reserved it for her personal disposal. It was the Lord Deputy or Viceroy, however, who made the actual recommendation to Queen Anne, and, in 1710, when the position became vacant, Benjamin Pratt was appointed. Pratt was well placed to occupy it. He was domestic chaplain to the second Duke of Ormonde, Lord Deputy of Ireland and chancellor of the University. Pratt was also a good friend of Swift, who described him in one of his pamphlets as 'a person of wit and learning'. However, the provost was also a man who liked to move in high society and he spent too many months at a time in London engaging in activities that had little to do with running the College. He appears in Swift's *Journal to Stella*, accompanying the satirist on expeditions to purchase old books or pictures, dining, or playing cards. It is not as if all were going smoothly at Trinity, for it was a period of faction fighting and plots between Whig and Tory supporters in the College, and there was concern about the succession to the Crown. The chancellor was forced to flee into exile in 1715, and though Pratt managed to get the Prince of Wales, the future George II, as chancellor, this was to no avail. Threatened with a 'visitation' over his absences in London, Pratt retired to the deanship of Derry in 1717.

The Burgh Library

During Pratt's provostship, an event of great significance took place, when construction of the great Burgh Library began. The Elizabethan buildings had contained a library above a residential block and Luke Challoner, together with James Ussher, made expeditions to England to stock it. However, when Sir William Brereton, who travelled extensively and recorded his impressions, visited Trinity in 1635, he was less than impressed by the Library: 'They glory much in their library, whereof I took a full view … not large, not well contrived nor well furnished with books'. Subsequently, Ussher's private collection, and Challoner's too, added greatly to the Library's holdings, so that an observer in 1680 could say that it contained 'the best and choicest books extant'. Though the Library survived the occupation by the troops of James II in 1689, the subsequent period was one of great privation and the Library fell into disrepair and misuse. In 1709 George Berkeley was appointed as Librarian.

George Berkeley (1685–1753), fellow of Trinity from 1707–24, is one of the world's greatest philosophers, ranking with Hume, Locke and Descartes. He is still read by physicists, for it is believed that he anticipated Einstein in deducing the relativity of space and time. His exposure to Locke helped him in his thinking, which culminated in *An Essay towards a New Theory of Vision* (1709) and *A Treatise concerning the Principles of Human Knowledge* (1710). His theory of vision is considered a classic by psychologists as well as philosophers, distinguishing between what we see and what we think we see or infer. The *Principles* represented his central philosophy, the complete and final expression

Figure 8. Col. Thomas Burgh, architect of Trinity College Library.

of his major principle: 'Esse is percipi' – to be is to be perceived. Pope credited him with 'every virtue under heaven'; he was a friend of Swift, who described him as an 'absolute philosopher'; but, idiosyncratically, he never accepted Newton's calculus and was a devotee of tar water as a 'cure-all'. In 1728 Berkeley went to America to found a college in Bermuda, but he did not travel further than Rhode Island. There he influenced the development of Yale and Harvard, becoming known as the father of American higher education, with the Berkeley campus of the University of California named after him.

It is Berkeley's role in the building of a new library that is important to us, however, for there are connections with Australia here that are indeed remarkable. Reflecting upon the parlous state of the Library, Berkeley began to campaign for a new library building. The times were propitious. Trinity had just demonstrated its loyalty to Queen Anne by stripping a graduate called Forbes of his degree for publicly expressing views about William of Orange that were at worst disrespectful. The College persuaded the Irish House of Commons to petition Queen Anne for £5,000 towards a College library on the grounds that the College stood for good literature and sound glorious revolutionary principles, citing the Forbes case. The stratagem was successful and the first stone was laid on 12 May 1710.

The architect chosen for the new library was Thomas Burgh of Oldtown, County Kildare. He entered Trinity at the age of fifteen, was commissioned in the army of William of Orange, serving in Ireland and on the continent and, at the age of thirty, he was appointed surveyor-general of Ireland, complementing his brother William Burgh of Bert, County Kildare, who was the accountant-general. Thomas Burgh designed a number of public buildings in Dublin before his commission to design a library for Trinity. He is thought to be the very first truly Irish architect.

Burgh's Library is modelled on Wren's Library at Trinity College, Cambridge, completed in 1699. It had open arches at ground level between the end pavilions to allow for the circulation of air to prevent rising damp. Originally faced with sandstone, the building had to be clad in granite in 1825, and in 1895 the arches were glazed in to provide for more book storage. The most spectacular feature of the Library is the Long Room. This extraordinary room, two hundred and eight feet long and forty feet wide, was built with a beautiful decorated plaster ceiling that remained in place until 1862 when, amid much controversy, it was replaced by the present barrel-vaulted oak ceiling that gives it its spectacular appearance. The vaulting increased the shelf space necessary to cope with the volumes pouring in as a result of the provisions of the *Copyright Act* of George III, which entitled the Library to receive a free copy of every book published in the United Kingdom from 1801.

Although building commenced in 1710, the Library was not finished until 1732. It is a masterpiece of the severe practicality that characterised Georgian good taste, and its sheer size contributes to its grandeur. It was called a 'powerhouse of learning', and it soon became one of the sights of Dublin, a popularity it has retained since then, and especially with the permanent display of the *Book of Kells*.

The Long Room was later to provide inspiration to Sir Redmond Barry, judge of Victoria's Supreme Court, when he was designing the Melbourne Public Library. The Queen's Hall Reading Room of the Library, opened in 1856, is clearly modelled on the Long Room, as it was in Barry's days as a Trinity undergraduate. But this is not the only link that the Library has with Victoria. The architect Thomas Burgh was an ancestor of the core group of the Irish cousinage in Victoria (see Chart 6, pp.108–9), and Sir Frederick Darley, chief justice of New South Wales, was descended from the stonemasons who built the Library. These were Henry and Moses Darley, father and son from a family whose association with Trinity College was to be long. A Frederick Darley became official College architect in the nineteenth century, and the granite and limestone for Trinity's great west front were supplied from Darley quarries, employing at the time of construction in the 1750s some one hundred men. The Darleys were originally from Arles, France, and they had settled in the English Midlands. Some migrated to Ireland in the seventeenth century and made a name for themselves as builders and stonemasons. As well as the Burgh Library, Henry and Moses worked on the Printing House and, later on, their sons worked on the Dining Hall in Front Square when, in 1761, the original, built by Richard Cassells, an architect of some note, had to be demolished after only twenty years.

Provosts MacDonnell and Gwynn

The fourth provost to be linked with Australia is Richard MacDonnell, who was appointed provost in 1852. His period of office coincided with the construction of the Campanile and the Museum. The Campanile, regarded as an architectural symbol of Trinity College, was the gift of Archbishop Beresford on his becoming chancellor of the University in 1851. Provost Sadleir, MacDonnell's predecessor, is said to have planted the idea of a new bell tower in Beresford's head, showing him the dilapidated structure that had housed the old College bell. The Campanile, a belltower for the old bell, rose close to the spot where the bell tower of All Hallows Monastery had stood two hundred and sixty years before. Designed by Sir Charles Lanyon, the Campanile is the embodiment of the consultant's recommendation that a small but highly architectural object with a central arched opening from east to west should be erected on the prominent site, 'with a low Campanile to receive the celebrated bell now so unworthily located'. The Campanile has become a symbol of the College and a challenge to clandestine College climbers since its completion. Although Sadleir put the idea for a Campanile bell tower into Beresford's mind, he died before it was begun, and it was Provost MacDonnell who saw it through to completion.

The museum building, designed by Deane and Woodward, the architects who successfully raised the roof on Burgh's Library, was built between 1854–57, also during MacDonnell's term of office. A landmark of Victorian architecture, it was designed to house geological specimens and the school of engineering. MacDonnell and his Board accepted the plans for this beautiful building, with its Venetian exterior and Moorish internal elements, in 1853, and the provost is mostly remembered for this bold architectural legacy. Later we shall consider

Figure 9. Richard MacDonnell, Provost of Trinity, 1852–67.

Sir Richard Graves MacDonnell, son of the provost, who became governor of South Australia.

The fifth provost to have a link with Australia, though beyond the colonial period, is Edward John Gwynn, an eminent Celtic scholar and advocate for constitutional reform, who served from 1927–37. He was the first provost to be appointed by the Government of the Irish Free State, which had inherited the prerogative from the English Crown. His father, John, was professor of divinity at Trinity and his mother was the daughter of William Smith O'Brien, leader of the 1848 Rebellion in Ireland. O'Brien was sentenced to death, but this was commuted to transportation to Van Diemen's Land. Gwynn's brother Stephen found fame as a biographer and literary historian, and his sister became the first 'Lady Registrar' of Trinity following the admission of women in 1904. It is with Provost Gwynn's other brother Charles that we find another significant link with Australia, this time after federation.

Figure 10. Edward Gwynn, Provost of Trinity, 1927–37.

Charles Gwynn (1870–1963) was commissioned into the Royal Engineers in 1889 and served in West Africa and Abyssinia before graduating from the Staff College at Camberley, with a subsequent year at London School of Economics. When the Royal Military College at Duntroon in Canberra was opened in June 1911, with Sir William Bridges as Commandant, Gwynn was appointed as director of Military Art, the senior of a small group of outstanding army officers appointed to key posts. His influence on the first intake of cadets, as on the College in general, was profound, for he spent much of his first year as acting commandant during extensive absences of Bridges. On the outbreak of war in 1914, Gwynn wished to join the Australian Imperial Forces, but he was ordered to England and then to Gallipoli to become general staff officer to Major-General Legge of the 2nd Australian Division. He commanded the 5th and 6th Brigades until the evacuation and was subsequently appointed as chief of staff to Lieut-General Sir Alexander Codley, commanding II ANZAC Corps.

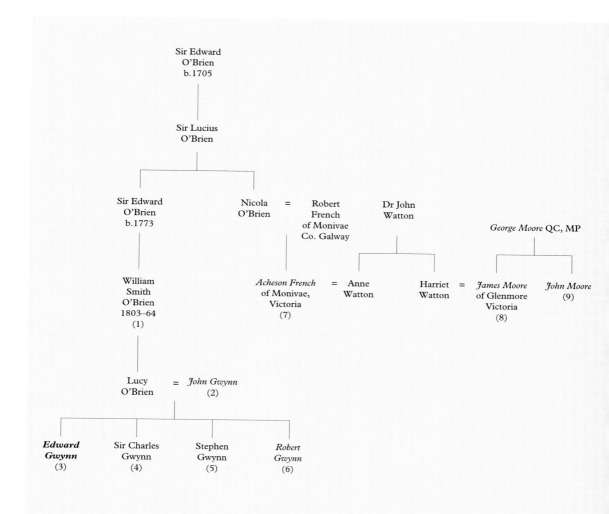

Chart 3. The O'Brien–Gwynn–French–Moore Links.

The following text appears within the chart area:

Sir Edward O'Brien b.1705

Sir Lucius O'Brien

Sir Edward O'Brien b.1773

Nicola O'Brien = Robert French of Monivae Co. Galway

Dr John Watton

George Moore QC, MP

William Smith O'Brien 1803–64 (1)

Acheson French of Monivae, Victoria (7) = Anne Watton

Harriet Watton = James Moore of Glenmore Victoria (8)

John Moore (9)

Lucy O'Brien = John Gwynn (2)

Edward Gwynn (3)   Sir Charles Gwynn (4)   Stephen Gwynn (5)   Robert Gwynn (6)

(1) Nationalist leader transported to Van Diemen's Land

(2) Professor of Divinity, TCD

(3) Provost of TCD

(4) Director of Military Studies, Canberra

(5) Author

(6) Professor of Hebrew, TCD

(7) Landowner, Victoria

(8) Landowner, Victoria

(9) Assistant Colonial Secretary, Victoria

Italics denotes attendances at Trinity College, Dublin.

Awarded the Belgian *Croix de Guerre* and the *Legion d'honneur*, Gwynn was appointed as commandant of the Staff College at Camberley in 1926 and knighted five years later. During his period at Camberley he had as instructors or students five future Field-Marshalls, including Brooke, Montgomery and Alexander, and many Duntroon graduates destined for high rank. Gavin Long, his biographer, notes that Gwynn won esteem by his learning, and high standards of discipline, behaviour and impartiality. His influence on Duntroon after its establishment was, according to Long, as potent as that of Bridges, and he was one of the outstanding staff officers of the British Army.

CHAPTER 4

The Outlaw Colony

New South Wales affords an excellent asylum for fools and madmen as well as rogues and vagabonds.

Governor Ralph Darling (1827)

The Principal Surgeon

The First Fleet of eleven ships under the overall command of Captain Arthur Phillip, RN, the first governor of the penal colony of New South Wales, sailed from Portsmouth on 13 May 1787. Sources differ on the exact number of people who sailed with the Fleet, but the most authoritative puts the figure at some thirteen hundred and fifty men, women and children. Captain John Hunter, who succeeded Phillip as governor in 1795, commanded the flagship HMS *Sirius*, and the complement included Phillip Gidley King, future governor; surgeon George Bouchier Worgan, who brought a piano; and two surgeon's mates, Lowes and Jamison. Thomas Jamison (1745–1811), son of the rector of Egremont in Cumberland, entered Trinity in 1763, became a scholar in 1766, and graduated BA two years later. In 1777, he received a warrant as naval surgeon and we next hear of him when he joined HMS *Sirius*. Joseph, Jamison's brother, had an outstanding legal career, graduating from Trinity in 1784 with BA and 1785 with LL.D. He was admitted to the Irish Bar, later becoming a King's Counsel.

On arrival in Sydney, Thomas Jamison was sent as assistant surgeon to the Norfolk Island penal colony, remaining there for eleven years. When relieved in 1799, he returned to Sydney briefly before setting out for England on one year's leave. While there he was appointed as principal surgeon for New South Wales, and in 1801 he again set out for the colony on board the *Atlas*, one of two convict transports, which set sail from Waterford and Cork with three hundred and twenty prisoners between them. The voyages of these transports were among the worst in the history of transportation. Sixty-five convicts on board the *Atlas* and sixty-two on the *Hercules* died of dysentery and starvation during the journey. Jamison quarrelled with Brooks, the captain of the *Atlas*, about the overcrowding, which was caused by the stowage of contraband liquor and other goods in the ship's prison and hospital. Jamison transferred to *Hercules* at Rio de Janeiro but found the situation on board that ship little better. On arrival in Sydney, the captain of *Hercules* reported a mutiny in which fourteen convicts were killed, and he was subsequently charged with the murder of ten of these. He was acquitted of these charges but found guilty of murdering one convict in cold blood after the mutiny had ended. The evidence was sent to England but no more appears to have been heard of the matter. Jamison brought a civil action against the captain of the *Atlas* for the neglectful way he had been treated, but lost on jurisdictional grounds. Governor King did, however, refund the cost of Jamison's passage from Rio de Janeiro to Sydney.

One of the more interesting convicts on board the *Atlas* with Jamison was Sir Henry Browne Hayes, an Anglo-Irish gentleman from Cork, who in 1797 abducted Mary Pike, heiress to a large fortune, and forced her to submit to a form of marriage. On her rescue, Hayes was declared an outlaw, but after a short period in hiding he lived quite openly, with seeming impunity. He gave himself up in 1800, presuming that his connections, his service in the South Cork militia, and his status as a freeman of the city of Cork, would save him. They did not. He was convicted and sentenced to death, with the sentence commuted to transportation for life, not because of the influence of his relatives, but because of his inability to consummate the 'marriage'. The commuting of his sentence attracted the ire of the Lord Chancellor, John Fitzgibbon, Earl of Clare and vice-chancellor of Trinity. Fitzgibbon, who may have been related to Hayes, was incensed, and compared the treatment of Sir Henry with that of a Mr Murphy who was hanged for a similar offence, the only difference being that Murphy succeeded in consummating his so-called marriage. 'It will be difficult to persuade the lower orders of society', he wrote, 'that equal justice has been administered to rich and poor'.

Hayes, in keeping with his unsavoury character, and that of the captain of the *Atlas*, negotiated a star passage to the penal colony for about three hundred guineas and, as a result, travelled and dined in relative comfort. Displaying what was described as 'irregular behaviour' and holding exaggerated views of his superior social position, Hayes soon antagonised Jamison by treating him 'in an improper manner', as the report on the matter put it. Jamison would not be treated insolently by a convict, however, and a violent incident on board cost Hayes six months imprisonment when he arrived in Sydney. He was later suspected of having taken part in the 1804 Irish uprising at Castle Hill, the first in the colony's history, but no proof against him could be found. Given his attitude and behaviour towards authority, it would not have been out of character if he had been involved behind the scenes in this abortive rebellion.

Despite being sent later to Norfolk Island, the notorious penal colony, and to the Newcastle coal mines for his cavalier attitude towards authority, Hayes still managed to live, between incarcerations, at the mansion he built on one hundred acres of prime Sydney harbourside land, bought for £100. He called the mansion *Vaucluse*, after the region in the south of France where Petrarch had a home. He surrounded the house with a moat of turf that he imported from Ireland, believing that this soil, blessed by St Patrick, would repel the snakes. Of course, no snakes have ever been seen around *Vaucluse House*! The house eventually passed to William Charles Wentworth, and the Australian Constitution was drafted in this historic mansion, which is now owned by the state government. Hayes was eventually pardoned and retired to Cork in 1812.

In 1804 Jamison, by this time principal surgeon of New South Wales in succession to William Balmain, collaborated with two assistant surgeons, John Harris and John Savage, to carry out the first successful vaccination for the prevention of smallpox. In that year, too, he wrote the first Australian medical research paper, 'General Observations on the Smallpox', published by the *Sydney Gazette* on 14 October 1804. This paper was accompanied by an offer to vaccinate children against 'this loathsome, disgusting and too often fatal disease'. Jamison's achievement was not without controversy, however, for Savage claimed that it was he who had carried out the first vaccination. Savage was a member of the Royal Jennerian Society set up in 1803 to promote the use of vaccination for the prevention of smallpox and the *Australian Dictionary of Biography* accepts the account he gave of his experimentation with cowpox and the first vaccination. Savage later claimed to have vaccinated or provided the material for vaccinating over one thousand children, and that his success alienated Jamison, whose own attempts, according to Savage, had been unsuccessful. In fact, the challenge to Jamison's role and priority in the vaccination achievements may have had more to do with the principal surgeon having court-martialled Savage in 1805 for refusing to attend women in childbirth

Figure 11. Thomas Jamison, Surgeon's-mate on HMS Sirius.

on the basis that midwifery was not part of his duties. Savage was found guilty and was cashiered, but Governor King, who thought well of him, gave him leave to return to England where his sentence was set aside. He did not return to New South Wales but spent his time writing a book on New Zealand, which he dedicated to Lord Fitzwilliam, his former militia commander and mentor.

Jamison, discontented with the lack of medical facilities and supplies, quarrelled with Governor Bligh and actively supported his enemies, D'Arcy Wentworth and John Macarthur, the founder of the fine merino wool industry in Australia. As a result, Bligh reported to London that Jamison was 'not an upright man, and [was] inimical to government as likewise connected to imported transactions'. There is no doubt that Jamison was involved in the illicit spirits trade, and Bligh attributed his discontent, and that of Macarthur and Wentworth, to the curbs he had introduced to the trade. Whatever the overriding motivation, Jamison played a leading role in deposing Bligh as governor on 26 January 1808. Appointed magistrate and naval officer by the rebel government, Jamison later sailed for England to be a defence witness at the court-martial of the leader of the revolt, Major Johnston, and did not return. He died in 1811 and his son John went to the colony to take up his inheritance of more than three thousand acres of farmland.

Sir John Jamison was born in County Antrim in 1776 and followed his father into the medical profession. In 1809, while serving as naval physician in the hospital ship *Gorgon*, with the Baltic Fleet, he was responsible for the containment of a serious outbreak of scurvy in the Swedish navy. Charles XIII of Sweden knighted him in 1809 for the achievement, as did the British Prince Regent in 1813. He was always grateful for this latter honour and called the mansion he built on one of his properties *Regentville*, in honour of George IV. It was on this property that in 1839 Henry Parkes, the 'Father of Federation', found his first employment as a labourer when he arrived in New South Wales. Sir John, known as the 'hospitable knight' for the lavishness with which he entertained his visitors, was not particularly generous to his labourers. Parkes reported home that the workers' rations were 'too frugal and too bland; the beef was unfit to eat; the rice was of the worst imaginable quality; the tea inferior; half the flour was ground rice and all was served without a leaf or a vegetable or a drop of milk'. As the assigned convict labour received only half of a free settler's allowance, one can imagine that Parkes may have fared rather better than his letters home would have us believe. He spent only six months on Jamison's farm but he never forgot it. The experience may have coloured his view of the Irish, which, for his entire political life, was negative.

Sir John Jamison also earned the displeasure of Governor Lachlan Macquarie because he objected to the liberal emancipist policies, 'the very impollitick levelling measures', expounded by the governor. Macquarie labelled Jamison as one of twelve 'intriguers' in the colony and at one time removed him from the lay magistracy. By 1826 Macquarie's successor, Governor Ralph Darling, had received instructions from London that on no account whatever should Jamison be employed in any civil office. It was not until the arrival of Sir Richard Bourke as governor that Jamison was restored to the magistracy; and in 1837 he was nominated to the Legislative Council of New South Wales. Over the years he had clearly modified his conservative views about the emancipists, for he was later described by Bourke as one of the many free immigrants of great wealth and intelligence who advocated liberal principles. He was a friend of William Charles Wentworth, D'Arcy's son, and was in the forefront of those, like Wentworth, who agitated for responsible government and trial by jury.

At this point it is appropriate to consider the state of the law in the colony and the role that Trinity-educated lawyers played in bringing respectability and equity to its administration.

The First Charter of Justice (1788–1814)

When the First Fleet arrived in Sydney, HMS *Sirius* had on board David Collins, the only law officer to sail with the Fleet. Curiously, he was called the 'deputy judge advocate'. As might be expected, the initial arrangements for administering justice were less sophisticated than those of England and Ireland, so that until 1814, when a 'Supreme Court' was established, the deputy judge advocate and lay magistrates dispensed justice. Until the advent of the Supreme Court, two courts under the presidency of the deputy judge advocate were established, namely the Court of Criminal Jurisdiction, comprising the deputy judge advocate and six military officers, and a Court of Civil Jurisdiction, also presided over by the deputy judge advocate, and which had two civilian members. There was also an Imperial Vice-Admiralty Court.

Collins, born in Exeter to an Irish mother, was a naval officer who had served at the Battle of Bunker Hill and who had no legal training whatsoever. Remarkably, he is said to have conducted the courts well, but when he departed for England in 1796 Governor Hunter wrote to the Colonial Office, 'I look forward with hope that the time may not be far distant when our courts will be settled more immediately upon the plan of our mother country'. It was to be many years until Hunter's wish came even close to being true, and the fact that it finally did owes much to the appearance on the scene of well educated Trinity men. Until their arrival, administration of the law was in the hands of a succession of what Governor Darling called 'fools and madmen'.

In 1796 Governor John Hunter, Arthur Phillip's successor, warmly welcomed the second deputy judge advocate, Richard Dore, who was, at least, an attorney (now solicitor), having been admitted by the Court of Common Pleas in England. Dore was a disappointment, however. Instead of having a law officer on whose advice he could rely, Hunter described him as 'a public pest, of a class of people ruinous to the colony', and 'too willing to give the aid of the law to petty private dealers'. Dore died insolvent in 1800 and was accorded the colony's first state funeral. Richard Atkins, a man described by John Macarthur, leader of the exclusives, as 'a public cheater, living in the most boundless dissipation', replaced him. Atkins, a former British military officer, went to Sydney in 1792, apparently to evade his creditors at home. He was said to be of gentlemanly birth, the son of Sir William Bowyer, but changed his name to take advantage of a will. His connections enabled him to obtain a position in

New South Wales as registrar of the Vice-Admiralty Court, despite a complete lack of a legal background. As registrar, he acted as deputy judge advocate between the departure of Collins and the arrival of Dore and, indeed, it was said of him during Dore's incumbency, 'though not a judge, he acted as a kind of deputy when Judge Dore was absent which was frequently the case, for when spirits were aplenty in the colony Dore was generally indisposed.' Atkins' lifestyle appeared to have been even more dissolute than Dore's, but somehow he survived for eight years until his recall 'by reason of his want of professional education, his practices and dissoluteness, which have had too great an inconvenience and injustice to suitors'.

The Second Charter of Justice (1814–23)

Governor Lachlan Macquarie arrived in Sydney in 1809 accompanied by Atkins' replacement, Cambridge-educated Ellis Bent, who, initially at least, got on fairly well with the governor. He and Macquarie undertook some reforms of the judicial system. The Criminal Court remained as before and a deputy judge advocate continued in this jurisdiction, but the Civil Court was split into a Governor's Court with limited civil jurisdiction and presided over by Bent, as the deputy judge advocate, and a 'Supreme Court' presided over by a Crown-appointed judge, assisted by two lay magistrates. A crown prosecutor was to be appointed and barristers and solicitors were to be admitted.

In 1814 Jeffrey Hart Bent, Ellis Bent's elder brother, a man filled with his own importance, quarrelsome and ill-mannered, was the first judge appointed by the Crown to the Supreme Court. Differences between Ellis Bent and the governor had by now developed and newcomer Jeffrey sided with his brother and refused to inaugurate the Court until all of his complaints about his personal affairs had been addressed.

Macquarie had welcomed Jeffrey Bent as warmly as Hunter had welcomed Dore, and the outcome was the same. This man, who he believed to be of considerable eminence as a lawyer, and of having good sense and a conciliatory manner, turned out to be a great burden. Writing to the secretary of state for the colonies, Lord Bathurst, Macquarie hoped that 'no other colony may ever have such a curse entailed on it as to have Mr Jeffrey Hart Bent appointed to any official position in it'. Jeffrey complained of many things including: the number of guns that should greet his arrival; the right to be called 'the honourable'; the inadequacy of chambers appropriate to his station in the courthouse; the lack of an official residence; and the preferment given to the 'notorious highwayman' D'Arcy Wentworth. Eventually the situation became untenable and Macquarie asked for the recall of the two brothers.

The immediate cause of the recall centred around three convict lawyers, Eager, Chartres and Crossley. Edward Eager, son of an Irish landowner, sentenced to transportation for life for forgery, was pardoned in 1813; George Chartres, son of a Dublin physician, practised as an attorney in Dublin before being transported for fraud in 1810. He was given conditional freedom called a 'ticket of leave' on arrival and set up in practice. George Crossley, a London attorney, was transported for perjury, arriving in 1799. He was pardoned in 1801 and two years later he began to practise as an attorney. In the absence of free settler attorneys, Ellis Bent had permitted these emancipist lawyers to appear before him in the Civil Court on condition that 'if His Majesty's ministers sent out at least two respectable solicitors' the privilege would be withdrawn. By mid-1815, when Jeffrey Hart Bent at last convened the Civil Court, only one of the two respectable attorneys, William Moore, who he had appointed in London as a government attorney before he set out for the colony, had arrived. The emancipist attorneys, therefore, petitioned for admission to practise before the Supreme Court with Governor Macquarie's support. Jeffrey Bent, angered by the governor's 'interference', was determined that these former convicts who were 'unfit for the situation of an attorney' would not appear. He was fearful, however, that his magistrate colleagues on the Bench would outvote him so he adjourned the court indefinitely. Before the adjournment, he admitted William Moore to practise, the first admission of a solicitor in Australia. Moore was not a success. A born intriguer, he was later described by Governor Macquarie in a despatch to London as 'a worthless and unprincipled reptile'.

Suspension of the court by Jeffrey Bent, and other intrigues by the Bent brothers, sealed their fate and they were recalled. Ellis died before the recall notice arrived from London and Jeffrey made as much trouble for the governor as he could before he reluctantly left for England in 1816, even offering his services to the Colonial Office as governor of the colony. He was appointed as chief justice of Grenada and died in the West Indies in 1852 after acrimonious relationships with a number of governors there.

The Bents' replacements carried on the tradition of incompetence and disruption. John Wylde, deputy judge advocate, and Barron Field, judge of the Supreme Court, both educated in Cambridge, quarrelled with each other and with the governor until they were both replaced in the organisational changes resulting from a third charter of justice. In 1819 the secretary of state had set up a Commission of Inquiry into the colony under John Bigge because 'the governor has many secret enemies as well as open ones who inundate the secretary of state's office with complaints'. Complaints against governors were endemic to the system and though they were taken seriously by the Colonial Office they were, at the same time, a source of irritation. Often taking more than a year to resolve because of distance, they could have a paralysing influence on government. During Bigge's inquiry, Sir Thomas Brisbane succeeded Macquarie as governor.

The Third Charter of Justice 1824

In his report, Bigge assessed the Supreme Court judge, Barron Field, who claimed to be a direct descendant of Oliver Cromwell, 'not to have that degree of temper and deliberation necessary to conduct the judicial business of the colony'. The governor, with whom Field quarrelled frequently, claimed that 'he embraced every opportunity of falsely slandering me and my government as contemptible to various individuals'. Wylde was no better. He attempted to thwart the governor's inclination to closely examine capital verdicts with a view to mitigation, and was responsible for gross miscarriages of justice involving such cases. Governor Brisbane tried to have him recalled but Bigge's report intervened, making Wylde's position redundant in any case. During his period in the colony, Judge Wylde refused to enter Government House, made numerous false and slanderous statements about the governor and allowed himself to become head of a faction. He later became a judge in Gibraltar and was described by Disraeli who observed him on a visit there as 'a noisy, obtrusive, jargonic judge ever illustrating the obvious, explaining the evident, and expatiating on the common-place.'

Bigge's report in 1823 resulted in the establishment of a full Supreme Court presided over by a chief justice. There was provision for the appointment of additional judges and two further courts were set up – the Court of Requests dealing with civil cases up to £10 and a Court of Quarter Sessions, for non-capital cases. The Act of 1823, 'for the better administration of justice in New South Wales and Van Diemen's Land and for the more effectual government thereof', provided for the appointment of an attorney-general and the establishment of a Legislative Council of up to seven persons appointed by the Crown. The governor, with the consent of a majority in the Council, could make laws and ordinances 'for the peace, welfare and good government of the colony provided these were not repugnant to the laws of England'. The chief justice was a member of the Council and had to confirm that any proposed laws were acceptable in this context. The Act tempered autocratic rule by governors with the need to consult, but it also created a second powerful position besides the governor, that of chief justice, whose relationship with the governor was a vital factor in the administration of the colonies.

In 1824 Francis Forbes, chief justice of Newfoundland, was appointed to be the first chief justice of New South Wales and in the same year the new Charter of Justice was brought to New South Wales by the colony's first attorney-general, Cambridge-educated Saxe Bannister. The governor now had two powerful figures with whom he had to contend, and the sorry saga of acrimony, ill-will, obstruction and personal vendettas continued unabated. Relations between Forbes as chief justice, and Brisbane's replacement, Governor Ralph Darling, were so poor that the secretary of state in London threatened to remove them both from office. Forbes objected to the requirement of his office to assess whether a proposed Bill was repugnant to the laws of England. He felt that this forced him to make political as well as legal judgements and this brought him into conflict with Darling, a military man used to exercising supreme authority and expecting compliance. Forbes instituted trial by jury in the Supreme Court and the Court of Quarter Sessions but jury membership continued to be restricted. His natural inclination was to try to reduce the governor's interference in the courts, and the conflicts that arose, together with the burdens of office, eventually forced his retirement.

Saxe Bannister, the attorney-general, was the first person to be sworn in as a barrister at the inaugural sitting of the new Supreme Court in May 1824. Following the familiar pattern amongst the lawyers in the colony, the attorney-general was, according to Forbes, 'incompetent, irascible and indecorous in court, and megalomaniac, or mentally deranged in some way'. The supposed inadequacy of his pay was a constant source of irritation to Bannister, and his private practice, which was allowed under the terms of his appointment, did not prosper. Eventually he informed the governor that if his emolument was not doubled he would resign his commission. Much to Bannister's chagrin the governor publicly accepted the resignation in 1826, giving him no chance to retract. To add to his woes, Bannister had taken proceedings against Robert Wardell, lawyer and publisher, for libel, and not being satisfied by the result he fought a duel with Wardell on the day before he was due to leave the colony. Shots were exchanged, they missed, and honour was satisfied. The governor was glad to see Bannister go: 'The apparent eccentricity of his mind and his want of experience in his profession prevented my depending on his counsel'.

Cambridge-educated Wardell and William Charles Wentworth were the second and third barristers to be admitted to practise in the Supreme Court. Wentworth had returned to the colony from Cambridge in 1824 with Wardell, and together they set up the *Australian* newspaper. With their admission to the Bar in England, each was entitled to practise as both attorney and barrister but, controversially, they then proceeded to try to deny others that privilege.

Wardell proposed that 'the gentlemen at present practising as attorneys and acting as barristers be compelled to retire from the Bar – confining themselves to their own province in the profession as attorneys'. It took some time, but in 1834 the Supreme Court created the division between barristers and solicitors that exists to this day in New South Wales. Wardell was murdered in the same year, not by disenfranchised attorneys, it must be said, but by convicts at large. He and Wentworth dominated at the Bar for ten years and their performances were in marked contrast to many of the law officers who continued to be sent out from England.

The second attorney-general, Alexander Baxter, was a most unfortunate choice. Within months of his arrival in 1827 it was clear that he was unable to perform the duties of his office. Governor Darling was of the opinion, which he expressed to the Colonial Office, that Baxter could never before have had a brief, as he was incapable of addressing either the court or a jury and was helpless against Wardell and Wentworth – 'whose effrontery and talent kept the Court and the Bar in subjection'. Baxter's only response to the governor's strictures was to ask for an increase in pay. Incredibly, he was appointed as puisne judge in Van Diemen's Land but when he went there, leaving his insane wife destitute in Sydney, Lieutenant-Governor Arthur, who called him a 'habitual sort', would not allow him to take his seat on the Bench. He had been bound over to keep the peace prior to departing for Hobart and, with his career now at an end, he returned to England where eventually he was imprisoned for debts. Darling's report to the Colonial Office reflected his frustration: 'Do not my dear sir', he wrote, 'suppose I am disposed to complain unnecessarily. I am fully aware of the difficulty you must experience in selecting proper individuals for offices here when it would appear that persons having claims on the government consider that New South Wales affords an excellent asylum for fools and madmen as well as rogues and vagabonds.' As Bennett, a historian of the law in New South Wales, has it, it was not until John Hubert Plunkett came that the government was well served. But this is somewhat unkind, as before Plunkett, John Kinchela and Roger Therry, the first of many Trinity-educated colonial lawyers, arrived in Sydney, the former as successor to Baxter as attorney-general.

A Deaf Attorney-General

John Kinchela (1774–1845) attended Kilkenny College, the school that also educated Swift and Berkeley. He entered Trinity in 1792, graduating BA in 1796 and LL.D in 1808. After being called to the Irish Bar he practised in the Court of Prerogative and all other ecclesiastical courts in Dublin. He later moved back to Kilkenny, entering local politics to become mayor of the city in 1819. Although he inherited considerable holdings of land he was, by 1829, seriously in debt. He asked Lord Ormonde to use his influence at the Colonial Office to obtain a position and the happy result for him was appointment as the third attorney-general of New South Wales. Apart from the fact that his debts were prodigious, the only difficulty with his appointment was that he was losing his hearing even before he arrived in June 1831. His deafness and inability to keep out of debt threatened to overshadow his clear ability as a lawyer and administrator. Although his disability prevented him from performing well in court, and made him the butt of many a joke there, he was a talented administrator – clearing the backlog of cases left by his incompetent and neglectful predecessors, settling arrears and filling the government's coffers with the proceeds.

Governor Bourke, who arrived some six months after Kinchela, was impressed by the new attorney-general's high principles, unusual at this time in a law official, by his diligence, and by his determination to give satisfaction. Bourke was less impressed by the effect Kinchela's disability had on his performance in the Legislative Council, of which he was, with the chief justice, an ex-officio member. But Bourke strongly supported him against his enemies and, as an example, suspended the government solicitor, the 'unprincipled reptile' William Moore, who insulted Kinchela because of the amount of work that the attorney-general had delegated to him. Moore had acted as attorney-general in the period between Baxter's departure and Kinchela's arrival, and resentment at not being offered the substantive position may have contributed to his animosity towards his new superior.

Moore had been the subject of a number of complaints by Ralph Darling, Bourke's predecessor, who, regarding him as 'one of the most idle men living, constantly bested in court by the barristers', had asked for Moore's dismissal. The Colonial Office waited until Bourke was appointed to call for an inquiry into his conduct. Bourke found Moore culpable and neglectful on many occasions but hoped that the influence of Kinchela would improve his work. When Moore was subsequently reprimanded by Kinchela for failing to properly prepare briefs for him, the letters of complaint that Moore sent to Bourke were so grossly insulting to Kinchela that Moore was immediately suspended as a government-appointed solicitor. He was never given the title of solicitor-general.

Kinchela, while acknowledging the effects of his disability on his court work, relied on his record as a first class legal adviser to justify his continued occupancy of the attorney-generalship. He had, he said, kept every department of government free of legal embarrassments and defeat in the courts, a not inconsiderable achievement in view of his disability, and in marked contrast to the total incompetence of his predecessors. Bourke appointed him as acting puisne judge in 1836 when Chief Justice Forbes went on leave to England. Despite his deafness, which caused delays only when he was sitting alone, he did well on the Bench and Bourke recommended him for a permanent judgeship in Van Diemen's Land. The secretary of state, irritated by Kinchela's creditors in London, who were causing embarrassment at the Colonial Office, refused to allow the promotion and asked that he be given a temporary appointment on the New South Wales Bench until a pension could be arranged. Kinchela served on the Bench for eighteen months in all, and was then given a sinecure as deputy commissary of the Vice-Admiralty Court, advisory crown counsel and master in equity. When he retired from the Bench he was lampooned by an 'exclusive' settler, James Mudie, in his *The Felonry of New South Wales*, published in London in 1837. Kinchela's son, James, defended his father's honour by a public horsewhipping of the unpopular Mudie. The fine imposed on the young man was immediately paid by sympathetic people who attended the trial.

Despite his unfortunate disability and inability to stay solvent, Kinchela brought to New South Wales a professionalism, legal knowledge and high principle that had not been seen before amongst the government legal officers. In reporting on Kinchela's work on the Bench, Governor Bourke, who admittedly may have had a sympathetic leaning towards Kinchela by reason of their common heritage, said that 'his legal knowledge and persevering research have been of essential service'. No other law officer to this time had received an accolade such as this from a governor. Indeed, the sentiments were usually quite the opposite. When Kinchela retired he was succeeded by his fellow Trinity man, John Hubert Plunkett, one of the reforming 'Irish triumvirate' of Bourke, Therry and Plunkett.

The Irish Reformers

John Hubert Plunkett (1802–68) was the first Catholic to reach high civil office in the colony of New South Wales. He was a member of an old English family centred on *Castle Plunkett* in County Roscommon, whose most famous member, Saint Oliver Plunkett, was executed at Tyburn in 1681. The estates of the Catholic section of the family had been forfeited to the Crown except for some properties held by Lord Crofton, a Protestant and family friend of Plunkett, to be handed back in more propitious times. As Cleary puts it in his *Irish Nation-Builders*, the patriotic movement of 1782 'hastened the brighter

Figure 12. John Hubert Plunkett, Attorney-General of New South Wales.

days', and John Hubert Plunkett was able to avail himself of 'the meagre opportunity opened to Catholics by Trinity College, Dublin'. He entered Trinity in 1820, graduated in 1824 and was admitted to the Irish Bar in 1826. Active in the Catholic Emancipation movement during a six-year period on the Connaught Circuit, he was appointed, through Daniel O'Connell's influence, as solicitor-general of New South Wales. A fellow Trinity graduate, Edward McDowell, had accepted the position in 1828 but had failed to take it up within the one-year time limit, and the offer was withdrawn. McDowell was left with little alternative but to take up the less lucrative solicitor-generalship of Van Diemen's Land.

Plunkett soon found that John Kinchela's hearing disability meant that many cases fell to him that would normally have been the responsibility of the attorney-general. On Kinchela's retirement Plunkett replaced him as attorney-general and also retained the position of solicitor-general. In this combined role, and with the support of Governor Bourke and Roger Therry, he launched upon reform of the laws in an attempt to bring to the colony some semblance of equality under the law. Even at this time the practice of the law was of a peculiar colonial variety, summed up in Governor Darling's later remarks that, 'Bearing in mind the description of people they had to deal with, I doubt whether the peace of the country is better preserved by rigid adherence to all forms of the law'. Lay magistrates drawn from the exclusive class dispensed justice with scant regard for the rule of law; illegal sentences were imposed; severe floggings with the cat o' nine tails were carried out, even on mere suspicion; what would now be regarded as trivial offences or even speaking one's mind, as happened with Sir Henry Brown Hayes, were punished by being sent to the hell hole of Norfolk Island, or the Newcastle coal mines; and executions and floggings were regular entertainment for the public, with little or no sympathy being shown for the unfortunate victims. The savagery of the law, and of those who executed the judicial decisions, seems incomprehensible now, but in the early days of the colony its survival depended upon mutual co-operation, stability and trust. Later on, as fortunes began to be made and the colony was supplying commodities to England, a docile convict labour force was also seen to be essential.

The 'Irish triumvirate' of Bourke, Plunkett and Therry, as Cleary has called them, was determined to make the system fairer, to impose the rule of law and, especially, to curb the excesses of the exclusives. Roger Therry, who was appalled by the amount of corporal punishment that was meted out, made an extraordinarily enlightened statement for the time, which reflects the thinking of the Irish triumvirate: 'Corporal punishment', he said, 'has been in its excessive inflictions, as instrumental as crime itself in multiplying victims for the scaffold. Of the hundreds of bushrangers who passed through our criminal courts I do not remember to have met one who has not been over and over flogged before he took to the bush'.

When Plunkett was given the dual role of attorney-general and solicitor-general in 1836, it was the hope of the exclusives that the workload would break him. As solicitor-general his views on the operation of the law were well known and, in 1835, he published the *Australian Magistrate*, the first Australian practice book, which was critically important in imposing procedural uniformity among the magistracy. Such was its popularity at the time that it was revised and reprinted in 1840. Plunkett abolished summary punishments by magistrates with the passing of the *Magistrates Act* (1837); rights to serve on juries were extended to emancipists; administration of justice in private houses, an intimidating and corrupt practice, was ended; the number of lashes that could be inflicted was limited to fifty; and, as the result of the notorious Mudie case, he succeeded in limiting landowners to seventy assigned convict labourers and servants.

James Mudie, considered previously as the antagonist of Kinchela, was a thoroughly disreputable officer of marines. Although cashiered in 1810, by 1828 he was a significant landowner with a large complement of convict labour. Six of his convicts escaped from the barbaric treatment they were receiving from Mudie and his overseer and while on the run they committed other serious crimes. They were arrested and charged with mutiny and robbery and were put on trial. Therry defended the convicts but he lost the case and three of the convicts were hanged. However, Therry's revelations about Mudie's treatment of his convict labour prompted Governor Bourke to ask Plunkett to conduct an inquiry into the behaviour of Mudie and his overseer. This inquiry was highly critical of the landowner, and led to reforms in the way convict labourers were treated. This only increased Mudie's vitriolic attacks on the Irish attorney-general and a pamphlet war erupted between Mudie and his opponents in the colony.

In 1838, one of the blots on Australian colonial history occurred, which was a watershed in the way crimes against the Aboriginal population were to be regarded. At Myall Creek in the north of New South Wales, twelve stockmen and their labourers massacred at least twenty-eight Aboriginal men, women and children, as a reprisal for sheep stealing. The perpetrators of the massacre were apprehended but did not expect to be punished for their crimes. It was presumed that the prosecution would fail as the entire Aboriginal group had been murdered, leaving no one to identify the culprits. Additionally, people were perplexed at the notion of whites being tried for the murder of blacks when the prevailing legal opinion, set out by the dissolute Atkins in 1805, was that, though the Aborigines were 'within the pale of His Majesty's protection, most would not understand the meaning of pleading to charges and would be totally ignorant of the nature of European law'. This insinuated that the laws could not encompass them and 'the only way of dealing with them, when they deserve it, is to pursue and inflict such punishment as they merit'. In other words, it was 'open season' on the Aborigines until Plunkett prosecuted the Myall Creek murderers and persevered even though they were acquitted at their first trial. He indicted them again on a charge of murdering an Aboriginal child and this time they were found guilty. Seven were hanged and this was the first time in Australia that white men were punished to the full extent of the law for murdering Aborigines.

Granted leave in 1842, Plunkett acted as adviser to the colonial secretary in London on a constitution for New South Wales, then under discussion. When Plunkett returned to the colony he became a nominee member of the partly elected Legislative Council, a body that signalled the beginning of representative government. In 1852, in preparation for responsible government which came into effect in 1856, a drafting committee for the constitution was formed, which included Plunkett and his Irish friend Sir Terence Aubrey Murray as members, and with William Charles Wentworth in the chair. Like Wentworth, Plunkett favoured the establishment of an upper house, with members holding hereditary colonial titles. In the event, two houses of legislature were established – a Legislative Council consisting of members nominated by the Crown, that is, effectively by the governor, and holding their seats for life; and a Legislative Assembly with a maximum five-year mandate, and elected by the votes of people who possessed freehold property to a certain value. Executive government was the responsibility of a cabinet chaired by a premier. The ministers comprising cabinet had to possess the confidence of parliament and were to be dismissed from office whenever that confidence in them was lost.

Plunkett, who had contributed so much to the drafting of the New South Wales constitution, stood for election to the Legislative Assembly and was opposed by a 'bunching' of Henry Parkes, Charles Cowper and two others who used Plunkett's Irish Catholicism as a weapon against him. Plunkett was defeated by one hundred votes. He later won a seat in the Legislative Council, and Cowper, the premier, invited him to be the first attorney-general under responsible government. He refused on the grounds that he was chosen only because there was no other lawyer with his experience in the Council. He did, however, become the first president of the Legislative Council under responsible government, a notable achievement. Plunkett won election to the seat of Sydney in the Legislative Assembly in 1858, took a popular position on the land question, which sped up the better distribution of land and break-up of the large estates, and supported the Ballot Bill, which introduced the secret ballot and manhood suffrage – 'one man, one vote'.

Plunkett was again appointed to the Legislative Council in 1860 and held office as a minister in the cabinet of Sir James Martin, the state's first Irish premier. When Martin's government fell in 1865, Plunkett accepted the attorney-generalship in its successor, headed by his old antagonist, Charles Cowper. Plunkett's subsequent resignation from the ministry precipitated the fall of the government in 1866. He left active politics then and settled in Melbourne, travelling to Sydney only for the parliamentary sittings.

Plunkett was the only high-ranking government official to oppose transportation, and when the campaign was successful in 1840 three gold medals were struck by Van Diemen's Land to celebrate this momentous achievement. These were for Queen Victoria, Plunkett and William Wentworth. As we shall see, Plunkett was also a member of the committee, chaired by William Wentworth, which established Sydney University. He was a founding member of the university senate and served as vice-chancellor from 1865 until 1869.

The First Irish Judge

We turn now to Roger Therry (1800–74), the second Trinity-educated Catholic to reach high civil office in the colony of New South Wales. Therry was born in Cork into an old English family that had settled in the area in the thirteenth century. Edmund Burke was a close friend of Therry's grandfather, and guardian of his father, John Therry. Burke played a similar role to that of Lord Crofton in the case of the Plunketts, when he acted as trustee for the Therry lands then centred on *Castle Therry*. The penal laws prevented Catholics like the Plunketts and Therrys from holding or inheriting property unless by the co-operation of a Protestant trustee. Burke saw to John Therry's education on the Continent and enabled him to read for the Bar in London. When introducing Therry to Henry Grattan – who in 1793 had secured for the Catholics the right to practise at the Irish Bar – Burke introduced John as 'a young barrister of the Catholic persuasion who, but for you, must have made a sacrifice of his conscience or of his faculties and education.' Burke's sensitivity to the issue probably arose from the fact that, though his mother was a Catholic, he had been brought up as a Protestant to enable him to enter Trinity and so to have a professional career open to him.

Roger Therry entered Trinity in 1818, the same year as Plunkett, but he did not graduate. Instead, he proceeded to Gray's Inn in London and was called to the Irish and English Bars in 1824 and 1825 respectively. Plunkett wrote later that Therry 'had given earnest and high promise of those talents and qualifications which later distinguished him'. He did not practise but instead took up law reporting for English newspapers and, in 1827, became private secretary to Whig prime minister, George Canning, and engaged in a project to prepare an edition of Canning's speeches. Canning died only months after assuming office and Therry continued to edit his speeches, seeking advice on them from Edward Huskisson, secretary of state for the colonies. Huskisson, impressed by Therry's ability, secured for him the post of commissioner of the Court of Requests in New South Wales, with the right of private practice. In

Figure 13. Sir Roger Therry, Judge of the New South Wales Supreme Court.

April 1829 he sailed with his wife Anne to Sydney in the convict ship *Guildford*, and in November became the first Trinity-educated lawyer to arrive in Australia.

It was widely acknowledged that Therry brought to the colony a broad knowledge of the law and legal procedure, and by 1834 the chief justice, Francis Forbes, expressed his admiration for Therry's knowledge as a lawyer and ability as an advocate and recommended him for early promotion. This was quite a change from the past: New South Wales was at last getting the honest lawyers that Governor Darling had requested years before. Justice Dowling, too, was impressed by Therry's ability at the Bar, and Deas Thompson, Bourke's son-in-law and colonial secretary, testified to the 'universal satisfaction that Therry brought to the suitors in his little court'. The government regularly asked him to prosecute crown cases, as the law officers were frequently 'indisposed' and were incompetent in any case. His defence of the convicts in the previously mentioned Mudie case, though not successful, resulted in the inquiry that led to Mudie's removal as a lay magistrate. Mudie's pamphlet attacks on Therry's character, for supposed neglect and delay of his public duties in favour of private practice, only called forth rebuttals from the judiciary. Judge Dowling, for example, wrote that Therry had, throughout his career, 'sustained that gentlemanly carriage and high tone which have ever distinguished the Bar'.

Bourke thought Therry well qualified to be the colony's first solicitor-general, but the secretary of state declined to appoint him; and by 1838, having advanced little despite the high opinions expressed about his work, Therry pressed very vigorously for promotion. While Therry was pressing his claims for advancement he was beginning to suspect that he was being discriminated against because of his Catholicism. In 1843 he stood for the seat of Camden in the part-elective Legislative Council and was duly elected despite opposition that was clearly based on his religion. He resigned his seat in 1845.

Though Therry had gained experience as acting attorney-general during Plunkett's absence on leave from 1841–43, a place on the Bench eluded him until 1845 when he was appointed as resident judge in Port Phillip District. The circumstances under which an appointment was necessary in Port Phillip will be considered in the discussion on the law in Victoria. At this stage, suffice it to say that Therry was a popular and effective judge but when the opportunity to return to Sydney presented itself he immediately left Melbourne behind. He became primary judge in equity and served on the Bench in Sydney until 1859.

In 1850 Governor Fitzroy appointed Therry to the first senate of Sydney University; in 1853 he was appointed to the National Commission on Education chaired by Plunkett; and in 1856 he became a nominated member of the first Legislative Council under responsible government, in his capacity as judge of the Supreme Court. He resigned from the Bench and the Council in 1859 and returned to England, where, in 1863, he published his valuable *Reminiscences of Thirty Years Residence in New South Wales and Victoria,* which received very favourable reviews in London and sold out. In New South Wales, however, it was almost unsaleable because of criticism of its content, which reflected badly on some of the important citizens of Sydney. Therry asked his publisher to return the unsold copies to England so that 'the people of Sydney may find something soon of more importance to think and trouble themselves about.'

Governor Gipps considered Therry and Plunkett to be the two most able barristers in the colony, but he also noted that 'the circumstances of

Mr Plunkett and Mr Therry being both Roman Catholics has, without any undue bias on the part of government, necessarily on occasion proved disadvantageous to the professional development of the latter'. He also made the comment that 'few things have given me more trouble in the administration of this government than the appointment of temporary judges'. He was referring to the acrimony surrounding such appointments in 1844. There were three judges on the Bench at the time, namely, the chief justice James Dowling, William Burton and Alfred Stephen. Stephen was on the Bench because Plunkett had refused a temporary judgeship in 1837 and Stephen had accepted it. When Burton was transferred to Madras in 1844 neither Plunkett nor Therry would accept a temporary position, but William a'Beckett did. On the death of Dowling in the same year, there was, as L.A.Whitfield has put it, a 'free for all' out of which Stephen, not Plunkett, emerged as chief justice. As we shall see with Therry, too, the chief justiceship of Victoria went to a'Beckett, not to him. It was not until 1886 that Trinity produced its first chief justice of New South Wales, Sir Frederick Darley, but before his career is described, it is appropriate to consider the appointment and contributions of other Trinity-educated judges in the colony of New South Wales.

An Injudicious Diarist

Thomas Callaghan (1815–63), district court judge, entered Trinity in 1832 and graduated four years later. He was called to the Irish Bar and for health and professional reasons he followed his brother Malachy, who had graduated from Trinity some nine years before, to New South Wales, with letters of introduction to leading lawyers, including Therry and Plunkett, and to Catholic clergy. He was entered as number eleven on the Bar roll shortly after his arrival in 1839, but, like a number of his contemporaries, Callaghan supplemented his income, initially by writing for newspapers. During his first six years as a resident, he kept a diary which not only recorded the mundane aspects of his life but also his impressions of colleagues, the people he met and his own hopes and disappointments. It is thought that his early struggle to get briefs and lack of recognition gave a bitter element to his recorded impressions of colleagues. He expressed rather a jaundiced view of the Therrys soon after his arrival in 1840. 'Mrs Therry', he said, 'has no head except for short-sighted cunning: however, she has great influence on her husband who is a vulgar shallow person: I do not think he is a man of more than ordinary intellect; he is certainly by no means a man of talent yet he is laborious and pushing, having also an admirable opinion of himself'. He goes on to indicate that John Hubert

Plunkett, too, had a poor opinion of Therry and of Edward Brewster, fellow Trinity man who, as we shall see, was the first judicial appointment in Port Phillip District and member for the district in the New South Wales Legislative Assembly. Callaghan's views of these two distinguished colleagues would not have been shared by others.

Callaghan eventually acquired the Crown appointments he so desired, first in 1841, as commissioner reporting on grants of land, then as crown prosecutor, and, finally, in 1858, as one of the first three judges of the District Court, set up when the Court of Quarter Sessions was abolished. He left his mark on the law of New South Wales by publishing a revision and consolidation of the Statute Law, called *Acts and Ordinances of the Governor of Council of New South Wales*, and *Acts of Parliament enacted for, and applied to the Colony*. He received a bronze medal at the 1851 London exhibition for these two volumes, which are known as *Callaghan's Acts*. Callaghan was a clever and capable barrister, though eccentric, and he built up a large practice before he became a crown prosecutor and judge. An obelisk testifying to his ability and judicial impartiality stands in Braidwood, New South Wales, where he was killed in a horse riding accident.

Leaders of the Bar

When the appointment of a chief justice to replace Sir James Martin was being considered in 1886, it was offered to Julian Solomons, who accepted it but who, due to a perceived lack of confidence in him by the other judges, resigned a few days later without taking the oath of office. As was usual at the time, the newspapers weighed in with all sorts of opinions as to the suitability or otherwise of Solomons for office. The *Sydney Morning Herald*, after previously offering lukewarm support to Solomons, pointed out that there was no shortage of men whose elevation to the chief justiceship would have provoked less disappointment and distrust than the unfortunate choice that had been made. 'Apart from Mr Faucett and Mr Darley', it intoned, 'Mr M. H. Stephen, Mr Owen or Mr W. J. Foster would, we believe, each be likely to command greater respect.' All of these named by the *Herald* except Stephen were educated at Trinity, and it is worth looking briefly at their careers.

A Judge of Earnest Tranquillity

Peter Faucett (1813–94), Supreme Court judge, represented Sydney University at the octocentenary of the University of Bologna in 1884 and at the tercentenary celebrations in Dublin in 1892. Born in Dublin, he entered

Trinity in 1837 and graduated with distinction in 1840. After spending time at King's Inns in Dublin and Lincoln's Inn in London, Faucett practised at the Bar in Dublin and on Circuit for seven years before migrating to Sydney in 1852. He soon followed so many of his Trinity-educated colleagues by entering politics, and was elected to the first Legislative Assembly under responsible government. He was offered the attorney-generalship in 1860 but declined. However, in 1861 Premier Sir James Martin, offered him, and he accepted, the solicitor-generalship, behaving in that role with 'the tranquil earnestness becoming the position of one whose sole concern is to have justice done'. As a parliamentarian he was plain-spoken, sober-sided and solid; and on the Bench, to which he was appointed in 1865, he was sound and careful, his judgements being rarely over-ruled. He was quite opposed to the *Matrimonial Causes Act* of 1862, which liberalised the divorce provisions, and carried on his protests in the Legislative Council to which he was appointed for life on retirement from the Bench in 1888. Unlike most of his Trinity colleagues, Faucett supported state aid for denominational schools and communities. He was a member of the Faculty of Law at Sydney University and became one of the longest serving members of the university senate – from 1859 until 1894. While a member of the Legislative Assembly, he moved a motion for a Bill to incorporate St John's, a residential Catholic college, into the university and served as a foundation fellow for five years. When Faucett retired due to ill health in 1894, Darley paid fulsome tribute to his industry and ability.

Water Jug Foster

William John Foster (1831–1909), Supreme Court judge, was the son of the Rev William Foster of Rathescar Co Down and Kate Hamilton, niece of the Duke of Wellington. Foster entered Trinity in 1848, spent four years there and left to go the Victorian goldfields without taking his degree. He did not strike it rich in Victoria, and after a brief visit to England he returned to Victoria in 1854, where his Irish cousinage connections (see Chart 6, p.109) procured for him an appointment to the public service. This he declined, however, and moved to New South Wales, where he farmed for a time. He studied further for the law under a Sydney barrister, was admitted to the New South Wales Bar in 1859 and was soon appointed as crown prosecutor, a position he held until appointed as member of the Legislative Council and attorney-general in 1877. Foster's support for the temperance movement earned him the nickname 'Water Jug' Foster and it is recorded that he took particular pleasure in implementing, as Minister of Justice, the *Licensing Act* of 1881. An evangelical Anglican, and member of both the Loyal Orange Order and the Lord's Day

Observance Society, Foster was a regular target for the press, which called him a 'fussy little brusher – the most singularly striking and original modern puritan prig'. In 1877 he said to the Anglican Synod that Orangeism had done more for religious liberty in New South Wales than all the laws, barristers and judges put together.

In 1880 Foster resigned from the Legislative Council and stood successfully for election to the Legislative Assembly, where he served as attorney-general in 1887. He declined the speakership in that year as it would affect his private practice, but his real objective was to be appointed to the Bench. He served as acting judge on a number of occasions and a permanent appointment to the Bench was his great ambition. When this was not forthcoming he created a great controversy by resigning from the government. He achieved his judgeship in 1888 from fellow cousinage member, Sir Frederick Darley, who praised him as a man of 'the most upright character, and the most unblemished honour'.

Chief Judge in Equity

Sir William Owen (1834–1912), Supreme Court judge, was the first of a remarkable legal family. Born in Wexford, the fourth son of a military officer, he entered Trinity in 1853, graduating in 1857 with a silver medal in ethics and logic and a prize for English prose. He completed his legal studies at Lincoln's Inn and King's Inns and, after being admitted to the Irish Bar, he migrated to Sydney in 1860. Immediately appointed as commissioner in the Court of Requests, he later accepted appointment as under-secretary of the Colonial Secretary's Department. Resigning to practise at the Bar, which he did with great success, Owen was a specialist in equity and drafted the legislation that resulted in the *Equity Act* of 1880. He became Queen's Counsel in 1882 and emerged as one of the leaders of the New South Wales Bar. In 1887 Owen was appointed to the Supreme Court as chief judge in equity and he later transferred to the common law and held the additional position of deputy-judge commissary of the Vice-Admiralty Court. He served as sole royal commissioner on investigations into the Lands Department, of which it was said, 'the fact that nobody got into gaol over the matter was certainly not the fault of Judge Owen'. He chaired a royal commission into the Railways Department and was knighted for his services in 1906. Owen was a reformer who, considering the equity legislation as backward and ruinous to plaintiffs, dilatory and expensive, tried twice to introduce legislation for a law reform commission. He reformed the operation of royal commissions, forcing the attendance of witnesses and the production of documents under threat of contempt, and his judgements were regarded as classic.

Owen's second son, Sir Langer Owen, educated at New College, Oxford, became chief judge of Matrimonial Causes of the New South Wales Supreme Court and was knighted in 1934. He was a founder of the Bar Association of New South Wales and was appointed CBE in 1918 for his work in organising and directing the Red Cross Information Bureau, which brought much help and consolation to the relatives of wounded soldiers, prisoners of war, and those missing or killed in action. He was president of the Bribery and Secret Commissions Prevention League, reflecting the strong position on morality in public office that his father pioneered.

An Old Irish Gentleman

The first Irishman to become chief justice of New South Wales was the son of poor Catholic parents from Cork. (Sir) James Martin migrated with his parents to Sydney in 1821 when he was just one year old. He was educated at great sacrifice by his family at the private Sydney College and was articled to a

Figure 14. Sir Frederick Darley, Chief Justice of New South Wales, 1886–91.

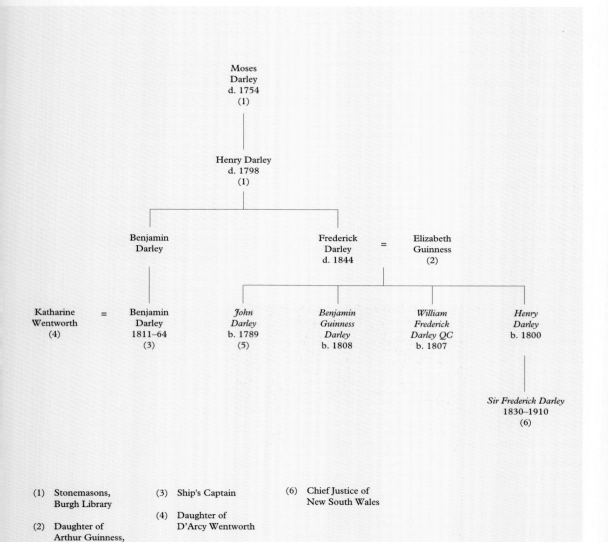

Moses
Darley
d. 1754
(1)

Henry Darley
d. 1798
(1)

Benjamin
Darley

Frederick
Darley   =   Elizabeth
d. 1844   Guinness
(2)

Katharine   =   Benjamin   *John*   *Benjamin*   *William*   *Henry*
Wentworth   Darley   *Darley*   *Guinness*   *Frederick*   *Darley*
(4)   1811–64   b. 1789   *Darley*   *Darley QC*   b. 1800
                  (3)   (5)   b. 1808   b. 1807

Sir Frederick Darley
1830–1910
(6)

(1) Stonemasons,   (3) Ship's Captain   (6) Chief Justice of
     Burgh Library   New South Wales
                         (4) Daughter of
(2) Daughter of   D'Arcy Wentworth
     Arthur Guinness,
     brewer   (5) Fellow of TCD

Italics denote attendance at Trinity College, Dublin.

Chart 4. The Darleys.

Sydney solicitor. Martin entered politics in 1848 and served as a member of the Legislative Council and of the Legislative Assembly. Between 1856 and 1873 he served as attorney-general for a short time and eventually became a somewhat authoritarian and unpopular premier. In 1873 he succeeded Sir Alfred Stephen as chief justice, an appointment that he held with some distinction until 1886 when, on his death, he was succeeded by another Irishman, Frederick Matthew Darley.

It has already been noted that during the provostship of Benjamin Pratt, the great Burgh Library of Trinity College was commenced and the stonemasons were the father and son team of Henry and Moses Darley. The quarrying and stonemasonry tradition was broken by Frederick Darley, grandfather of the chief justice, who became chief magistrate of police and an alderman of Dublin, and married the sister of Arthur Guinness, founder of the well-known brewery. Frederick sent his four sons to Trinity: Benjamin Guinness Darley, who graduated BA and MB; John, who became a scholar and fellow of Trinity; William Frederick Darley, judge and Queen's Counsel; and Henry, who graduated in 1821 and went on to achieve a significant reputation as one of the six clerks of Chancery in Dublin's Four Courts.

Henry's son, Frederick Matthew Darley (1830–1910), was born in Wicklow and educated at Dungannon College, where a relative, John Darley, was headmaster. Frederick's schoolmate at Dungannon was George Higinbotham, who, as we shall see, became chief justice of Victoria in the same year as Darley accepted the chief justiceship of New South Wales. Darley and Higinbotham entered Trinity in 1848 and, after graduation in 1851, Darley was called to the Bar at King's Inns. He read in chambers in England, was called to the English Bar at Lincoln's Inn, and on returning to Ireland he practised on the Munster Circuit.

In the *Sydney Quarterly Magazine* in 1887 it was said of Darley that, despite his commanding talent securing him full employment in Ireland and the possibility of a judgeship, 'his mind though great was capricious, and, contrary to all expectations he turned his attention to a new sphere of labour in the antipodes'. In 1860, while in England for a time, Darley met and married Lucy Forrest Brown, sister of Thomas Alexander Brown, better known as author 'Rolf Boldrewood'. A chance meeting in London with Alfred Stephen, chief justice of New South Wales, convinced Darley to emigrate. Like others before him, the crowded Munster Circuit was not giving him the income he desired and in 1862 he and his wife set sail for Sydney, calling en route at Melbourne, where they visited George Higinbotham and Lucy's Irish cousinage relatives. Darley subsequently went into partnership in a pastoral property with Molesworth Greene, his and Sir William Stawell's brother-in-law.

Darley's success as a barrister in Ireland was not immediately repeated in Sydney and he lost many of his cases. He later said that the first eleven years at the Bar in Sydney were the most difficult of his life. By 1878, however, when he was elevated to Queen's Counsel, his practice was thriving to such an extent that when first offered the chief justiceship he declined because of the financial sacrifice.

In 1868 Darley began a new phase of his life, entering parliament after some persuasion by Sir James Martin. His parliamentary career as an appointed member of the Legislative Council was unremarkable. He remained an independent no matter who was in government and his major role was that of standing counsel to the parliament, responsible for drafting legislation. His first efforts were concerned with reforming the criminal code and amelioration of prison discipline. His most famous statutes referred to the *Equity Act* and the *Matrimonial Causes Act*, which gave the wife equal rights to those of the husband and allowed marriage with a deceased wife's sister. Darley became vice-president of the Legislative Council in the Parkes Ministry of 1881 and represented the Council on the senate of Sydney University.

Darley had a highly developed sense of public service and in 1886 he accepted the chief justiceship of New South Wales despite the financial sacrifice, believing that he could use his abilities to make a positive and lasting contribution. The decision cannot have been an easy one as his pastoral pursuits had not been profitable, and that, together with the relatively low remuneration of the public post, meant that, according to him, his income was now half that to which he had become accustomed.

As one who upheld the independence of the judiciary against the encroachments of government, Darley was popular amongst the other judges and within the profession; and it was said of his distinguished appearance that he wore his robes as though born to them. When Sir Alfred Stephen resigned as lieutenant-governor in 1891, Darley was appointed as his replacement. In the absences of the governor he served as administrator of the colony with such effect that his appointment as governor was widely canvassed. He was acting governor from November 1900 until May 1902, and upon him fell the duty of swearing in Lord Hopetoun in Sydney as the first Governor-General of the Commonwealth of Australia on 1 January 1901. Darley was proud of his heritage and, as noted previously, he wished only to be remembered as 'an old Irish gentleman'.

Darley brings to a close our consideration of the influence that Trinity men had on the development of, and reforms to, the law in New South Wales, and to the administration of the law. Some of those mentioned served on the senate of the first university to be established in the colonies, and it is to the key role played by one Trinity man in particular to the foundation of that university that we now turn.

The First Colonial University

In 1850 the first colonial university was founded in Sydney. In reflecting on its foundation, Sir Francis Merewether, a member of the first senate and later chancellor, could find no reason for the foundation of the university other than the enthusiasm of Dr Henry Grattan Douglass, who, in 1848, re-awakened in William Charles Wentworth an interest that he had some eighteen years previously when the military vacated their barracks in the centre of Sydney. Wentworth had been unsuccessful in his bid to have a university founded on the site at that time and consequently lost interest in the idea of a university altogether.

When Douglass's mind turned to such a possibility he first approached Merewether, son-in-law of John Hubert Plunkett and clerk to the Legislative Council, to use his influence on Governor Fitzroy and Edward Deas Thompson, the colonial secretary, to obtain political support for the foundation of a university. Merewether thought that the governor and colonial-secretary were not yet ready to consider a proposition like this and referred Douglass to Wentworth. 'I ventured to add,' said Merewether, 'that if Mr Wentworth could be induced to take the matter up, and gain the necessary support of the Legislative Assembly he would have the support of the government'. Wentworth immediately and enthusiastically embraced the idea and the establishment of Australia's first university, by a Trinity-educated doctor and the son of an Irish doctor with historical connections to Trinity, was underway.

Henry Grattan Douglass (1790–1862), named in honour of the great Irish politician, Henry Grattan, received his early medical education in Dublin, served as assistant naval surgeon in the Peninsular War during 1809–10, and then in the West Indies in 1811. Invalided home, he became medical superintendent in Cahir Hospital in County Kildare, becoming a member of the Royal College of Surgeons in Ireland. During a typhoid fever epidemic Douglass published a pamphlet entitled *The best means of securing against the prevailing epidemic*, which formed the basis of his thesis on the typhus, successfully submitted to Trinity for the MD degree. At the age of thirty this brilliant doctor was elected as a member of the Royal Irish Academy, an

Figure 15. Henry Grattan Douglass, a founder of Sydney University.

honour at the time equivalent to Fellowship of the Royal Society of London. In 1821 he migrated to Sydney and was appointed as superintendent of the Glenelg Hospital at Parramatta.

Douglass immediately set out to foster the sciences in the colony, playing a key role as founding secretary in establishing the Philosophical Society, the first colonial scientific organisation. Governor Brisbane strongly supported Douglass by appointing him to the magistracy and then to the Court of Requests. He sent him to England to consult at the Colonial Office on the functions of the court and while there Douglass's enemies amongst the powerful and corrupt exclusive class, who he had antagonised by his emancipist sympathies, plotted against him. They made use of revelations that in 1821, as a serving officer, he had flouted military discipline by travelling without permission to Sydney. On his return to Sydney, again without permission, he was persuaded by a reluctant Governor Brisbane to step down as magistrate. Being generally well regarded at the Colonial Office, however, he immediately received an appointment from the home government as clerk to the Legislative Council and then to the Court of Requests. Brisbane's replacement, the despotic Governor Ralph Darling, was not so well disposed towards Douglass, his attitude having been prepared by the exclusives and by Barron Field, now in England, who was well used to slandering people, having been sued in his own court by Edward Eager for such an offence. An incident at a Turf Club dinner where Douglass made injudicious remarks about the governor gave Darling the excuse to dismiss him from his official positions and he left the colony in 1828.

Douglass spent the next twenty years in England and then France, returning to Sydney in 1848 as assistant surgeon superintendent on the emigrant ship *Earl Grey*. He soon became honorary physician to the Sydney Hospital and one of the first teachers of clinical medicine in Australia. It was at this time that he began to promote the idea of a university and Merewether wrote of him that the foundation of a university became the chief object of his thought and 'he discoursed on it frequently and earnestly'. Wentworth's Bill to establish the University of Sydney was passed through the Legislative Council in April 1850. Like Wentworth, Douglass held no official post on the senate, but he served as a member for twelve years. Douglass is remembered in the university by his coat of arms in stone at the entrance to the Great Hall and in a stained glass window in the main building. He served as a member of the New South Wales Legislative Council, where he tried to introduce a Bill to regulate the qualifications of medical practitioners and pharmacists, and he helped the university's second provost, Charles Nicholson, re-establish the Philosophical Society, which later became the Royal Society of New South Wales.

Douglass was a brilliant man who became a victim of the vicious politics of the exclusive class in Sydney during his first sojourn there, and who demonstrated many of the positive qualities attributed to the middle class Irish who migrated to Australia. He had a concern for the welfare of the convicts and a strong sense of equality under the law. His actions in pursuing members of the exclusive class in the courts, and imposing fines and confiscations upon them, brought him powerful enemies whose campaigns against him succeeded, at least initially. His second period in Sydney brought no such controversies, only remembrance as the founder, with Wentworth, of the University of Sydney, and a reputation for 'benevolence, kindly humour, fullness of temper and instructive conversation'.

A Mere Extravagance

The senate of Sydney University held its first meeting in the Speaker's Room of

Figure 16. William Charles Wentworth, a founder of Sydney University and statesman.

the New South Wales Legislative Council in February 1851, with William Wentworth in the chair. John Hubert Plunkett and Roger Therry were members but Douglass was not. He had to wait until 1853 before he was appointed to fill a casual vacancy. Despite his seminal role in establishing the university, Wentworth was not elected as the first provost, a title that was subsequently changed to chancellor. This honour went to pastoralist Edward Hamilton, a former fellow of Trinity College, Cambridge, who took little interest in the university and resigned two years after his election. Although now wealthy and Cambridge-educated, Wentworth, the son of a convict mother and highwayman father, did not even become vice-provost of the new university. That position went to Charles Nicholson, another Cambridge man, interested in classical studies and ancient history, and possessing a rare collection of manuscripts and antiquities. Nicholson subsequently succeeded Hamilton as provost and the path that the university would initially follow was set.

Although Wentworth had enjoyed his period in Cambridge, he thought that the University of London or the Queen's Colleges in Ireland provided better models of a university education, with their practical orientation and non-denominational organisational structure. Religious controversies would be avoided by the creation of a secular examining university where the students would be taught in colleges, which might be secular or denominational. The university developed along different lines, however, and was described by historian F.B.Smith as an Oxford-Cambridge mule. When Nicholson became provost, he looked to the ancient universities for his inspiration, even securing a coat of arms which had, as Smith says, 'the Cambridge lion and the Oxford book pasted on a cross of St George with a Latin motto which translated as *the same under different stars*'. Nicholson sought special legislation requiring British subjects throughout the world to recognise Sydney degrees but failed in this endeavour because, as pointed out to him, there was no legal requirement for anyone to recognise the degrees of any university. He did, however, obtain a royal charter that gave to the University of Sydney the same authority to confer degrees as had been granted to the University of London. In the Great Hall, stained glass windows commemorate ten centuries of English history with the founders and arms of Oxford and Cambridge colleges prominently displayed.

Wentworth's idea of a university as expressed in the Bill was entrusted to a senate, whose members were overwhelmingly in the 'Oxbridge' tradition. Of the sixteen members, five were educated in Cambridge, three in Trinity College, Dublin, one each in Oxford and Edinburgh, and five had never attended a university. Even the foundation professors were to be restricted to Oxford or Cambridge graduates despite the objections of Plunkett and Therry. Nicholson and, surprisingly, Douglass, in setting out the requirements for the professors to the selection committee in England, stipulated that they should be gentlemen scholars, graduates of Oxford or Cambridge, who could lead the colonials to appreciate the noblest creations of the human intellect. Three professors were appointed by 1852, two of whom were educated at Oxford and the third at Cambridge. By 1880 only six professors had been appointed, half of whom were from Oxford or Cambridge and the rest from Scottish universities. Peter Faucett, member of the senate for thirty years and reader in law, is recorded as one of only two Trinity men to be involved in teaching at Sydney University up until the end of the century.

Nine years after its foundation and following widespread criticism of the university led by William Cape, headmaster of the private Sydney College, the parliament set up an inquiry into the university. Turney and his colleagues, in

Australia's First, describe well the subsequent events. Cape had written to the *Sydney Morning Herald* that all that the colony had to show for its enormous investment in providing colonial youth with superior or modern university education was a staff of three professors, a few subordinate teachers, a fine 'commodious' building yet to be finished, and an empty cash box. The curriculum, he said, was 'ten years behind the age in which we are living'.

Henry Parkes, too, was scathing in his criticism, and in his newspaper, the *Empire*, called the university 'a mere extravagance isolated on its hill above Sydney town'. 'Oxford and Cambridge', he sneered, 'the source of its inspiration, were places famous for their lordliness in knowledge, in ignorance, in vice and in antiquated statutes and sectarian illiberality'. Parkes preferred the idea of a people's college 'serving the actual business of life'.

It was against this background of public disquiet and criticism, with low student numbers and meagre output, that Sir Terence Murray, landowner and member of the Legislative Council, was asked to chair the parliamentary inquiry into the university. Sir Terence, born in County Limerick to a Catholic land-owning family, had come to New South Wales in 1842. He received grants of land near present day Canberra, which he called *Yarralumla*, and where the governor-general of Australia now resides. He married Agnes Gilbert, cousin of W.S.Gilbert of Gilbert and Sullivan fame, in 1860 and their son, Sir John Hubert Murray, named after Murray's hero, John Hubert Plunkett, became administrator of Papua. The second son, Gilbert Aimé Murray, became regius professor of Greek at Oxford; and the third son, James Murray, graduated MD by diploma from Trinity and went to Sydney in 1828. He became surgeon at Sydney Hospital, assistant surgeon to the penal colony at Moreton Bay in Queensland, and then superintendent of the Goulburn Hospital in New South Wales. In 1839 he gave up medical practice and settled on a property that he called *Woden*, now a major suburb of Canberra. He was elected to the New South Wales Legislative Assembly in 1855 but died shortly afterwards.

When the parliamentary inquiry was announced in September 1859, Sydney University had 38 students, a large annual government subvention and allegedly low standards. Although the university had been set up as a secular institution, the senate had introduced by-laws that in effect imposed religious tests on certain students before they could be admitted to their degrees. John Hubert Plunkett, then vice-chancellor, welcomed the inquiry and was asked to join the committee, which he did.

The committee concluded that the University of Sydney had failed to fulfil the expectations held out for it by the public. The senate's priorities were questioned and especially its concentration on grand buildings modelled on those of the ancient institutions. It asked how the 'griffins, unicorns and other monstrous shapes which have been selected as decorations suitable for the university could possibly cultivate and improve the taste of colonial youth'. A scheme for the establishment of affiliated denominational colleges was condemned as a grievous mistake, unnecessary and a violation of the great principle of secular education; appointments to the senate on the basis of social position, not literary attainment, was questioned; as was the government grant being spent on buildings not yet needed, and which were 'on a scale of magnitude which in other parts of the world has almost invariably been the growth of ages'.

In his response to the findings, Provost Nicholson could only invite Sir Terence to 'go to the old country where he would find his aspirations and feelings powerfully affected by contemplation of the magnificent piles of buildings and other works of art to be found in the ancient institutions'. The cultivation of the mind rather than the transmission of useful knowledge was re-affirmed by Nicholson as the principal purpose of a university! 'We attempt', he said, 'to found the university here on the principle which is generally received at home, the ruling object in the examination for the BA degree being first to train the mind – not necessarily to give any large amount of information which would be immediately available.'

The response of the newspapers was to condemn the report itself for not going half far enough. Parkes's *Empire* claimed that the inquiry had condemned the university as an utter failure; a sham; a delusion and a swindle; and 'a monstrous plunder of the public conducted by a clique who had perpetuated the miserable snobbery of disfiguring the university building from top to bottom with their coats of arms', and who 'amused themselves by robbing the public purse to perpetuate abortions in stone which stamp us for ages to come as a set of vandals'. The Murray Report of 1859 was quietly shelved. It was not until the 1870s and 1880s that the university established the professional courses that might have allayed public anxiety about its expense and demonstrated its usefulness to society. By 1881, thirty years after the first meeting of the university senate, there were only fifteen teachers and one hundred and fifty students enrolled in the university. By then Melbourne University, as we shall see, was thriving, and Sydney lagged behind Melbourne right to the end of the century. In Melbourne, Trinity men were not only involved in the university's foundation but they were also key participants in the direction it took and in the creation of its international academic reputation.

CHAPTER 5

Van Diemen's Land

> *Many people go to court for no other purpose than the amusement afforded by the chairman.*
>
> **George Boyes (1826)**

Aspects of the Law

In response to fears that the French might colonise Van Diemen's Land, now Tasmania, the governor of New South Wales, Philip Gidley King, established a settlement there in 1804 under the command of David Collins, the former deputy judge advocate of New South Wales. Collins settled on the site of the present capital, Hobart, and remained there as lieutenant-governor until his death in 1810. He had earlier failed to establish a colony on the south end of Port Phillip Bay and the first law officer to be sent to Hobart, Samuel Bate, was intended for that new colony had Collins been successful. The appointment of Bate as the first deputy judge advocate of Van Diemen's Land continued the trend established in New South Wales, of total incompetents and misfits being appointed to legal positions. With no established courts, Bate could only function as a magistrate, and this he did very poorly. Governor Macquarie described him as 'much addicted to low company, totally ignorant of law, a very troublesome and ill-tempered man'. He was dismissed when a new charter of justice in 1814 established a Lieutenant-Governor's Court.

Edward Abbott, former soldier and magistrate in New South Wales, a man with 'a small knowledge of the law and large concern for the welfare of his own family', replaced Bate. Judged by Governor Macquarie to be very unequal to the duties of the position, Abbott often declared that he was no lawyer himself and 'would not bother with the law'. He served as deputy judge advocate, using convicts and emancipists to act for litigants in the absence of free attorneys, until the Supreme Court was established in 1824.

John Lewes Pedder, the first chief justice of the Supreme Court, was educated at Cambridge and was described in newspapers as 'a passionate, violent-tempered man who acted under the influence of an infirmity of temper to which he is unhappily – equally for himself and for the public over whom he is the highest minister of law – uncontrollably subjected'. In 1825, Van Diemen's Land was declared a separate colony with Sir George Arthur, 'one of the wiliest men that ever administered public affairs', installed as the first independent lieutenant-governor. Arthur was to become embroiled in many disputes, one of the most vindictive being that which involved the Irish contingent in Van Diemen's Land.

With the Supreme Court came the law officers. The first attorney-general, Joseph Tice Gellibrand, was both distrusted and disliked by Arthur and so he appointed Alfred Stephen as solicitor-general, to provide alternative advice. Arthur dismissed Gellibrand in 1826 for professional misconduct, including, in some cases, acting for both the plaintiff and defendant at different stages of the proceedings. We next encounter him in Port Phillip District.

In 1826, too, Joseph Hone, the first commissioner and chairman respectively of the newly established Courts of Requests and of Quarter Sessions, was appointed as acting attorney-general. Hone was an eccentric who waved his arms about and made diabolical faces in court to the amusement of the gallery, so that people went to the court just to enjoy the spectacle. Gilbert Robinson, editor of the *Colonist,* described Hone in his paper as 'universally looked-upon as only a few degrees removed from an idiot'. Yet he served as law officer in a variety or roles for thirty years. McCleland, Gellibrand's replacement, was clearly insane on his arrival in 1827 and quite unable to perform the duties of attorney-general, and Algernon Montagu was sent out to replace him. The law historian L.A.Whitfield says that with Montagu's arrival it was now a question as to who, out of the various legal or pseudo legal personages sent out from England, 'should take the palm' as the maddest of them all. Montagu arrived in 1828 and served as attorney-general until 1832, when he was elevated to the Bench. He was passionate and eccentric, hurled abuse at those who appeared before him, railed against journalists like the Irish McDowells, and quarrelled with the attorney-general, Alfred Stephen, with such fury that both were admonished by the Legislative Council. Montagu was told to be more guarded in his court behaviour and Stephen advised to show more respect towards the judge. Later, when Stephen was appointed to the Bench in Sydney, he explained his behaviour with respect to Montagu as due to a disease that made him excitable and unstable. Montagu was eventually removed from office in 1847 for using his position as judge to avoid paying his debts.

The general incompetence, disloyalty and eccentricity of the lawyers sent out to the colonies prompted Governor Ralph Darling in Sydney to call for respectable men to be sent out for service in New South Wales, including Van Diemen's Land. One of the first of these to arrive was John Hubert Plunkett, who, as we have seen, was appointed in 1832 as solicitor-general of New South Wales. The position had previously been offered to another Irishman, Edward McDowell, but he forfeited it when he failed to arrive within a reasonable time. McDowell was then offered the first solicitor-generalship of Van Diemen's Land and arrived on time in January 1833.

The First Solicitor-General

As far as we know, Edward McDowell (1798–1860) was the first Trinity-educated lawyer to set foot in Van Diemen's Land. McDowell entered Trinity in 1815 but did not graduate. Called to the Bar at Middle Temple in 1824, he practised on the English Midland Circuit until he left to take up the solicitor-generalship of Van Diemen's Land in 1832. Four years later he succeeded Alfred Stephen as attorney-general.

McDowell did not embellish Trinity's reputation as his contemporaries on the mainland had done. His brother Thomas, a reporter in London, joined him in 1839 as Editor of the *Hobart Courier*. Thomas adhered to the anti-government 'Arthur faction' to which his brother Edward had become close due to his marriage to the daughter of a leading member of the faction, banker Charles Swanston. The faction supported the conservative and rigorous administration of Lieutenant-Governor Arthur, who was replaced by Sir John Franklin in 1837. Sir John, who had endless difficulties with the faction, believed that Edward McDowell inspired his brother's articles against the Franklins and the government.

A dispute between Edward and his successor as solicitor-general, Herbert Jones, which raged through the pages of the rival newspapers, led to the downfall of both Jones and McDowell as law officers. They were both dismissed and for three years McDowell practised at the Bar, quite successfully. In 1845 he returned to government service as commissioner of the Insolvency Court and in 1851 he was appointed crown solicitor. Though he achieved high office, McDowell was not well regarded, and the close relationship he had with his brother was notorious for the dissension it created. The McDowells find their place in the history of Van Diemen's Land as men who wanted to defend what they considered to be the realistic, though conservative, policies of Sir George Arthur, which were being compromised in their eyes by a weaker Franklin. This view of Franklin came to be shared in London and he was recalled in 1843.

If Edward McDowell was a ruthless and ambitious intriguer, who brought little credit to his *alma mater*, the one other notable Trinity lawyer to achieve high office in Van Diemen's Land did quite the opposite. When Sir John Pedder, the first chief justice, retired in 1854, Governor Denison appointed Valentine Fleming to the post. Fleming (1809–84), the son of army captain Valentine Fleming of Tuam, County Galway, was educated in England and entered Trinity in 1829, graduating in 1832. He was called to the Bar in 1838 and two years later he migrated to Van Diemen's Land as commissioner of the Insolvent Debtors Court. He was soon promoted to solicitor-general. Both he and Thomas Horne, the attorney-general, provided legal advice to the governor and the Legislative Council on matters of considerable significance, especially in relation to the removal of errant judges. When Judge Montagu was dismissed in 1846, on advice from Horne and Fleming, Horne was promoted to the Bench and Fleming became attorney-general and member of the Legislative Council. In 1853 Fleming was appointed to a select committee established to draft a constitution for Tasmania in preparation for responsible government, and the *Constitution Bill* was passed a year later. Fleming played a prominent role in drawing up the committee's recommendations and in drafting the Bill.

On Pedder's retirement, Governor Denison preferred to appoint Fleming as chief justice over Horne despite the latter's experience as a judge and attorney-general. Denison believed that Horne's penchant for not paying his debts might compromise his independence as chief justice. There had been much criticism of Horne's appointment as a puisne judge when Montagu was dismissed in 1848, as it was not clear that Horne was much better than Montagu in relation to the management of his financial affairs. Denison's instincts were right. In 1860 Horne was up before the acting chief justice of Victoria, Robert Molesworth, in a lawsuit in which he was accused of exercising undue influence on a relative in the matter of a will. Molesworth found against him; and at the same time, Horne was accused of soliciting a loan from a plaintiff in a case to be heard by him. To avoid dismissal, Horne resigned.

Fleming's appointment as attorney-general was confirmed, despite protests

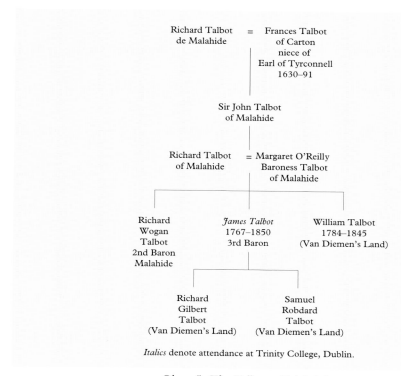

Chart 5. The Talbots of Malahide.

at the time by Horne and his supporters, and he was knighted shortly thereafter. He was, by then, the second Trinity-educated lawyer to be appointed as a chief justice in the Australian colonies and he served in the position until 1872, when he retired to England. Fleming was recalled to Tasmania, however, to be acting chief justice from 1872–74 during the absence on leave of his successor, and was also deputy-governor for a time. Fleming went again to England in 1874 and served as a magistrate for Surrey. On his retirement, expressions of esteem and appreciation of his care, courtesy and impartiality were made by the Tasmanian Bar and the Executive Council, celebrating no doubt that the colony was at last getting some honest lawyers.

Pastoral Pursuits

The first notable Irish family to settle in Van Diemen's Land with connections to Trinity were the Talbots of Malahide. William Talbot (1784–1845) arrived in 1820 and received a grant of two thousand acres assigned to him on the basis of the significant capital he had brought with him. William was the youngest son of Richard Talbot of *Malahide Castle* near Dublin and his wife Margaret O'Reilly, the first Baroness Talbot of Malahide, who belonged to the ancient Milesian House of Breffny. The Talbots were one of the oldest and most distinguished of the old English families in Ireland, having occupied the family seat at Malahide continuously from 1174.

The earliest Talbot recorded as having attended Trinity is Richard, grandson of Sir William Talbot of Malahide, who entered in 1596, four years after the foundation of the College. Few Talbots subsequently attended Trinity or took an interest in it, but one who did was Richard, Earl of Tyrconnell (1630–91). The fellows might have wished that he had not, however, for it was he who turned them out in 1698 to make way for his cavalry, and he treated them quite cruelly. In her history of Trinity College, Constantia Maxwell tells of the conditions endured by the fellows and others who were confined in the College prior to expulsion, and which were recorded by William King, Dean of St Patrick's Cathedral thus: 'September 27th 1698 – Mr Pierson came up and gave us an account of his confinement in the College, "yt he had bin clapt up before and bailed but yet was taken again. Twenty of ym were put into ye same room without fire or beds and yt powder was laid in the room under ym and they were told yt if they stirred they should be blown up".'

Tyrconnell installed Michael Moore, a Jesuit priest, as provost and, as already mentioned, it was he who persuaded the troops not to burn down the Library with its precious Ussher collection and *Book of Kells*. Tyrconnell fought for James II at the Battle of the Boyne and his wife has become famous for her response to the King following his defeat at the hands of William of Orange in 1690. Complaining to her in Dublin after the battle about the readiness of her husband's battalions to flee, Lady Tyrconnell reminded him of the fact that he had arrived in Dublin before them.

Two main branches of the Talbot family were united with the marriage of Tyrconnell's niece, Frances, to Richard Talbot of Malahide, and it is from those Talbots of Malahide that the Tasmanian pioneer William is descended (see Chart 5, p.89). William's brother James (1767–1850) entered Trinity in 1788 and went to the Bar, inheriting the title and estates in 1849. Two of James's sons, Richard Gilbert Talbot and Samuel Robdard Talbot, joined William in Tasmania to work the family estates.

William Talbot undertook a three year grand tour of Europe and the Middle East before migrating to Van Diemen's Land. Even though his grant of land was moved to another location by a vindictive Governor Arthur, he prospered in what is known as the Fingal region. Samuel Robdard Talbot inherited the

Tasmanian *Malahide* on William's death in 1845 but he, too, returned to Ireland in 1850 and the estate, by now some forty thousand acres, was managed by Richard Gilbert Talbot, who stayed and was appointed as a member of the Legislative Council in 1852.

The Bryan Complex

The Talbots were clearly influential in persuading others to go to Van Diemen's Land, including Samuel Bryan (1794–1862), member of a family whose estates in Spring Valley, County Meath, adjoined the Winters' in Agher. In his application to the Colonial Office in 1822, Bryan had stated that he wished to join his 'friend Mr Talbot' in Van Diemen's Land. His brother William arrived in Van Diemen's Land two years later with a letter of recommendation from Colonel Talbot of *Malahide Castle*. Samuel Bryan, one of four sons to be educated in Trinity, entered the College in 1811 and graduated in 1816. On his arrival in Van Diemen's Land, Samuel was granted two thousand acres of land and prospered. He persuaded the great pioneering Henty family to move their enterprises from Western Australia to Van Diemen's Land and consolidated his position by marrying Jane, daughter of Thomas Henty.

When William joined his brother in 1824, he suffered a delay of nearly a year in obtaining a grant of one thousand acres from Governor Arthur, who appeared to have no affection for the Talbots or the Bryans. By 1831 William had acquired eleven thousand acres and significant businesses, but then his troubles began with the governor and the inimitable Judge Montagu. Bryan had many convict servants and, because of a shortage of free settlers who might become tenant farmers, he entered into questionable share-farming agreements with at least two of them. It was also alleged by his neighbours that he allowed his servants to collect wild cattle, some of which belonged to them. Cattle duffing – the changing of brands or branding of unmarked neighbours' cattle – was still a capital offence, since Van Diemen's Land was considered a penal colony by the authorities. The Bryans and the Talbots regarded the colony not as a prison but as a rich resource and opportunity for them to become landed proprietors. When the allegations of illegal practices were brought to Arthur's attention it seemed to him that the very foundations of the penal colony were being threatened.

One of Bryan's neighbours was William Thomas Lyttleton, a *poseur* who claimed to be related to Lord Lyttleton of Hagley Hall in Worcestershire. He called his property *Hagley* and used the Lyttleton crest. He also claimed to be an army captain whereas he did not proceed beyond lieutenant. Lyttleton's daughter, Maria, married Robert Rowland Davies, a Trinity graduate of 1827 and a descendant of Rowland Davies, Dean of Cork and chaplain to the Williamite army at the Battle of the Boyne and the Siege of Limerick. Davies was eventually to become Anglican Archdeacon of Hobart Town. Lyttleton's Irish connections did not prevent him from improperly impugning the reputation of William Bryan, following a trial in 1833 in which one of Bryan's convict servants, Samuel Arnold, was before the court for cattle stealing. The trial was conducted by Judge Montagu and Arnold was found guilty. On passing sentence of death, the erratic judge commented that he was surprised the master was not also in the dock. After the trial, Lyttleton expressed a similar view outside the court and the hot-headed Bryan sent his friend Thomas Lewis to Lyttleton to demand an explanation. When none was forthcoming, Lewis issued a challenge to a duel on behalf of Bryan. Lyttleton, despite his claim to be a gentleman, refused the challenge and reported Lewis to the attorney-general, who indicted him for inciting a breach of the peace. At the trial, at which he represented himself, Lewis was warned by Montagu that he would be fined every time he made an irrelevant statement. When Lewis then made what Montagu considered to be an unwarranted statement about another case, he was immediately fined £10. In the light of Montagu's behaviour Lewis was quite unable to conduct his defence; he was found guilty, sentenced to eighteen months gaol and fined £150. Lewis referred his case to the secretary of state, as a result of which Montagu's extraordinary behaviour was censured, Lewis was released, and he received compensation for wrongful imprisonment.

Meanwhile, Bryan had written to Arthur resigning as magistrate, since he would no longer sit on the Bench with Lyttleton. Arthur refused to accept the resignation, instead sacking Bryan and attempting to ruin him by withdrawing all of his convict labour at harvest and shearing time. Arthur had a reputation for vindictiveness and for being relentless in the pursuit of those who had offended him. His technique of waiting patiently until he had enough evidence against his opponents and then acting against them was known as 'Colonel Arthur's hellish system of getting up cases'. Bryan considered that in his particular case the vindictiveness was stimulated by a successful appeal he had made to the secretary of state when Arthur refused to grant him additional lands. Insulted by his sacking as magistrate, Bryan instituted proceedings for defamation and conspiracy against Lyttleton, applying for the case to be heard in Hobart, where Lyttleton had no control over jury lists. His application failed and he abandoned the suit. His convict servant Arnold and other convict servants made depositions, which supposedly revealed that for three years Bryan had conspired with them in cattle duffing, sharing the proceeds with them and with his nephew Robert Bryan. Arnold's sentence of death was, as a result, commuted. Bryan protested his and his nephew's innocence and decided to proceed to London to seek redress and to conduct a campaign for Arthur's recall. He left for England in November 1834, never to return. His nephew Robert Bryan was indicted for cattle stealing before Chief Justice Pedder. Robert, uneducated, illegitimate son of Bryan's brother Richard, a clergyman in Ireland, was found guilty and sentenced to death, but family influence ensured that the sentence was commuted and Robert served six years at Port Arthur prison. Arthur was recalled in 1836 and it is claimed that this was due to the campaign against his administration mounted by Bryan and others. Parliament did formally hear the complaints and they may have contributed to the recall, but on his return to London Arthur was completely cleared of any misdemeanour by the colonial secretary. The case has become known in the legal history of Van Diemen's Land as the 'Bryan Complex'.

The Pratt Winters of Murndal

As William Bryan was preparing to leave for England, Samuel Pratt Winter, the descendant of the two Trinity provosts (see Chart 2, p.40), had already arrived in Hobart, sent out from County Meath by his uncle and guardian Francis Pratt Winter. Samuel was named after his father, who graduated from Trinity in 1800 (see Chapter 3), was sent to England after graduation to work as an assistant in business, and by 1808 had returned ill and without the £3000 capital he had been given. The subject of our interest, Samuel Pratt Winter, the third of eight children, was sent to school in Yorkshire, and while there his father and mother died in Dublin within one month of each other. Whereas his brother George as well as his father and uncles had all studied at Trinity, Samuel was unable to proceed beyond school. Entrusted to the care of his uncle, the Rev Francis Pratt Winter, it was soon clear that young Samuel would have to emigrate. He was sent out to William Bryan in Van Diemen's Land in 1834 with considerable capital, as a down payment on his inheritance. Bryan was, of course, embroiled in his dispute with Governor Arthur and left for England only five months after Samuel's arrival. With William Bryan gone, his overseer Robert Bryan in gaol, and Samuel Bryan engaged in his own pursuits with the Hentys and on his Van Diemen's Land estate, Samuel Winter was able to gain valuable experience in operating a large property. He might have gained this experience at home had the inheritors of *Agher* and *Garradice*, the Winter and Pratt estates respectively, been successful in keeping them profitable. After three years of successful operation of the Bryan holdings, Samuel's brother Trevor joined him; and in 1839 Trinity-educated George arrived with his sister Arabella, who had insisted on emigrating despite opposition from the family.

In 1837 Samuel, inspired by the Hentys, decided to move to the Victorian mainland and he established himself first at Portland Bay with a small flock of merino sheep and then moved north to the Wannon River, in the fine country of the Western District of Victoria. The Aborigines called the area *Tahara* and that is the name Winter chose for the land he and Trevor occupied in partnership with George. His move to *Tahara* was only made possible when he received further funding from Ireland, sent out with his nephew, Benjamin Pratt Winter.

Benjamin (1808–44), who graduated from Trinity in 1832, had been appointed as deputy surveyor for the South Australian Land Company and arrived in 1838. He decided to take up a pastoral run in the Wannon region in 1843 but after only a year on the property he called *Norbury* he became ill and died at the age of thirty-six. The disposition of Ben's estate on his early death

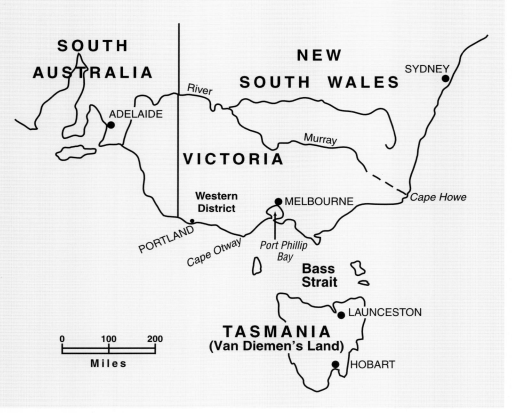

Figure 17. Van Diemen's Land and the Western District of Victoria.

was to be the cause of an estrangement between the brothers, Samuel and George, and this resulted in the division of the property, with George retaining a part that he continued to call *Tahara* and Samuel taking possession of Spring Valley, which later became *Murndal*, the Aboriginal name for the area where Samuel chose to build his homestead in 1848. Leaving *Murndal* in the charge of his station manager, Samuel travelled widely, to North and South America and to Europe, where he began his collection of paintings, many of them copies of masterpieces, and he also built up a large library. He returned to *Murndal* in 1854, acquired the freehold to almost twenty thousand acres and licensed a further twenty thousand. The *Murndal* homestead was extended and beautified with acres of trees, including cypresses from seeds brought from Italy. *Murndal* was long considered to be one of the most beautiful places in the Western District. In 1839 Arabella Pratt Winter married Cecil Pybus Cooke and *Murndal* is still in the hands of the Winter Cooke family. A copy of Samuel Winter's portrait (see Fig. 6, p 37) hangs in the *Murndal* homestead.

CHAPTER 6

Fostering in this Land of Victoria

> There are too many Fosters fostering and festering in this Victorian land.
>
> **Raffaelo Carboni (1853)**

Settlement

The fear of encroachment by other powers on unoccupied parts of the Australian continent led not only to the establishment of a settlement in Van Diemen's Land but also to the extension of settlement to the Port Phillip District of New South Wales, later to become the colony of Victoria. In April 1802 Matthew Flinders, who had circumnavigated the continent in the *Investigator*, had encountered the French ship *Geographie* under the command of Nicholas Baudin in the subsequently named Encounter Bay, located at the mouth of the Murray River near present-day Adelaide. Though Baudin was on a purely scientific mission, it was not unreasonable for the British to assume that his discoveries would be relayed to Paris, then at war with Britain. A record of Baudin's voyage published in France showed the coast of Australia from Port Phillip District to the head of the Great Australian Bight as *Terre Napoleon*. In 1800 the brig *Lady Nelson* had been sent out from England under the command of James Grant to assist in the work of exploration being undertaken by Flinders and she passed through Bass Strait going east, observing the opening at the head of Port Phillip Bay. The *Lady Nelson* was sent to further explore this inlet and in February 1802 the little ship sailed into Port Phillip Bay. The Union Jack was duly hoisted on land at the southerly end of the bay on 8 March 1802, proclaiming possession on behalf of King George III.

Encouraged by reports on the quality of the soil along the shores of Port Phillip Bay, Lieutenant-Colonel David Collins arrived in 1803 with a company of three hundred including marines, administrators and convicts. He did not attempt to penetrate the great bay but landed at its mouth. He was not impressed. 'Every day's experience', he said, 'convinces me that it cannot nor ever will be resorted to by speculative men'. Ironically one of Melbourne's principal streets is now named in honour of Collins. He was permitted to abandon the little colony in June 1804, moving the whole company to a site in Van Diemen's Land where Hobart is now located. The area around Port Phillip remained unsettled until 1834 when the Hentys and Samuel Bryan chartered the schooner *Thistle* in Launceston, filled it with livestock and all kinds of implements and set out to establish the first permanent settlement in the Western District of what is now Victoria. They were the first 'squatters', occupiers of Crown lands without title.

In 1834, too, John Batman, convict's son born in 1801, and Joseph Tice Gellibrand, the dismissed attorney-general of Van Diemen's Land, landed in the northerly extreme of Port Phillip Bay. In an impressive looking 'treaty' drawn up by Gellibrand, Batman and his syndicate purported to buy from the local Aboriginal tribes an area of six hundred thousand acres in exchange for a quantity of blankets, looking glasses, clothing, knives and flour. When Batman presented his treaty to Governor Bourke, he hoped 'that the British Government will duly appreciate the treaty I have made with these tribes and will not molest the arrangements I have made'. Bourke not only molested the arrangements by repudiating the 'treaty' but he issued a proclamation that declared Batman and his syndicate to be trespassers on crown land. A short time later, on an expedition into the bush, Gellibrand was killed by Aborigines.

Batman had taken his ship's boat up the river situated at the head of Port Phillip Bay to a point where Melbourne now stands. 'This will be a place for a village', he wrote, and marked on his charts the spot to be 'reserved for a township and other purposes'. Meanwhile, another party under the command of John Pascoe Fawkner sailed in the *Enterprize* from Van Diemen's Land and this signalled the beginning of sustained settlement in the Port Phillip District. By May 1836, when Bourke sent a police magistrate to assess the situation, there were one hundred and seventy seven settlers with more than twenty five thousand sheep on land around the township. They were occupying their lands illegally and in that rough settlement it soon became apparent that there was a need for the establishment of official law and order.

In August 1836 Bourke sent Captain William Lonsdale of the 4th King's Own Regiment to Port Phillip District. Lonsdale sailed from Sydney on the frigate HMS *Rattlesnake* under the command of Captain William Hobson, who was born in Waterford in 1793, the son of a Trinity family. His father, Samuel Hobson, entered Trinity in 1767 and went to the Irish Bar in 1778. His brother, Richard Jones Hobson, graduated from Trinity in 1806, subsequently becoming Archdeacon of Waterford. William, however, entered the navy in 1806 and after his sojourn in Port Phillip he was sent to New Zealand. There he was appointed British consul in 1838 and lieutenant-governor in 1840. He persuaded some fifty Maori chiefs of the North Island to sign the famous treaty of Waitangi by which, in return for British protection, the chiefs signed over the lands to Queen Victoria. When New Zealand separated from New South Wales Hobson became its first governor. The Melbourne suburb of Williamstown, named by Bourke in honour of William IV, is situated on Hobson's Bay, which commemorates the name and achievements of William Hobson.

Captain Lonsdale, the first law officer to arrive in Port Phillip District, was to take general superintendence in the new settlement of all such matters as required the immediate exercise of the authority of the government. He also exercised the ordinary functions of resident magistrate and his conduct of the law was much like that exercised by a military court, dispensing justice and punishment, accompanied by a soldier and a 'scourger'. The first practising solicitor, a William Meek, arrived in 1838, by which time the settlement had grown to a population of fifteen hundred. Bourke had already visited the Port Phillip District in 1837 and named the village Melbourne after the then British Prime Minister. Lonsdale administered the little colony until 1839, when the superintendent of the District of Port Phillip in the colony of New South Wales, Charles La Trobe, arrived. In the same year, John Hubert Plunkett, the attorney-general of New South Wales, proposed to Governor Bourke that, as the new settlement at Port Phillip was 'almost without the pale of law', it would be necessary to add a fourth judge to the Bench of the Supreme Court of New South Wales so that one would be available for the holding of assizes twice a year at Port Phillip. Bourke gave the proposal his support but the appointment of a fourth judge was not approved by the Colonial Office. Instead, a Court of Quarter Sessions was established in 1839 with Dr Edward Jones Brewster as its first chairman. Trinity's extraordinary connection with the Bench and the Bar in Victoria had commenced.

The Early Bar

Edward Jones Brewster (1812–98) entered Trinity in 1830, graduated in 1835 and was called to the Irish Bar. As he recalled later, he frequently had time on his hands, which he occupied in reading at the magnificent library at Trinity. 'One day', he says, 'while so engaged – doubtless by providential direction – I took up a book, lately published by Mr William McArthur, of Camden, New South Wales, giving a most favourable account of Australia'. Brewster noted in particular that Macarthur's book pointed to good openings for barristers. The overstocked condition of the Irish Bar persuaded Brewster that he should go but the final decision was not made until he had consulted with his uncle, Anthony Brewster, QC, soon to be Lord Chancellor of Ireland. With positive advice from his uncle and armed with recommendation from his uncle and letters of introduction to Plunkett, Brewster set sail on the *Alfred*.

His travelling companions were Sir Francis Forbes, chief justice of New South Wales, Richard Gilbert Talbot, third son of Lord Talbot of Malahide, and James Graham from Ennis, who was to have a distinguished career as pastoralist and politician in Sydney. Brewster landed in Sydney in September 1838 and presented his letters of introduction to Plunkett, who, in consultation with the new Governor Gipps, appointed him as chairman of the Court of

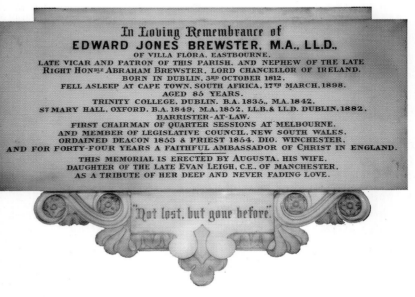

Figure 18. Memorial tablet to Dr Edward Jones Brewster.

Quarter Sessions in Port Phillip District. One year after the court began its work a Court of Requests with jurisdiction up to £10 was established, and Brewster was appointed as the first commissioner of that court, as well. He held the two posts until 1841, when the appointment of a resident judge to deal with Port Phillip District cases was approved. Brewster's chairmanship of the Court of Quarter Sessions became a part of the resident judge's responsibilities, leaving Brewster as commissioner of the Court of Requests. He was notable for his severe judgements and was frustrated especially by the administration's inability to accommodate bankrupts in gaol, forcing their release. He resigned from his position in late 1841 to practise at the Bar, and to engage successfully in land speculation. When reforms were made to the New South Wales Legislative Council in 1843 Brewster was elected as one of the six members for Port Phillip District of the Colony of New South Wales. During his time as a member of the Legislative Council Brewster introduced Bills to simplify the legal process and reduce costs: to simplify conveyancing so that educated legal clerks could effect the sale of property; to make solicitors provide bills of costs; and to facilitate recovery of property from defaulting tenants. Notably, and for this he is remembered in the annals of the law in New South Wales, he introduced a Bill to amalgamate the professions of barrister and solicitor. He was supported strongly by the powerful politician Robert Lowe, who later became chancellor of the Exchequer in England, but he did not get the support of William Wentworth and the Bill failed. A Bill similar to Brewster's was passed in Victoria in 1891. In 1853, considering that he had 'finished his course in Australia', Brewster returned to England, where he was ordained as a clergyman of the Church of England by the Bishop of Winchester in 1853. He became curate at St Helens, Isle of Wight, and eventually vicar of the parish church at Leyton, Essex, where a memorial in the Church remembers him. Trinity admitted him to the degree of LL.B and LL.D in 1882 and on his death the *Times* gave him the credit for laying the foundation stone on the first bridge over Melbourne's River Yarra.

Edward Brewster was the first barrister to arrive in Melbourne and it was not long before he was joined by three others from Ireland, two of whom, James Croke and Redmond Barry, were educated at Trinity. They arrived in 1839. James Croke, born in 1794, entered Trinity in 1817 and practised on the Munster Circuit for eighteen years before deciding to emigrate. He was selected to be the first crown prosecutor for Port Phillip District and standing legal advisor to the government representative there. He subsequently presided over the Court of Requests, was appointed as member of the Legislative Council and was solicitor-general of Victoria. Croke was a man of great independence of spirit and he clashed more than once with the resident judge. He exhibited fiery characteristics even before he arrived in Melbourne. In the Court of Petty Sessions in Limerick he had dissented loudly and vigorously from a ruling by the magistrates, was placed in the dock and invited to apologise for his candid views about the ruling. Forced to apologise, the standing of Croke and his family was such that the Lord Chancellor was informed and the magistrates involved were rebuked. The magistrates' response to the reprimand was apparently quite libellous and Croke sued. His case was heard before the Lord Chief Justice and Croke won a large sum in damages. In Melbourne Croke's appearances before the irascible Judge Willis were always noteworthy.

When Brewster resigned he was succeeded as commissioner of the Court of Requests by Redmond Barry from County Cork. Barry, who accompanied Croke on the journey to Sydney and Melbourne, revealed his Trinity origins when he called the Court of Requests his 'Little-go', a term used in Trinity to denote the compulsory examination at the end of the second undergraduate year. An ordeal for some, and an irritating obstacle for others on their way to the final 'moderatorship' examination for the BA degree, Little-go was abolished in 1952.

As noted, Bourke and Plunkett favoured an addition to the Bench in Sydney specifically for the Port Phillip jurisdiction, but they wanted the judge to be resident in Sydney to preside over the Port Phillip district cases as well as undertaking specified duties attaching to the role in Sydney. The fourth judge was approved but not for residence in Sydney. Bourke and Plunkett had in mind the appointment of John Kinchela, the attorney-general who was, of course, hard of hearing. But the need to get rid of John Walpole Willis, then judge of the Supreme Court of New South Wales, was more pressing. Gipps, Bourke's successor, made no secret of the reasons for foisting this judge on the Port Phillip District. 'Willis', he said, 'was afflicted with an infirmity of temper which goes far to unfit him for the calm and dispassionate administration of justice'. Gipps simply wanted to put an end to the dissension that had arisen on the Bench in Sydney as a result of Willis's irascibility.

In order to enforce the orders of the new 'Supreme Court' in Melbourne, Samuel Raymond, Trinity graduate and son of the colonial postmaster-general in Sydney, was appointed as deputy sheriff of the Court. Raymond served in this role for one year before entering practice in the country districts and then returning to Sydney as protonotary of the Supreme Court there. He was born in Limerick in 1808 and graduated in 1830. In 1837 he was admitted to the Trinity LL.B and LL.D degrees. Willis and Raymond arrived in Melbourne in

March 1841 and at the first sitting of the Supreme Court Redmond Barry, Edward Jones Brewster, James Croke, Archibald Cunninghame and R.W.Pohlman were admitted as the first five barristers. In the following year William Foster Stawell was admitted and the local Bar was dominated by Trinity men. A new courthouse was commissioned for Willis but by the time it was finished in 1843 he had been removed from office. The acoustics were so poor that witnesses could hardly be heard, even when a large curtain was hung on the wall behind the judge and the timber ceiling perforated to reduce echoes off the high stone walls. Ned Kelly was tried before Barry in this court in 1880 and it is suggested that the conflicting accounts of his exchanges with Barry were due to the inability of the reporters to hear the exact words said. In 1884 the present Supreme Court, which took some of its features from the Four Courts in Dublin, was commissioned and architects Smith and Johnston kept an illustration of the Dublin building in their office.

The Resident Judges

The first resident judge, John Wilberforce Willis, was educated at Trinity Hall Cambridge and appointed as judge of the Supreme Court of Upper Canada in 1827. He was removed from office there following a dispute with the governor and then received a judicial appointment in British Guiana. He arrived in Sydney in 1838 as puisne judge of the Supreme Court and friction immediately developed between him, Chief Justice Dowling and everyone who had anything to do with administration of the law. Sydney's problems were, of course, resolved by his appointment in Melbourne in 1841. When he and his wife went to Melbourne they took with them two horses, a goat, a dog and forty-three tons of possessions. The colonial treasurer queried the cost but it was gladly paid by Governor Gipps. He was only too pleased to be rid of the difficult judge.

The erratic and explosive behaviour of Judge Willis is legendary in the annals of the Victorian Bench. Edmund Finn, chronicler of early Melbourne who wrote under the pseudonym 'Garryowen', had this to say about Wills: 'Such was his irascibility and so often was the court a scene for unseemly squabbles that people who had no business there attended to see the fun for, as there was no theatre in town, Judge Willis was as good as a play'. The diarist, George Boyes, of course, had written in similar terms about Joseph Hone in Van Diemen's Land some ten years before. By May 1843 four different 'memorials' had been sent to Gipps seeking Willis's recall. On being offended by Willis in court, Crown Prosecutor Croke bowed to the Bench and left the court followed by all the barristers. A manifesto supporting Croke was drawn up by the barristers, which paid tribute to his upholding the dignity of the court and Willis's failure to do so. Willis's response was typical: the court could get on very well without any barristers at all. The last straw was Willis's treatment of prominent businessman J.B.Were, whom he accused of prevarication as a witness. To help Were's memory, Willis gave him two months imprisonment. When Were protested at the injustice being done to him he received another month. By the end of the court proceedings Were had been sentenced to six months imprisonment in all. Bailed, he complained to the Executive Council in Sydney and Willis was summarily removed from office. Willis left for London in July 1843 to lodge an appeal with the Privy Council and a barrister from Sydney, William Jeffcott, replaced him.

William Jeffcott (1800–55), the second resident judge, was born in Tralee, entered Trinity in 1821, and was called to the Irish Bar in 1828. He practised at the Bar and acted as legal counsel to the Dublin Castle administration before setting out for Sydney in 1843. Within weeks of his arrival Gipps sent him to the Port Phillip District as Willis's replacement. Jeffcott arrived in Melbourne as Willis was leaving, to be greeted by newspaper reports of his brother John's misfortunes, of which we shall hear more later. The newspapers described William Jeffcott as a vast improvement on Willis. 'Court business is no longer a series of gratuitous farces for public amusement', wrote the *Argus*. 'From a beer garden it has become a decent balanced place.' However, when Jeffcott learned that Willis had appealed against his removal from office he became very concerned. Fearing that the appeal might succeed, and that his judgements therefore might be subject to appeal – too late for capital punishments already carried out – Jeffcott resigned. His fears were not shared by La Trobe, Gipps or anyone else and, in the event, though Willis's appeal was upheld he was not re-instated and no appeals against Jeffcott's judgements were made. Jeffcott returned to Dublin to practise and in 1849 he was knighted and appointed as recorder in Singapore and Malacca. In 1855 he was appointed to the Bench in Bombay but died before he could assume office.

The third resident judge was Roger Therry, whose family history has been traced in the discussion on the law in New South Wales. Recommended to La Trobe as a well-disposed man and, 'though an Irishman and a Catholic, discreet and moderate', he arrived in Melbourne in July 1845 to what was described as the coldest reception experienced by any public officer under similar circumstances. Succeeding the popular Jeffcott, Therry overcame the prejudices against him and when he left the district in 1846 the Bar regretted 'the loss of a judge whose assiduity in the unaided discharge of his duties has upheld the dignity of the Bench and whose extreme urbanity of deportment, invariable courtesy and considerable attention to the members of the Bar, have rendered less difficult the discharge of their professional labours.'

When he left the district to take a seat on the New South Wales Bench Therry was replaced by William a'Beckett and it is ironic that, like Plunkett, Therry took a step that would deny him the opportunity to become chief justice. William a'Beckett was the last resident judge to be appointed to the Port Phillip District. Born in London, he was called to the English Bar in 1829 and, possibly because of his lack of success at the Bar, he migrated to Sydney in 1837. By 1841 he had assumed the role of acting solicitor-general followed by acting judge in 1843. The Colonial Office refused to confirm his appointment to the New South Wales Bench and suggested that he transfer to Melbourne as resident judge. Therry in his *Recollections* claimed that he and a'Beckett agreed to exchange jobs and this is possibly the case. William a'Beckett served as resident judge from 1844 until the separation of Port Phillip from the colony of New South Wales in 1851, when he became the new colony of Victoria's first chief justice, a position he held until 1856 when ill health forced him to retire. William Foster Stawell succeeded him.

The Irish Cousinage

William Foster Stawell was a key member of a highly influential group of Victorian Anglo-Irish, linked by blood, marriage, upbringing, religion, friendship and business partnerships, which became known as 'the Irish cousinage'. Many were educated at Trinity or came from families who had a long association with the College. The Fosters and the Stawells were post-Cromwellian settlers in Ireland who intermarried with the old English Burghs, one of whom, Thomas Burgh, surveyor-general of Ireland, was the architect of Trinity's Library. As Chart 6 pp.108–9, shows, there were two branches of the Burghs, the Bert branch deriving from William Burgh, accountant-general of Ireland, and the Oldtown branch, which has Thomas Burgh at its head. We shall consider each branch in turn.

The first cousinage members to arrive in Australia were James Moore and Charles Griffith. Moore (1807–95), son of George Moore, QC, and MP for Dublin City, claimed descent from Garret Moore, first Viscount Moore of Drogheda, whose son Charles married Alice, the youngest daughter of Sir Adam Loftus. By 1725 the Moores had acquired all the Loftus estates in Rathfarnham, near Dublin, by further intermarriage. James Moore graduated from Trinity in 1828 and then spent twelve years studying and travelling in Europe. Admitted to the English Bar in 1840 he did not practise but went immediately to Melbourne with Charles Griffith. It is said that he was also a

Figure 19. Walter Hussey Burgh, Chief Baron of the Irish Exchequer and ancestor of Irish Cousinage in Victoria.

friend of Redmond Barry and William Stawell, contemporaries of his at Trinity. Moore, an enthusiastic colonist, encouraged Stawell and others to join him. He quickly formed a partnership with Griffith in a pastoral station, which they named *Glenmore* and, in 1842, together with Molesworth Greene and Griffith, explored the Portland Bay region where others had already found lush pastoral lands. Nothing came of this expedition.

Moore subsequently sold his interest in Glenmore to Griffith and later, troubled by all the changes taking place as a result of the 1850s gold rush, he returned to England to study theology at Caius College, Cambridge. The clerical life did not appear to suit him, however, for in 1856 he returned to Victoria, where he acquired more pastoral stations. He became comptroller of the Melbourne Savings Bank, where his business acumen came to the fore, as he took the bank to become one of the world's leading savings banks. Moore was related by marriage to Acheson French (see Chart 3, p.47), who settled on a property adjacent to the Winters in the Western District of Victoria, and French, in turn, was related to William Smith O'Brien and the Gwynns. Moore's brother John, who graduated from Trinity in 1824, became proctor in the Ecclesiastical Courts in Victoria and assistant colonial secretary. As the latter, he signed the proclamation that raised official alarm at the events unfolding in Ballarat prior to the Eureka Stockade uprising (see Fig.24, p.123).

Moore's friend Charles Griffith (1808–63) was the doyen of the Irish cousinage. He was the fifth son of Richard Griffith, MP for Kildare, and Mary Hussey Burgh, daughter of Walter Hussey Burgh, chief baron of the Irish Exchequer, whose portrait hangs in Trinity's Dining Hall. As Chart 6, pp.108–9 shows, the Burghs were of that powerful Norman family that gave rise to so many of the Irish cousinage. Charles Griffith graduated from Trinity in 1829, one year after Moore, and was admitted to the Irish Bar. He migrated with Moore in 1840 and, after Moore sold his share of *Glenmore* to him, Griffith went into partnership with his nephew Molesworth Greene. During this time Griffith kept a diary, which presents a valuable insight into contemporary Melbourne society; and while on his pastoral lease he also wrote a guide for intending migrants, which was published in Dublin during a visit he made there in 1845. On separation of the Port Phillip District from New South Wales in 1851, Griffith entered politics as a nominee to the new Legislative Council. Two years later he became an elected member, serving as commissioner and later president of the Sewerage and Water Supply Commission. He was a high Tory: adopting a severe attitude towards the miners in their quest for relief from the tyranny of the licence system; favouring an Irish-style aristocracy where the nobility would sit in the upper house; and advocating state aid for religious and country schools, protection of squatters' licences, and representation of particular interest groups rather than of the population in parliament. In 1856 Griffith was defeated for the speakership of the Legislative Assembly by fellow Trinity man (Sir) Francis Murphy. Deeply religious, Griffith helped persuade his cousin, Hussey Burgh Macartney, another key member of the Irish cousinage, to emigrate from Ireland to Melbourne. Griffith helped found the Melbourne Church of England Grammar School and his devotion to the Anglican cause was rewarded when Bishop Perry appointed him chancellor of the Melbourne Diocese. He resigned from parliament in 1858 to visit England and on his return he became the chairman of the Common Schools Board and commissioner of Land Titles.

Griffith's cousin, Hussey Burgh Macartney (1799–1894), was the son of Sir James Macartney and Catherine Hussey Burgh, another daughter of Walter

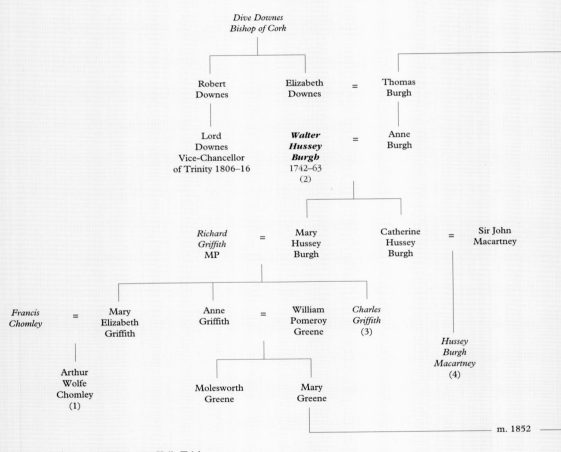

Dive Downes
Bishop of Cork

Robert
Downes

Elizabeth
Downes = Thomas
Burgh

Lord
Downes
Vice-Chancellor
of Trinity 1806–16

Walter
Hussey
Burgh
1742–63
(2) = Anne
Burgh

Richard
Griffith
MP = Mary
Hussey
Burgh

Catherine
Hussey
Burgh = Sir John
Macartney

Francis
Chomley = Mary
Elizabeth
Griffith

Anne
Griffith = William
Pomeroy
Greene

Charles
Griffith
(3)

Hussey
Burgh
Macartney
(4)

Arthur
Wolfe
Chomley
(1)

Molesworth
Greene

Mary
Greene

m. 1852

(1) Prosecutor, Kelly Trial

(2) Chief Baron Irish Exchequer

(3) Pastoralist, politician

(4) Dean of Melbourne

Italics denote attendance at Trinity College, Dublin.

Chart 6. The Burgh–Foster Families.

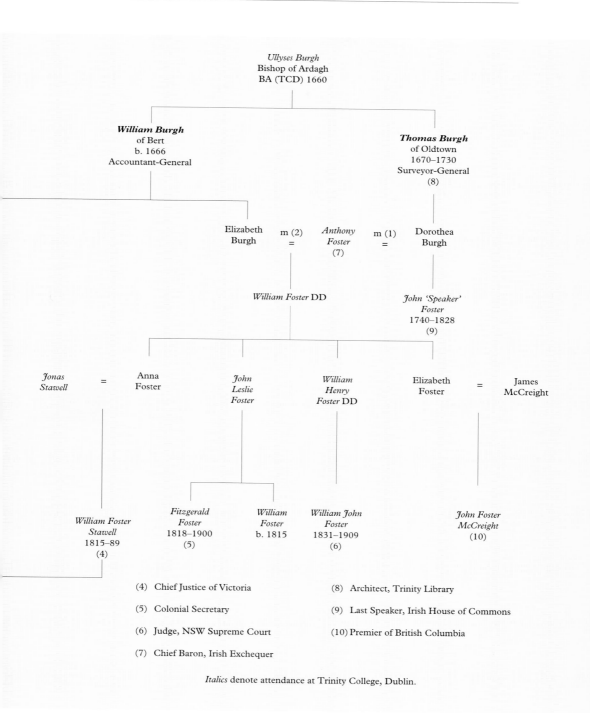

Chart 6. The Burgh–Foster Families.

Figure 20. Hussey Burgh Macartney, Anglican Dean of Melbourne.

Hussey Burgh. He graduated BA from Trinity in 1821 and was admitted DD in 1847. Because of ill health he needed to live in a warmer climate and when Griffith persuaded him to go to Melbourne he sailed in 1848 on the *Stag* with the party of John Perry, the newly appointed Bishop of Melbourne. In 1852 he became dean of Melbourne and eventually served as vicar-general. He refused the bishopric of Melbourne when Perry retired in 1876, on the grounds that he was too old, but he carried on as administrator of the Diocese in between bishops until he was eighty. Active in founding Melbourne's St Paul's Cathedral, Macartney died in 1894 at the age of ninety-five. In good cousinage tradition his son Edward married Georgina Moore, daughter of James Moore.

The Browns and the Greens

The Macartney and Griffith families belonged to the Bert side of the Burgh family. They were related by marriage to the Browns and the Greens, and by

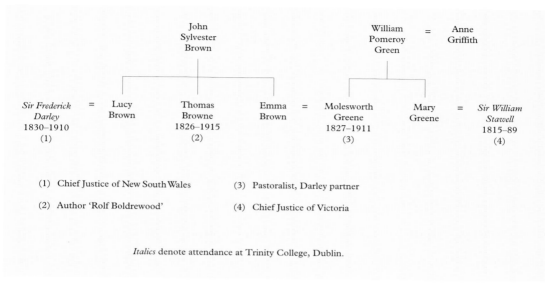

(1) Chief Justice of New South Wales   (3) Pastoralist, Darley partner

(2) Author 'Rolf Boldrewood'   (4) Chief Justice of Victoria

Italics denote attendance at Trinity College, Dublin.

Chart 7. The Brown–Green Family Links

business partnership to the Moores. The Brown family, originally from County Galway, arrived in Australia in 1831 aboard the *Proteus*, owned and captained by Sylvester John Brown, a ship's master who had served with the East India Company. They settled in Sydney where Sylvester built a stone mansion, which he called *Enmore*, a name that is now given to the suburb that grew up around it. In 1838 the family, with the exception of Thomas Alexander Brown, overlanded with stock to Melbourne where they bought a pastoral property at Mount Macedon of modern *Picnic at Hanging Rock* fame, and started a steam ferry between Williamstown and Melbourne. In 1846 Thomas Alexander joined his father, mother and six sisters in the Portland District, previously explored by James Moore and Molesworth Greene. He added 'e' to his surname and ran a pastoral station with his brothers-in-law, Greene and Darley. Adverse conditions forced them out in 1869 and Browne returned to Sydney, becoming a police magistrate and gold commissioner in the country.

Browne's pastoral experiences and country life provided the inspiration for his writing career. Adopting the pseudonym 'Rolf Boldrewood', he first wrote a serial *The Squatter's Dream* in 1878 and then his famous novel *Robbery Under Arms*. 'Boldrewood' is a place in the New Forest in Hampshire, which features only once in one of Sir Walter Scott's lyrical poems. *Robbery Under Arms* gained for Boldrewood an international reputation. In 1851 Boldrewood's sister

Emma married Molesworth Greene, and Greene's sister Mary married William Foster Stawell a year later. As Charts 6 and 7 (pp.108–9 and 111 respectively) illustrate, the Browns had joined the cousinage, and the Greenes had re-united the Bert and Oldtown branches of the Burgh family.

In 1842 Lieutenant William Pomeroy Greene, a retired naval officer, and his wife Anne, sister of Charles Griffith, made the decision to emigrate from Ireland to Port Phillip District. The reports coming back from Charles Griffith and James Moore encouraged them to make the move and the former mariner chartered the vessel *Sarah*, setting out with their six sons, including Molesworth and George, their sixteen year old daughter Mary, and a relative, one of the Oldtown branch of the Burgh family, William Foster Stawell. Also on board were a governess, groom, useful boy, gardener and his wife, laundress, man cook and his wife, housemaid, and child's nurse; in addition, there were two thoroughbred horses, a Durham cow, two bulls, a library and a portable house. The house, *Woodlands*, was erected near Melbourne and is now a historic homestead.

Molesworth Greene, the eldest son, became head of the household when his father died in 1846. He had acquired James Moore's share of *Glenmore* and ran it with his uncle, Charles Griffith. Unlike many of the cousinage members, Greene did not go into politics. He became a justice of the peace, trustee of the Melbourne Public Library and chairman of the South Broken Hill Mining Company. He was unique in being the brother-in-law of two Trinity- educated chief justices, Darley and Stawell.

Alphabetical Foster

We turn now to the Oldtown branch of the Burgh family from which derived the Fosters and the Stawells. On his mother's side, William Foster Stawell's ancestry can be traced to Ulysses Burgh, Bishop of Ardagh in County Kildare, who graduated from Trinity in 1660. Stawell was the second son of barrister Jonas and Anna Foster, daughter of William Foster, DD, Bishop of Kilmore. Stawell was the most illustrious of the Irish cousinage and his career will be considered presently. Stawell's first cousin was the influential John Leslie Fitzgerald Vesey Foster. Known in Melbourne as either 'Alphabetical' or Fitzgerald Foster, he was second son of John Leslie Foster, chief baron of the Irish Exchequer, and Letitia Vesey Fitzgerald, sister of Lord Fitzgerald. He will be referred to here as Fitzgerald Foster. It is of interest to note that Fitzgerald Foster's grand-uncle was Irish statesman John 'Speaker' Foster, the last speaker of the Irish House of Commons. In accordance with Lord Fitzgerald's will, Fitzgerald, his brother William, and their mother, adopted the surname Foster-

Vesey-Fitzgerald after 1860 causing great confusion in the records. William, a pastoralist, who emigrated from Ireland to Victoria with his brother, returned to Ireland in 1843 as heir to Lord Fitzgerald's estates.

Fitzgerald Foster (1818–1900) studied law for a time following his graduation from Trinity in 1839, and, in 1841, he travelled to Sydney and then 'overlanded' to Port Phillip District, where he took up a pastoral run in 1842. Two years later he went into partnership with Stawell, in a station that they called *Rathescar* after a Foster estate in County Down. Identified with the aristocratic class and the squatters, Foster was a member of the New South Wales Legislative Council as Port Phillip District representative in the period 1846–50. He was an adherent to the code of honour and, whilst a magistrate in early Melbourne, he publicly horsewhipped Scotsman Farquhar McCrae, and his mount, over a dispute surrounding the purchase of land by McCrae. McCrae had wanted the dispute dealt with by an 'honour court' but Foster issued a challenge to a duel. McCrae, fearing he would never be paid if Foster lost, declined the challenge and suffered the usual fate of a coward, a good horsewhipping. He had Foster charged with assault and the resulting court case was presided over by William Jeffcott, the resident judge. Foster was defended by Redmond Barry, who himself had fought a duel in 1838, and it might have been thought that the Scotsman's case would have been overwhelmed by the Trinity-educated judge, defence counsel and defendant. It was not to be. Jeffcott, whose brother's life had almost been destroyed by the honour code, had no time for duelling and horsewhipping and found Foster guilty, fining him £10 and awarding the large sum of £250 in damages to McCrae.

At the end of his second term of office as member of the Legislative Council, Foster sold his share of *Rathescar* and returned to Ireland, where he wrote *The New Colony of Victoria, formerly Port Phillip*, as a guide to migration agents and prospective migrants. He returned to Victoria in 1852 as colonial secretary, administering the colony between governors and becoming a member of the committee formed to draft the Victorian constitution. This, when it became law, was a conservative document which generally protected the squatters' interests. As colonial secretary, Foster was held responsible for the colony's financial difficulties arising out of alleged excessive public expenditure. His remedies, including appropriation of land and an immigration fund, found no favour. He also proposed that the miner's licence, which the miners considered exhorbitant and unfair, should be replaced by a gold export licence. This, too, was rejected, and the vigorous pursuit of licence revenues was a factor in the Eureka Stockade uprising. Foster's resignation as colonial secretary

Figure 21. Fitzgerald Foster, Colonial Secretary.

after Eureka was accepted by Governor Hotham on condition that Foster would be compensated. In the end, Foster was made the scapegoat for the rebellion and public sentiment prevented Hotham from honouring his commitment. Foster was elected to the Legislative Assembly for the seat of Williamstown in 1856 and served as treasurer in the government of Sir John O'Shanassy, which survived for only one month in 1857. He was a foundation member of the council of Melbourne University from 1853 until 1857, when he then returned to England.

Overshadowed by his cousin Stawell, Foster's contribution to the development of the colony, albeit from a Tory conservative stance, was never adequately recognised. We have already noted the career of his first cousin, William John Foster, who served as attorney-general and judge in New South Wales. Another first cousin, John Foster McCreight, eldest son of Rev James

McCreight and Elizabeth Foster, entered Trinity in 1850, was called to the Irish Bar in 1853 and travelled to Melbourne in 1854. He was clerk and then crown prosecutor in the Attorney-General's Department until 1860, when he migrated again, this time to Canada. He was premier of British Columbia in 1871–72. The greatest of the cousinage was William Foster Stawell, and his appointment as the second Irish chief justice of Victoria returns us to further consideration of the Bench and the Bar in the colony of Victoria.

Chief Justice Stawell

William Foster Stawell (1815–89), the most distinguished member of the Irish cousinage, entered Trinity in 1833 and graduated with honours in classics four years later. He studied law at King's Inns in Dublin and at Lincoln's Inn and was called to the Bar in 1839. After travelling in Europe he practised on the Muster Circuit until he was encouraged to go to Victoria where Barry, Croke, Moore and Griffith had already settled. As we have seen, he sailed on the *Stag* in the company of the sixteen-year-old daughter of Captain William Pomeroy Greene, who would become his wife ten years later. On arrival Stawell was called to the Bar, and went into partnership with Fitzgerald Foster in *Rathescar*. He was never very active in the partnership and disposed of his interests in 1853. A leading barrister, Stawell cut a fine figure. More than six feet tall and of strong physique, he was an accomplished horse rider and won a local Grand National held at *Woodlands* on his horse *Master of the Rolls*. Although he was initially an agnostic, and engaged in what is usually described as dissolute behaviour when he first arrived in the colony, he was converted in 1848 by a sermon preached by Bishop Perry and became devoutly Anglican.

In 1850, an Act *"for the better Government of Her Majesty's Australian Colonies"* was passed by the parliament in London, which provided for the separation of Port Phillip District from the colony of New South Wales and the establishment of the new colony of Victoria. This was an event long awaited by Stawell, who was appointed as the colony's first attorney-general and as an official member of the Legislative Council. The Act also provided for the future constitutional development of the colonies along democratic principles, the so-called 'responsible government'. Redmond Barry became solicitor-general and both he and Stawell worked together on the development of a judicial system for the colony. In the Stawell-Barry report, they recommended that a Supreme Court be set up with a chief justice and two puisne judges, and this was done. In January 1852 Sir William A'Beckett became the first chief justice and shortly thereafter Redmond Barry was appointed to the Supreme Court as the first puisne judge.

Figure 22. Sir William Foster Stawell, Chief Justice of Victoria, 1857–86.

Fitzgerald Foster, in London at this exciting time, determined to return and he secured the post of colonial secretary. On his return to Melbourne, he and Stawell worked together on the Constitution Bill, earning for themselves the jibe from a later Eureka rebel, Rafaello Carboni, 'There are too many Fosters fostering and festering in this Victorian land'. The draft constitution had an upper house, the Legislative Council elected by property owners, clergymen, doctors, lawyers, university graduates and officers of the army and navy; and a Legislative Assembly also with a restricted franchise, requiring £2000 worth of property to qualify for election. The parliament reproduced the main elements of the Westminster system except that no colonial peerage for the upper house was proposed. This is not because Stawell and Foster did not favour hereditary nobility for the colony. They did, but the treatment of the proposed 'bunyip aristocracy' by an Irish politician, Daniel Deniehy, in New South Wales put an end to that idea for Victoria as well as for New South Wales. The Bill, which essentially protected conservative and landed interests, was approved by the British Parliament in 1855. Lieutenant-Governor La Trobe retired in 1854 and Sir Charles Hotham became the first governor under responsible government.

Stawell's influence on Hotham was as great as it had been on La Trobe. Hotham's policies and values were Stawell's, and these included a land policy favourable to the squatters, strict and harsh enforcement of law and order in a primitive and lawless society as he saw it, and direct raising of revenue from the gold rush boom by the imposition of licence fees. When the new Constitution came into effect in November 1855, bringing responsible government to Victoria, Stawell was elected to one of the five seats for Melbourne in the Legislative Assembly. He retained the attorney-generalship, and his seat, until 1857 when, on the resignation of William a'Beckett, he was appointed as the second chief justice of Victoria. It had been known for a time that a'Beckett wanted to retire on the grounds of ill health. The logical choice for chief justice would have been the hard working Justice Redmond Barry; and Barry had canvassed for the position with Premier Haines, but to no avail. The appointment of Stawell caused a rift between him and his friend Barry, and Stawell's conversion to Anglicanism and the prudery that accompanied it only served to embellish Barry's stories about the youthful misdemeanours of the chief justice. They did work well together, however, in establishing the university and the Melbourne Public Library, both monuments to Barry's diligence and effort; and Stawell was the last person to visit Barry before he died in 1880.

It is now generally accepted that Stawell was the right choice for chief justice. As historian of the Victorian Bar, Sir Arthur Dean, has said, 'it was the good fortune of the colony that it should in its formative years have had a man of Stawell's stature presiding over its highest judicial tribunal'. He has the distinction of being the longest serving chief justice in Australian history, presiding over the Supreme Court for twenty-nine years. In those years only one major controversy surrounded his judgements, a celebrated case involving an entrepreneur and speculator named Hugh Glass with whom Stawell had had business dealings. This case is described later in this chapter.

In 1873 Stawell took leave and visited Ireland where he was admitted to the LL.B and LL.D degrees by Trinity. He was recalled from leave by Governor Sir George Bowen to take on the acting governorship for a lengthy period. In his voluntary service Stawell was a member of the first council of Melbourne University and succeeded Redmond Barry as its second chancellor. He lasted for only one year as chancellor as his style did not suit the councillors, who found him autocratic, dogmatic and unheeding. It is said that Stawell had learned the art of chancellorship from Barry, but times had changed. Stawell was also president of the Philosophical Institute, later to become the Royal Society of Victoria, and he chaired the Exploration Committee superintending the arrangements for the ill-fated Burke and Wills expedition to cross Australia from south to north. Stawell led the parade to see the expedition off, and Burke bequeathed to him his watch and papers. In 1886 Stawell resigned as chief justice and was appointed as lieutenant-governor. He was succeeded as chief justice by fellow Trinity graduate, George Higinbotham, a man whom he considered to be a dangerous politician, but who commanded great respect. As Sir John Young records, Higinbotham, presiding over the famous Toy vs Musgrove case in 1888, aptly and rather lengthily summed up Stawell's great contribution to Victoria when he said:

> 'In this place and by members of the profession of the law it is not, and I hope it never will be, forgotten, that the foremost *longo intervallo* of the pioneers of Victorian legislation, foremost in capacity, in public spirit, and in unselfish devotion to exacting duties and to unremitting and stupendous labours, was he who afterwards as Chief Justice of this Court administered for twenty-nine years the general body of Victorian laws, most of which he had himself designed, prepared, and carried into legislative effect'.

In 1871 the name of Stawell was given by Premier Charles Gavan Duffy to a town in western Victoria previously known as Pleasant Creek.

The First Puisne Judge

The Stawell-Barry report on the administration of justice in the new colony of Victoria provided for a chief justice and two puisne judges. With a'Beckett in place as the first chief justice, the choice of the first puisne judge fell naturally upon the solicitor-general, Redmond Barry. Barry (1813–80) was born in Cork, the third son of Major-General Henry Barry. Sent to a minor private school in England that specialised in training boys for a military career, Redmond returned to Ireland in 1829 hoping for an army commission. This did not eventuate and so he entered Trinity to read history and classics, graduating in 1837. He was admitted to King's Inns while still an undergraduate and, as it was necessary at the time to have been admitted to one of the English Inns of Court in order to practise as a barrister in Ireland, Barry attended at Lincoln's Inn for six terms, the minimum time required, and was called to the Irish Bar in 1838. After vacationing in Europe Barry decided to go to Australia. His decision came as a surprise to his family but the death of his father and the passing of the family estates to his eldest brother prompted his decision.

Barry sailed on the *Calcutta* in April 1839 with James Croke as fellow passenger, and who Barry described in his diary as 'refined'. A shipboard romance with a married woman, pursued even after his arrival in Sydney, left Barry without preferment there and he left for Melbourne with Croke after only four weeks. Arriving on 13 November 1839, Barry celebrated this day with friends on each anniversary. He commenced work as a barrister but from the start he was seeking an official post. As standing counsel for the Aborigines from 1841 until his appointment as solicitor-general, Barry was never able to overcome the prejudice of the settlers against the native population. He did, however, ensure that they had good representation. In 1843 an official post came, with appointment as Brewster's successor as commissioner of the Court of Requests, and as the historian of the Bar in Victoria, fellow Trinity man J.L.Forde, expresses it, 'Barry disposed of the business of his 'Little-go' with all the care, patience and dignity and conscientiousness which he displayed long after when he was a judge'.

The Court of Quarter Sessions, presided over by Brewster, had, of course, been abolished with the arrival of Judge Willis and, in the two years that he appeared in Willis's Court, Barry conducted himself with great dignity and decorum in the face of the judge's onslaughts. Barry usually overcame Willis with his unctuous politeness, and Willis even praised him as an eloquent young advocate. Barry was no mere sycophant, however. When Willis was dismissed he simply noted 'te deum laudamus' in his diary. On separation of Port Phillip District from New South Wales in 1851, Barry was appointed over Croke as solicitor-general and, after only six months in that position, he was appointed to the Supreme Court.

Described by Garryowen as 'the most remarkable personage in the annals of Port Phillip', Barry founded the Melbourne Public Library, the University of Melbourne, the Ballarat School of Mines, the Philosophical Society, and much else besides. He was an example of the well-educated second or third son of the minor gentry in Ireland, adopting manners that were designed to demonstrate their superiority over other more 'ordinary' colonists and holding attitudes that reflected their upbringing as the sons of the garrison in a hostile environment. His dress was particularly noteworthy, especially the bell topper, or 'Barry' hat, with its distinctive tapering cone and level brim. When he fought a duel with Peter Snodgrass in 1841 his style of dress was almost as remarked upon as the duel itself.

The duel between Barry and the Scot was fought on a challenge by

*Figure 23. Sir Redmond Barry, Judge of the Victorian Supreme Court
and Chancellor of Melbourne University.*

Snodgrass over some insult to his dignity contained in a private letter written
by Barry to a member of the Melbourne Club. Barry's not too discreet
confidante showed the letter to Snodgrass and in the early morning on a
winter's day in 1841, the duel was fought. Barry dressed well for the occasion,
possibly to unnerve an already nervous Snodgrass. He wore the bell topper,
swallowtail coat, strap trouser, white vest, gloves and cravat. Bowing to his
opponent, Barry calmly awaited the order from the second. As reported in the
papers, 'Snodgrass fussed and fidgeted a good deal. It was his over-eagerness on
such occasions that caused his duelling to eventuate more than once into
fiasco.' His fidgeting may also have been due to other causes, for he confessed
to Judge Willis in another case that he was always 'tight' in the mornings. In
his nervous state the hair trigger of his pistol discharged the weapon
prematurely into the ground. Barry fired in the air and honour was satisfied. It

is sometimes said that Snodgrass shot himself in the foot during the encounter with Barry. Contemporary records show that this is not the case. Snodgrass shot himself accidentally in the toe in a duel with squatter William Ryrie. Ryrie too, fired into the air. Although duelling was against the law it was still looked upon as an acceptable way for gentlemen to settle disputes. Derived from trial by combat, duelling was a peculiarly upper class activity. By the mid-1840s public opinion in England was turning against the practice. Pistols had become more accurate and fatalities were common. People with no 'honour' to protect but anxious to emulate their upper class 'betters' were foolishly engaging in duels; and revision of the articles of war in 1844, which ruled that an officer who refused a challenge could not be punished for cowardice, was a breakthrough in completely abolishing the practice, which, to all intents and purposes, ended in the 1850s.

As a barrister, Barry was not considered to be particularly gifted, but it is recorded that he was unparalleled in working a jury. His private life was rather unusual for a man in such a public position in that at the age of thirty eight he formed a relationship with an Irish Catholic married woman, Louisa Barrow, who bore him four children. Mrs Barrow, the wife of a labourer who died in 1859, is buried beside Barry but her name does not appear on the gravestone; and their four children were given their mother's name.

As a judge Barry was considered harsh, intolerant and unfeeling. One of his more notorious cases, which is said to illustrate his penchant for passing the death sentence, involved the impromptu killing of a brutal overseer named Price at the prison hulks in the port of Williamstown. After severe provocation Price was struck down by a group of convicts and seven were subsequently indicted for murder. Barry, the trial judge, was unmoved by the evidence that not all of the seven struck Price; to Barry this was immaterial since all had a common purpose. Denied counsel since they were convicts, and despite recommendations for mercy for two, one of whom was a boy of sixteen, all were sentenced to death and hanged. He also presided over two of the most famous trials in Victoria's history, the Eureka and the Ned Kelly trials.

Eureka

One of the defining events in the history of Australia was the rebellion at the Eureka Stockade in 1854 and the subsequent trials of thirteen of the ringleaders, with Barry as trial judge for most of them. The harsh and repressive regime endured by miners in Ballarat and elsewhere because of the government's decision to raise money from licence fees has already been mentioned. Digger hunts were frequent and often brutal; and because the fines for evasion were shared between the administration and the arresting officer, coercion and corruption were rife. After the burning of licences at a mass meeting in Ballarat in December 1854 and Peter Lalor's mounting a stump to proclaim 'liberty', confrontation was inevitable. Lalor was the brother of James Fintan Lalor, the young Irelander who was a passionate advocate of armed insurrection in Ireland to force return of the land to the Irish people. James was planning armed resistance in Ireland up to the time of his death in 1849 and he had designed a fortified circular enclosure for the purpose. The Eureka Stockade where the miners made their stand may have derived from James's design. The stockade was attacked by government troops on the morning of Sunday, 3 December 1854 and twenty-two miners and six troopers were killed. Lalor was wounded but escaped from the stockade and remained at large until an amnesty was declared. Governor Hotham received the news of the building of the stockade on the morning of the attack but not the news of the attack itself. On hearing of the fortification, he, Stawell and Foster prevailed upon the assistant colonial secretary, John Moore, Trinity-educated brother of James Moore, to issue a proclamation calling upon 'all British subjects to abstain from identifying themselves with the evil disposed persons at Ballarat'.

Although people of many nationalities were involved in the agitation and rebellion at Eureka it is usually considered to be a very Irish affair, a continuation of the battle for freedom from British rule in Ireland. The watchword at the stockade was 'Vinegar Hill', reminiscent not only of the 1798 battle in Wexford but also of a small rebellion in New South Wales in 1804, which resulted in the death of nine Irish rebels armed with pikes, the arrest of Sir Henry Brown Hayes on suspicion, and the execution of a further nine rebels. Government thinking at the time of Eureka was expressed by the Ballarat goldfields commissioner, William Rede, who said that 'the licence is a mere watchword of the day, a cloak to cover a democratic revolution'. But Lalor was not a revolutionary, even though he was brought up in a radical environment at the 'big house', *Tenakill*, in County Laois where his father Patrick Lalor was MP. Patrick, a staunch nationalist, leased *Tenakill* and was an active supporter of his landless countrymen. He led the opposition to the collection of tithes by the Church of Ireland, and was an associate of Daniel O'Connell.

Although his other brothers actively supported James Fintan Lalor in his rebellious activities, Peter remained apart. He attended Carlow College and then studied civil engineering in Dublin, either at Trinity or in the charge of a Trinity tutor. Meanwhile, James helped to organise the Young Ireland Movement with John Mitchel and William Smith O'Brien and contributed articles to the *Nation*, established by Thomas Davis, John Blake Dillon and

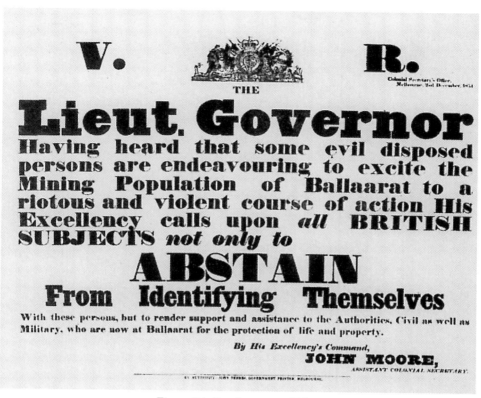

Figure 24. Proclamation, 1854.

Charles Gavan Duffy. Mitchel entered Trinity in 1831, established the revolutionary Irish confederation in 1847 and, after his arrest and trial in connection with his seditious activities, was transported to Tasmania. He escaped in 1853, settled in America and eventually returned to Ireland in 1875 to become MP for Tipperary. Mitchel was a nephew of Sir William Irvine, premier and fifth chief justice of Victoria.

Cambridge-educated William Smith O'Brien, related to the Gwynns and to Victorian pastoralist Acheson French, and, through him, to Irish cousinage member James Moore (see Chart 3, p.47), was sentenced to death after the 1848 rebellion but his sentence was transmuted to transportation to Van Diemen's Land for life. He was conditionally pardoned in 1854 and returned to Europe, passing through Melbourne on his way. While in Melbourne a great banquet hosted by John O'Shanassy, a future premier of Victoria, was held in his honour and he was presented with a nugget of gold weighing nine pounds by the miners of Ballarat. This was cast into a magnificent cup now in the National Museum of Ireland. He was unconditionally pardoned in 1856.

Charles Gavan Duffy, too, was arrested in Ireland but the juries disagreed at his trials and after the fifth trial he was released. He became MP for New Ross in Ireland but, in 1856, he set out for Australia with Moses Wilson Gray. Editor and co-founder of the *Nation*, Gavan Duffy became premier of Victoria in 1871–72, and third speaker of the Legislative Assembly from 1880 until 1887.

The Trials

On the day of the attack on the Eureka Stockade, one hundred and twenty diggers were arrested, of whom thirteen were brought to trial in Melbourne. Six of these were Irish. There was a reward posted for the arrest of Lalor but he was protected by his many supporters and often appeared in public during the period before an amnesty was declared. The thirteen miners were indicted on a charge of high treason and the selection of this charge by the then attorney-general, William Stawell, was a gift to the defence. It represented a complete over-reaction to what was essentially an armed affray. The indictments were heard before the chief justice, William a'Beckett, and a summary of the four counts of high treason was read to the defendants who were represented by Trinity men, Richard D. Ireland and Joseph Henry Dunne. They and a number of other barristers gave their services to the miners free of charge. The others were Archibald Mitchie, Butler Cole Aspinall, A.C.Cope, H.S.Chapman and James Grant, all of whom were sympathetic to the miners' cause and were later to achieve eminence at the Bar or the Bench. Grant, according to historian Margaret Kiddle, had an alarming habit of referring to guillotines, lamp posts and other French revolutionary accoutrements in his court appearances for defendants indicted by the Crown or being sued by the 'squattocracy'. The first two defendants were tried before a'Beckett, and Stawell himself prosecuted, determined to stamp out the sedition, lawlessness and treason that he saw in the miners' action at Eureka. He was assisted by the solicitor-general, fellow Trinity man Robert Molesworth. Depending on who is analysing the trial, Stawell either prosecuted with 'cold, detached single-mindedness', or, 'with courage and determination'. One can imagine the ridicule that the brilliant defence lawyers poured upon charges such as that laid against John Joseph, the first defendant to be tried. Joseph, an American negro was accused, in part, of waging war against her Sovereign Majesty the Queen. He was acquitted. So too was John Manning, an Irish nationalist defended by Ireland and Mitchie.

A furious Stawell adjourned the trials for a month while he empanelled a new jury. Barry was judge for the resumed trials and Timothy Hayes, defended by Ireland and Cope, was tried next. To his great credit, Barry reversed the main thrust of a'Beckett's summing up in the case of Joseph and Manning, in which a'Beckett had ruled that it was for the accused to satisfy the jury of his innocence once the Crown had proved facts incriminating him. Barry made it clear that the burden of proof lay with the Crown. Hayes, too, was acquitted and the crowds bore him shoulder high through the streets. Then Raffaelo Carboni appeared. Italian immigrant and later a follower of Garibaldi, he was famous for the disparaging remark about the Fosters, one of whom, William Foster Stawell, was now his prosecutor. Ireland and the brilliant half-Irish Butler Cole Aspinall defended Carboni, and Ireland asked the jury if they realised that if found guilty of high treason Carboni would be hung, drawn and quartered and the four parts of his body 'stuck up on top of the gates of the town'. Carboni, rising to the occasion, and playing upon the lack of suitable sites for the grim purpose, asked 'how the deuce can they hang up my hindquarters on the gates of Ballarat township?'

In due course all of the defendants were acquitted. After the trials the licence fee was abolished and replaced by a miner's right with an annual fee of thirty shillings instead of £1 a month for the licence fee. Miners were given the title deeds to their claims and won the right to vote for candidates in the elective Legislative Assembly, formed on the granting of responsible government in 1855. Lalor was the miners' representative in the Assembly, succeeding Duffy as speaker in 1880.

In 1865 the colony was divided into districts in each of which there was a mining board elected by those holding a miner's right. In each district, too, there was a Court of Mines presided over by a county court justice. The chief judge of the Courts of Mines for thirty years was Sir Robert Molesworth and he laid down the law on the questions submitted to this court. The first chief justice of the High Court of Australia, Sir Samuel Griffith, said of Molesworth, 'It is a well known fact that the mining law of Australia was practically made by Mr Justice Molesworth'. In Forde's *The Story of the Bar* he called his fellow Trinity man, Molesworth, 'The noblest Roman of them all'. Molesworth was the fourth judge to be appointed to the Victorian Supreme Court.

When Sir Arthur Dean, historian of the Victorian Bar, set out to give an account of the principal figures of the Bar, he illustrated his selection by recounting some cases of public importance and general interest. Most of the examples featured what Forde had called 'a remarkable group of Irish lawyers'. We shall consider five of these cases to illustrate the Trinity influence, and the first of these concerns Judge Molesworth himself.

The Molesworth Case

When the Victorian Supreme Court was established in 1852 a'Beckett and Barry were the first two judges to be appointed. Barry's successor as solicitor-general, Edward Eyre Williams, became the second puisne judge, and James Croke was appointed as solicitor-general from then until his retirement in 1855. Then Croke was succeeded by Robert Molesworth, the son of Hickman Blayney Molesworth, solicitor and great grandson of the first Viscount Molesworth. The Molesworths were an illustrious family tracing their lineage to Sir Walter de Molesworth, a soldier who accompanied Edward I to the Holy Land in the fourteenth century. A descendant, Robert Molesworth, who served with Cromwell, obtained two thousand five hundred acres in County Meath and his son, Robert, became Viscount Molesworth in 1716 (see Chart 8, p.129). The viscount's second son, Richard, found fame at the Battle of Ramillies by rescuing the Duke of Marlborough when he was unhorsed and in danger of his life from a French detachment. Richard Molesworth subsequently became commander-in-chief of the King's forces in Ireland, sent his son to Trinity in 1765, and married his daughter to William, second Earl Fitzwilliam.

Our subject, Robert Molesworth (1806–90), graduated from Trinity in 1826 and was admitted to the Irish Bar in 1828, in the same term as William Jeffcott. Molesworth practised on the Munster Circuit until 1852 when he and his seventeen-year-old wife, Henrietta, left for Adelaide. A year after their arrival they moved to Melbourne, where the Supreme Court had just been established; and interestingly, within months of his arrival in 1853, he was appointed as acting chief justice, in the absence of a'Beckett, even though he had no government post. At the beginning of 1854 he became acting solicitor-general and was embroiled in Stawell's prosecution of the Eureka rebels a year later. He secured permanency as solicitor-general and, in 1856, was elevated to the Supreme Court as the third puisne judge.

The chroniclers of the Bar and judiciary in Victoria consider Molesworth to have been the colony's greatest judge. Forde said, without hesitation, that 'in every judicial attribute he was indeed great.' Sir Arthur Dean, too, writing in 1968, said that 'no one can deny Molesworth was one of our greatest judges if not the greatest – still another outstanding man from Trinity College, Dublin'. On the Supreme Court he became primary judge in equity and then chief judge of the Court of Mines. In dealing with this new area of the law he established a code of precedent which became a guide to the rest of Australia and overseas. He sat on the Bench until his death in 1890.

Molesworth's career was placed in jeopardy, however, in the early 1860s by

Figure 25. Sir Robert Molesworth, Judge of the Victorian Supreme Court.

a sensational matrimonial case involving him and his wife. Suspecting that she was engaged in an affair with Richard Ireland, he expelled Mrs Molesworth from the home in 1855. She returned to England with an allowance that she considered inadequate, and returned to Melbourne early in 1856. She did not seek reinstatement in the home but, from time to time, sought increases in her allowance from Molesworth. Little is known of her life from her return until 1861 when, with the passage of the *Divorce and Matrimonial Causes Act*, Molesworth presented a petition for divorce on the grounds of adultery, with Ireland as co-respondent. The petition was rejected on a technicality by the remainder of the court comprising Stawell, Barry and Williams, with Chief

Justice Stawell dissenting. The brilliant Irish barrister Charles Alexander Smyth and three other lawyers appeared for Ireland; English barristers Dawson, Wood and Fellowes appeared for Mrs Molesworth. Billing and Mitchie appeared for Robert Molesworth.

Mrs Molesworth went to England again in 1862 where she allegedly gave birth to a son. On her return to Melbourne she presented a petition for judicial separation on the grounds of cruelty, and an interlocutory application for alimony pending the suit. She was represented in this application by George Higinbotham, and won a large increase in alimony, awarded by acting justice Henry Chapman, later to be Richard Ireland's brother-in-law. Meanwhile, Molesworth filed a cross petition for judicial separation on the grounds of adultery.

The petition and cross petition came on for hearing before a judge and a special jury of twelve in November 1864. Stawell, who in the very first petition in 1861 appeared to favour Molesworth, was the judge; Mitchie, already a Queen's Counsel, and Billing, afterwards to be elevated to that rank, appeared for Molesworth; Ireland, also now a Queen's Counsel, was not indicted as co-respondent as this was not possible in a case for judicial separation. He was allowed to appear as witness on behalf of Mrs Molesworth and to deny that adultery had taken place between them. In so doing he referred to Mrs Molesworth as 'an eccentric, hasty, peculiar, good-natured sort' who drank too much on occasions. Mrs Molesworth was represented by two English barristers, Wood and Dawson. George Higinbotham had become attorney-general in 1863 and one of his first acts was to advance Ireland to Queen's Counsel in August of that year, before the listed hearing began.

As Dean, who recounts the trial in detail, puts it, 'Here was a *cause célèbre* if ever there was one. A Supreme Court judge was the respondent to proceedings in his own court before his chief justice in which his conduct and his credibility were involved; and a leading member of the Bar of that court, a Queen's Counsel, a former attorney-general was alleged to have committed adultery with the wife of that judge. One can readily imagine with what zest the press reporters sharpened their pencils, and how rapidly the points wore away!' Dawson, opening for Mrs Molesworth did not spare the judge and told the court of Molesworth's physical ill-treatment of his wife when she came to ask for an increased allowance, and of his fights with Richard Ireland. Billing was brilliant in cross-examination and provided photographic evidence that Mrs Molesworth did indeed have a child in England. The jury found against her; Judge Molesworth, who was cleared of the charge of cruelty, was granted a decree for judicial separation on the grounds of his wife's adultery with a person

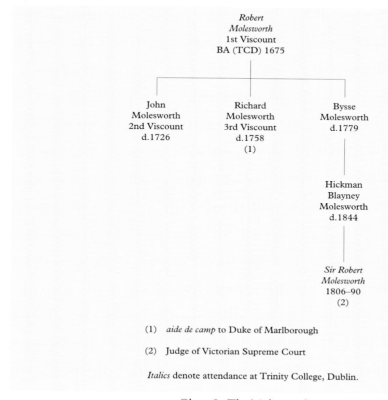

Robert
Molesworth
1st Viscount
BA (TCD) 1675

| John Molesworth 2nd Viscount d.1726 | Richard Molesworth 3rd Viscount d.1758 (1) | Bysse Molesworth d.1779 |

Hickman
Blayney
Molesworth
d.1844

Sir Robert
Molesworth
1806–90
(2)

(1)   *aide de camp* to Duke of Marlborough

(2)   Judge of Victorian Supreme Court

Italics denote attendance at Trinity College, Dublin.

Chart 8. The Molesworths.

unknown; Stawell commented that if, in 1855, Mrs Molesworth had sought re-instatement instead of alimony her situation might have been very different; and Ireland emerged as quite the hero in the newspaper reports. The jury found that, though Mrs Molesworth's conduct was not adulterous, she was 'unduly familiar for a married woman'. Ireland was portrayed as the victim of the inappropriate attentions of Mrs Molesworth and the brutality of her husband. Robert Molesworth was castigated for allowing the scandal to develop when more money would have kept Mrs Molesworth quiet. Mrs Molesworth appealed against the findings to the full court but her petition was dismissed.

George Higinbotham, the attorney-general, wrote to Molesworth suggesting that he should not conduct matrimonial cases in the future, and the *Argus* claimed that Molesworth had been asked to resign. Molesworth responded to Higinbotham's 'singular communication' by reminding him that he had no right to interfere in the distribution of business among judges; the chief justice undertook that task. In any case, Molesworth had already asked Stawell not to give him matrimonial cases again. Higinbotham's role, first in acting as counsel for Mrs Molesworth in the alimony matter of 1862, then in elevating Ireland to Queen's Counsel while the allegations against him were unresolved, and, finally, in attempting to admonish Molesworth by suggesting that he might be unfit to take matrimonial cases, showed his antipathy towards the aristocratic Molesworth. But it also showed the tension that often arose between attorneys-general and the judiciary. This tension between attorney-general Higinbotham and the judges also surfaced during a celebrated dispute, discussed presently, between him and Barry in 1864.

In giving details of the Molesworth trial, the legal historian Arthur Dean deplored the extravagant and colourful language used against a justice of the Supreme Court, especially by Dawson, who went well beyond the evidence called and who abused the judge in the most extraordinary way. This was, after all, a trial for judicial separation, not divorce. What is just as remarkable is the extent of Trinity-educated and Irish lawyers and judges in the case. Trial judges Stawell and Barry, defendant Molesworth, attorney-general Higinbotham, barristers Billing and Smyth, and former attorney-general, Richard Ireland, were all, except Smyth, part of the Trinity group. The judiciary and the law were brought into ridicule and scandalous attention over a period of some years. It is extraordinary that all reputations survived, except, of course, Mrs Molesworth's, which did not. She returned to England and died there in 1880 at the age of fifty-seven. Richard Davies Ireland, whose role in this affair added to the reputation he had for fast living, deserves special mention.

Richard Davies Ireland

The lead defence counsel for many of the Eureka rebels, and one of Melbourne's most celebrated barristers and politicians, Richard Davies Ireland (1816–77) was born in County Galway, the son of an army captain. He graduated from Trinity in 1837, the same year as Stawell, was called to the Bar, and practised in Dublin. He was drawn to the turbulent politics of the time and supported the Irish confederation in 1847. When Thomas Meagher, a leader of this revolutionary group, was arrested for sedition Ireland provided bail and, with Isaac Butt and Sir Colman O'Loghlen, was defending counsel at his trial. Meagher was found guilty and transported to Tasmania from where he escaped to America. Ireland himself left for Melbourne with his family in 1852 and was almost immediately drawn into the defence of the Eureka miners. Carboni in his book on the Eureka rebellion compared him in eloquence with Daniel O'Connell and surmised that he would always cast a spell over a jury; indeed, few could resist his potent mixture of eloquence, wit and vituperation. Sir Arthur Dean considers him to have been the greatest advocate of his day and this reputation began to emerge after the Eureka defence.

Ireland entered the Legislative Assembly in 1857 and represented a series of electorates over an eleven-year period. He became solicitor-general and then attorney-general and, while in that capacity in Sir John O'Shanassy's ministry of 1861, it was agreed that William Hearn, professor of political economy at Melbourne University, would draw up a land bill for the sum of £500, in accordance with cabinet specifications. The charge of opportunism levelled at Ireland derives from his handling of this episode and from other instances of some sharp practice. Both his and O'Shanassy's sympathies lay with the squatters whose tenure on their properties would be threatened by the reform legislation. The legislation was introduced in 1862 by the minister for lands, Charles Gavan Duffy, who was surprised to find later that the squatters could easily exploit loopholes in the Act by which they would be able to hold on to their estates. Duffy accused Ireland of knowing about the loopholes and Ireland admitted as much several years later in a debate in the Legislative Assembly. He believed that the Act was unworkable in any case, relying for his judgement on the notion that to ignore the interests of the squatters was to fly in the face of the existing facts. Though a supporter of the Irish confederation, he was also a member, with William Smith O'Brien, Isaac Butt, John Mitchel and Sir Colman O'Loghlen, of the Irish Council, the object of which was to present a benign face of the wealthy land-owning classes in Ireland.

It is as a barrister rather than politician that Ireland is best remembered, especially in his role as advocate for the Eureka rebels. When Stawell asked one of the defence witnesses at that trial what had happened at the meetings of miners on the day before the rebellion, the answer was that three cheers had been given for Ireland, who had already involved himself in the Ballarat turmoil by defending three miners accused of burning down James Bentley's Eureka Hotel. Bentley, a most unsavoury character, had been indicted with two others for the murder of a miner trying to gain admission to his hotel. He was acquitted, and an angry mob burned down the hotel. The three arrested were defended by Ireland and, though his defence was persuasive, they were found guilty but sentenced to short gaol terms. According to the *Argus*, 'the law had been upheld but the government had been disgraced'.

Ireland's defence of the 'blackbirders', Mount and Morris, many years later brought less joy. This is a famous case of the trial of two men involved in a slave trade expedition in 1871 to the South Pacific Islands. While at sea the captured natives became very threatening and many were shot. When the ship

Figure 26. Richard Davies Ireland, Attorney-General of Victoria.

returned to Sydney the captain and mate were tried and executed. Two other instigators, a Dr Mount and Mr Morris, were arrested in Victoria and put on trial before Stawell. Ireland acted for the defence and the case was prosecuted by Travers Adamson and Sir Bryan O'Loghlen; thus the entire proceedings were conducted by legal men educated in Trinity. Due to Ireland's brilliant defence, the defendants were found guilty of manslaughter only, and sentenced to seven years penal servitude. Ireland, however, was able to have them freed on a writ of *habeas corpus* on a technicality, a result that caused outrage and censure of the government in parliament. The Privy Council reversed the decision of the full court to release the men but, by then, they had left the colony.

Ireland was a larger than life character, a brilliant barrister, who claimed to have made and lost several fortunes in the course of his life. He is considered by Geoffrey Serle, in *The Golden Age*, to have been a liberal opportunist who made little impact on the politics of the colony during his period in office, as solicitor-general in one conservative government and attorney-general in a radical administration. His admission that he was aware of the errors in the land Bill lost him selection for a parliamentary seat in 1867. He gave his services free to the Eureka Stockade rebels, yet he would defend with equal brilliance the likes of Mount and Morris. Serle believes that Ireland left no mark on the politics of the colony, but there is no doubt that he found a significant place in the history, and especially in the legal history, of Victoria.

The Case of Dr Mackay

This case, considered to be important in the continuing battle between freedom and responsibility in press reporting, involved George Mackay, born in County Meath in 1815. A Trinity graduate of 1839, who was advanced to LL.D in 1848, he was admitted to the Irish Bar and migrated to Victoria in 1852. Appointed as crown prosecutor in 1854, he was conducting prosecutions before Judge Pohlman in Geelong, where the *Geelong Advertiser and Intelligencer* reported in the convoluted prose of the time that he was 'under the influence' in court: 'When a crown prosecutor vibrates', the paper reported, 'and executes sundry mandarin movements and runs a whole sentence into one thick word compounded by gutturals, lispings and an incessant hiccup, it must be presumed that symptoms indicative of drunkenness in another individual tell with equal effect against a crown prosecutor'. The government called upon Mackay to sue for libel, which he did, and the case came before Judge Williams of the Supreme Court in Melbourne. The legal firepower ranged against Harrison, the hapless editor, comprising Ireland, Aspinall, Mitchie and Robert Fellowes, 'a cold venomous old Etonian arch-Tory', was formidable. Harrison claimed he could find no one to represent him. Mackay admitted that he had been to a race dinner the evening before the court case in question and was still recovering on the next day. The evidence against him, including Judge Pohlman's, was overwhelming, yet Mackay won, and was awarded £800 in damages. The Lord Mayor of Melbourne convened a large meeting at which motions of support for editor Harrison were adopted and the Melbourne *Argus* published a long leader defending the freedom of the press and repeating the libel – 'The crown prosecutor has been made £800 richer by being drunk in court'; Mackay did not tempt fate a second time and he ignored the libel. But Richard Ireland and his colleagues had triumphed again, and Ireland's luck held, just as it was to do in the Sir Robert Molesworth case.

The Hugh Glass Case

In 1869 allegations of corruption and bribery were made against Hugh Glass, a wealthy squatter and businessman. It was believed that members of parliament were involved and a select committee found that Glass was a member of a squatters' association who bribed members of the Legislative Assembly. Glass and another association member were brought before the Bar of the Legislative Assembly and it was ordered that they be gaoled. The speaker, Sir Francis Murphy, signed the warrant; Richard Ireland then presented a writ of *habeas corpus* to the gaol on behalf of Glass; Glass was produced in the Supreme Court before judges Stawell, Barry and Williams; Richard Ireland, Travers Adamson and William Hearn appeared for Glass; and Richard Billing and Archibald Mitchie, QC, appeared for the speaker. Ireland succeeded in having the warrant declared invalid and the popular Glass was released to the great jubilation of the crowd. But in parliament there was outrage, especially by George Higinbotham, the former attorney-general, who considered the Supreme Court's judgement to be hasty and ill-considered, and the fact that Stawell had business dealings with Glass in the past added fuel to the fire. On appeal to the Judicial Committee of the Privy Council, the Supreme Court's verdict was overturned and the important constitutional doctrine was affirmed in the colony – that the parliament in respect of its privileges stands above the courts. All of the legal actors in this drama, except Williams and Mitchie, were Trinity educated.

The speaker, Sir Francis Murphy (1809–91), from Cork, graduated from Trinity in 1829 and went on to London to complete his medical studies. He emigrated from London to Sydney in 1836 and was appointed by Governor Bourke as colonial surgeon in a country district. He acquired pastoral and agricultural interests and in 1846 he moved to Port Phillip to take up a large pastoral lease. There he was elected to the Legislative Council at the first elections after the separation of Victoria from New South Wales in 1851, and in 1856, under responsible government, Murphy was elected to the Legislative Assembly, narrowly defeating Charles Griffith for the speakership. Unlike Griffith, Murphy undertook to abide by English precedent by not entering into debate, and thus he held the speakership for the first fifteen years of the parliament's existence.

Richard Billing (1814–82), the fifth Queen's Counsel to be appointed in Victoria, graduated from Trinity in 1836 and was called to the Irish Bar. He practised in Ireland and in 1856 sailed for Melbourne. As we shall see later, Billing was a reader in law at Melbourne University until 1882, when he was appointed as a county court judge.

Travers Adamson (1827–97) was born in County Meath and entered Trinity in 1844. After graduating in 1852 he practised at the Bar in Dublin until his appointment as crown prosecutor in the north-east district of Victoria. He held on to this position for some time despite being elected to the first Legislative Assembly. He was dismissed in 1858, however, 'in the interests of the public service', and became solicitor-general in 1859. In 1860 Adamson resigned from the parliament and practised law until 1866, when he again became crown prosecutor. As such he featured in one of Sir Arthur Dean's notable cases, that of Dr Beaney, who was charged in 1866 with murder following an inquest on a patient, Mary Lewis, on whom he had attempted an abortion. He was tried by Barry and the jury could not reach a verdict. Tried again before a different judge, the prosecutors were Adamson and fellow Irishman Charles Alexander Smyth. The defence team was Aspinall and Henry Wrixon. This time Aspinall's brilliance prevailed and Beaney was acquitted. This was a celebrated case relying very much on expert evidence, which Adamson and Smyth presented very well. Beaney, very showy and flamboyant, went on to make a fortune despite all the odium visited upon him. He became a member of the Legislative Council, and left a large sum to the Mayor of Canterbury in England, the city of his birth, to establish the Beaney Institute for the education of the working man.

The Kelly Trial

We now come to the trial of Ned Kelly, another defining event in the history of Australia. The numbers of Trinity men in positions of power and influence were declining but, even in 1880, four out of the five Supreme Court judges were Trinity-educated. One of them took the Kelly trial; one of the two prosecutors and the defence counsel were the sons of Trinity-educated judges and the lead prosecutor was an Irish barrister from County Longford.

Edward (Ned) Kelly, son of John and Ellen Kelly from Tipperary, was tried for murder before Judge Redmond Barry in October 1880. Found guilty of murdering Constable Lonigan at Stringybark Creek in Victoria two years before, Kelly was hanged at Melbourne gaol in November 1880. The mythology that has grown up around the Kelly story includes the supposedly prescient statement that he made to Barry when sentence of death was pronounced upon him. When Barry intoned 'may God have mercy on your soul', Kelly replied, 'I will go a little further than that, I will meet you there where I go.' Barry died from complications arising out of his diabetic condition two weeks after Kelly's execution.

Born in Beveridge, Victoria, in 1855, Kelly began his life of crime at the age of fourteen and had served a number of prison sentences by the time he finally went on the run in April 1878. The immediate cause of his taking to the bush was an accusation of attempted murder of a trooper named Fitzpatrick, who had been sent to the family home to arrest his brother Dan. The facts of this murder attempt were never properly established because the trooper in question was an unreliable and unsavoury character who was later dismissed from the police force. Kelly's mother was convicted with others, before Justice Barry, of attempting to murder Trooper Fitzpatrick and sentenced to three years gaol. Warrants were issued for the arrest of the remaining Kellys and at Stringybark Creek in October 1878 Ned shot and killed three of the four policemen sent to apprehend him and his gang. The gang then went on a campaign of bank robbery and Ned was eventually captured in a shootout at Glenrowan in country Victoria. Ned's confrontation with the police, protected by armour fashioned from plough mould boards, in the early morning of 30 June 1880, has been immortalised in the paintings of the Kelly gang by Sir Sidney Nolan. The armour was not quite protective enough, as Ned was brought down by shots to the legs.

The trial was set down for 18 October 1880, but Kelly's initial defence team of Gaunson and Hickman Molesworth presented an affidavit to Judge Barry giving details of the family's financial difficulties and requesting an adjournment until the question of fees had been satisfactorily settled. Barry rejected the affidavit on the grounds that the family had known about the trial for two months and had sufficient time to arrange for a properly briefed defence counsel. Barry, did, however, arrange for a ten-day adjournment to allow Molesworth to prepare the case. The Kellys were unable to raise the fees that Molesworth could command and the most junior barrister in Melbourne, Henry Bindon, took the case. Molesworth and Bindon were the sons of Trinity-educated judges Sir Robert Molesworth and Samuel Bindon. The prosecutors ranged against Bindon were Charles Alexander Smyth, crown prosecutor and future King's Counsel, who was born in County Longford, and Arthur Wolfe Chomley, nephew of Charles Griffith and a member of the Irish cousinage. Smyth was a leader at the Bar and Chomley was appointed as a county court judge five years after the trial.

The inexperienced, but apparently over-confident, Bindon was no match for Smyth and Chomley. He called no witnesses, failed to make use of evidence that might have helped Kelly's case, effectively questioned the competence of Justice Barry in asking for a referral to the full Supreme Court, and was quite ill-prepared for the case. On the basis of Redmond Barry's summing up and directions to the jury, John Phillips, in his *Trial of Ned Kelly*, reaches the 'inescapable' conclusion that Ned Kelly was 'not afforded a trial according to the law'. Dean, in his *A Multitude of Counsellors*, points out that Barry, in sentencing Kelly's mother earlier for the attempted murder of Fitzpatrick, had expressed the view that if her son Ned had been in court he would have made an example of him. If that were so, then Barry should have disqualified himself from presiding at the Kelly trial.

Ned himself, when allowed to speak after the guilty verdict was delivered, expressed a lack of confidence in Bindon. He said that 'he knew nothing of my case' and that 'a different picture would have emerged had I been allowed to give testimony'. Ned spoke of his easy mind in respect of events that had taken place at Stringybark Creek, whereupon Barry condemned him for blasphemy. 'You appear to revel', Barry said, 'in the idea of having put men to death'. Unwisely, and in a clear reference to Barry's reputation as a 'hanging' judge, Ned replied, 'More than me have put men to death'. Appeals for clemency were ignored, as were public petitions and a rally at the Hippodrome organised by Bindon's attorney Gaunson. John Phillips is unsure as to whether the verdict would have been different if Kelly had received a trial according to the law, but the outcome provided in Kelly a symbol of resolute courage and daring in the face of persecution by authority. Bindon's reputation never recovered from a trial where he could have made his name; and Barry's death only twelve days after Ned is seen as an indictment of the judge who, it is thought, saw Ned and his gang's lawlessness as an example of the rural violence that he had left behind in Ireland and which needed to be stamped out at all costs. As with the other important cases that have been recalled here, the Kelly trial was a very Irish affair on both sides of the Bench.

George Higinbotham

If Sir Robert Molesworth, third puisne judge to be appointed to the Supreme Court of Victoria, was the 'noblest Roman of them all', George Higinbotham was the most radical and the most complex of all the men educated at Trinity College, Dublin, who held the stage in Victoria. This complexity was obvious in his two major careers, as parliamentarian and as chief justice of Victoria .

George Higinbotham (1826–92), the youngest son of merchant Henry Higinbotham and Sarah Wilson, daughter of the United States consul in Dublin, was educated at the Royal School, Dungannon, where one of his schoolmates was Frederick Darley. The Higinbothams were of Dutch origin, tracing their ancestry to an officer in the army of William of Orange, and all except one of four sons were sent to Trinity. In 1843 Higinbotham won a major five-year scholarship and entered Trinity in 1844. His undergraduate studies

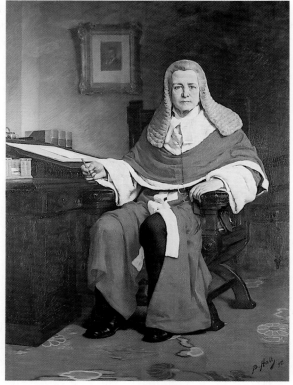

Figure 27. George Higinbotham, Chief Justice of Victoria, 1886–92.

were in classics, mathematics and philosophy and, though he did well, he had to take a pass degree in 1848, as his father's business was being affected by the famine. In Dublin, George became friendly with Jane Brougham, sister of Hussey Burgh Macartney, and it is through her influence that he became interested in Australia. Her cousin, Charles Griffith, and some of his friends were already in Melbourne and Mrs Brougham was keen to see her own sons associate themselves with the Higinbothams. One of her sons, Henry, a fellow student of George at Trinity, became Anglican Dean of Lismore in New South Wales.

In 1845 Higinbotham enrolled as a student-at-law at Lincoln's Inn and while reading for the Bar he supported himself as a parliamentary reporter for the *Morning Chronicle*, the leading liberal newspaper, which counted Thackeray and Dickens amongst those who had worked for it.

Sensitive to the relatively low status of the profession of journalism, George, having been admitted to the English Bar, left for Victoria. He intended to prospect for gold at first and it is reputed that he met his wife Margaret on a trip to the Ballarat goldfields.

He was admitted to the Victorian Bar on his arrival in 1856 and, to supplement his income, he wrote for the *Melbourne Morning Herald* and then the *Argus*, of which he became the editor. Meticulous and rather pedantic, he resigned from the editorship on a matter of principle, believing that an editor should have complete independence, even from the owner of the newspaper. His disagreement with the owner, Edward Wilson, revolved around the inequity of the special representation of property interests in parliament. His view, which differed from Wilson's, was that rich and poor had an equal share in good government, whereas the representation of minorities favoured the rich. It was said of him that he addressed himself to an ideal public, and gave it virtues, intellectuality and high moral purpose that it did not possess. The idealist dominated the practical man.

In 1887 his brother Thomas joined him in his new home in the suburb of Brighton, which still has many reminders of the family, including a Higinbotham Meeting Hall, and the two brothers lived in the same house for the rest of their lives. Thomas, the only son not to go to Trinity, became engineer-in-chief of the Victorian Railways and was responsible for the introduction of the Irish wide gauge railway to Victoria. Though the gauge was the safest, it was also more expensive than the narrower gauge adopted in neighbouring New South Wales. The result was that rail communications between the two states were to be interrupted at the border until 1962.

The Dangerous Politician

George Higinbotham's first foray into politics was short-lived. He was elected to the Legislative Assembly in 1861 but the government fell in that year. He was defeated in the new election but managed to get elected shortly afterwards and was appointed as attorney-general in 1863. As attorney-general he was the leading radical in the colony, making adjustments to his thinking as he gained experience. Though he supported Gavan Duffy's land Bill in 1862, he confessed two years later to his mistake in supporting a Bill that essentially gave security of tenure to those whom he called 'the wealthy lower orders'. Ten years later he had progressed to the notion that property was robbery and that Crown lands should only be available on thirty-three year leases, and with a property tax imposed.

His stand on state aid for education, too, altered over the years. In 1861 he was advocating a private approach where parents would initiate new schools and the government would give financial support to them, but by 1867 he was convinced that the state should take full responsibility for national education and withdraw aid to the sectarian schools. He chaired a royal commission in 1866 to prepare a public instruction Bill and the commission, wanting education rather than mere instruction, allowed a place for common Christianity but not the sectarian kind. The proposed Bill was withdrawn but Higinbotham's royal commission had prepared the way for adoption of a secular instruction Bill of 1872. By 1880, when he left parliament to become a puisne judge of the Supreme Court, he was arguing that all Christian references should be removed from school textbooks as these offended adherents to other religions.

As a politician Higinbotham believed in the common man as the source of political authority; he disliked the party system, advocating that parliamentarians should vote on every issue by conviction and conscience, not according to the party line but in support of competent and honest government. He was able to overcome his dislike of the party system as attorney-general by uniting his followers against the common foe – the Legislative Council. His dislike of the principle of an upper house and the qualifications necessary for election to it, and his antagonism towards Colonial Office interference in domestic affairs, were a part of his strategy to achieve supremacy for the Legislative Assembly. He consolidated the Victorian statutes in 1864–65, and again in 1890 while chief justice, receiving a vote of thanks, unique in Victoria's political annals, from both houses of parliament.

Higinbotham's resistance to imperial interference by the Colonial Office in domestic affairs did not imply that he was intent on promoting total independence. He was determined that the colonies should fulfil their obligations to the imperial government and to the governor as its representative. In the notorious *Shenandoah* case in 1865 Higinbotham, as attorney–general, advised against the United States consul's request that the American confederate ship *Shenandoah* be seized as a pirate ship after it had put into Melbourne for repairs and to take on supplies. Higinbotham's advice was to treat the *Shenandoah* as a ship-of-war of a belligerent power and, as Great Britain was neutral, it should not be seized. While in Melbourne the ship's officers were entertained by the Melbourne Club at a function attended by a number of judges, but after the ship left Melbourne it sank thirty-seven American ships. When the war ended the United States made claims on the British Government for $19 million in damages. In the subsequent settlement the British government had to pay more than £800,000 in compensation. The issue was complicated by the fact that the *Shenandoah* had recruited men while in Melbourne and these were on board when she sailed. This compromised any defence against the so-called post Civil War Alabama claims. Higinbotham, in his own defence, and not covering himself with glory, argued that in this case he and the ministers were acting as advisers and were not responsible for the governor's decision. Subsequently, four men were tried for having been unlawfully on board the ship while it was in port. One was an American and was discharged; the others appeared before Molesworth with Higinbotham prosecuting and Wrixon and Aspinall for the defence. Aspinall made much of the fact that one of the men was a cook. 'Did the jury suppose', he asked, 'that Her Majesty was trembling on her throne because Charley was frying potatoes on the ship?' The men were given ten days in gaol. The case was important for its ramifications in international law and the laws involving neutrality.

In the early 1860s the issues of free trade and tariff protection were very much to the fore in the Victorian Parliament. In 1864, believing that the Legislative Council would not pass a Bill to impose tariffs, the premier introduced to the Legislative Assembly, and had passed, an appropriation Bill, to which had been added a customs tariff and other measures to raise revenue. The Legislative Council had the option to reject all of the Bill or to pass it without amendment. Higinbotham wrongly gave the assurance to the premier that he was acting lawfully, but the Bill was laid aside and an impasse ensued that resulted in the government resorting to the premier's bank to pay salaries, and by a device that was clearly illegal. It was not until April 1866 that the issue was fully resolved.

The Colonial Office had followed these events in Victoria with mounting alarm. The secretary of state for the colonies had been annotating despatches from Melbourne with comments on Governor Charles Darling's 'want of judgement' in accepting Higinbotham's advice. They advised the governor that the device used by the premier to obtain funds, and sanctioned by him as governor, was illegal, and recalled him. Asked in parliament why the governor was being recalled, Higinbotham responded full of rage and indignation, revealing his antagonism to the Colonial Office and the Legislative Council. Darling, in Higinbotham's view, had been recalled because he dared to support the Legislative Assembly in its struggle with the Legislative Council, 'the stronghold of the obscurantist squatters, the grasping merchant princes – a faction that was the very vilest by which this country has been cursed'. 'They could', he said, 'have papered the walls of Government House with all the illuminated addresses that poured in protesting the recall; and the Colonial

Office could have done the same with the protests it received'. Darling's recall had as much to do with the open disapproval he expressed of members of the Opposition as it had with his acceptance of Higinbotham's advice.

Another constitutional crisis emerged as a result of Darling's recall when the Legislative Assembly voted £20,000 to Lady Darling and prepared an address of sympathy and gratitude to her husband. Richard Ireland denounced the grant while Higinbotham vigorously supported it. The Legislative Council rejected the appropriation Bill; Lady Darling said she would not accept the grant anyway and Sir Charles Darling took up another post.

In a re-elected parliament in 1869, Higinbotham refused to serve as attorney-general again in a ministry that precluded him from submitting his case for independence from the Colonial Office. He had drawn up five resolutions to prevent such interference, provoked into this by a group of conservative Victorian colonists in London, who had called a conference on colonial affairs. A debate occurred in the House of Lords where the existence of responsible government in the colonies was implicitly denied. Only Lord Chancellor Cairns, Trinity graduate, chancellor of Trinity from 1867–85 and half-brother of William Wellington Cairns, governor of Queensland, held fast to the principle of responsible government so dear to Higinbotham. He said, 'If it was to be laid down that the secretary of state at home was to hold in leading strings the ministry of the colony, then the pretence of free colonial institutions was simply a delusion and a mockery'.

Higinbotham considered the London conference to be a gross interference in colonial affairs by irresponsible expatriates and demanded that its deliberations not be sanctioned. He also proposed, and had accepted in the Legislative Assembly, that Victoria wished to remain within the empire; that imperial legislation should not interfere with the colony's internal affairs; that the Colonial Office had no right to instruct the governor in domestic issues, but could merely advise on the royal assent to colonial Bills; and that the Assembly should support its ministers in designing measures to establish an independent colonial legislature. Higinbotham's point was that the notion of responsible government as it stood was a charade, since a foreigner – the secretary of state in London, on the advice of the Colonial Office, 'the poodle dog of a courtesan' – could accept or reject colonial legislation. Higinbotham, in his unrelenting battle against the Colonial Office, believed that it had no right to interfere in colonial affairs by giving coded instructions to the governor, which meant that the most senior official was being directed from London and not by the colony's ministers. In his opinion, the activities of the Colonial Office, 'that straw image of official intrigue and arbitrary unlawful interference', made the idea of self-government a farce. The Darling case showed him to be right. He resented despatches being sent by the Colonial Office to the governor to be passed on to the ministers, and this influenced his later behaviour as chief justice. When Lord Canterbury succeeded Darling as governor in 1866, he realised that the government in London was under-estimating Higinbotham's popular support, and he advised London to give more substance to the idea of responsible government. By the 1890s the principles of self-government that Higinbotham had expounded had become a reality.

In 1871 Higinbotham lost his seat in the Assembly by fourteen votes but was elected to another constituency two years later. In 1876 he decided to leave politics and return to practice at the Bar, but he was not highly successful. The doctrine to which he held, that a barrister owed a double duty, to the client and to the truth, did not help him make a fortune of the kind that Ireland, Mitchie and others were earning. He never sought to become a Queen's Counsel, even though this would have been easily achieved.

The Fearless Judge

In 1880, at the age of fifty-four, Higinbotham entered a new phase of his life. He was invited by the premier, James Service, to accept appointment as a puisne judge of the Supreme Court. It was ironic that he accepted the appointment because in 1864, as attorney-general, he had reprimanded Redmond Barry for failing to recognise the supremacy of his office over the judges. Barry had informed the governor by letter that he was taking leave to go to Sydney on holiday. The letter was referred by Governor Darling to Higinbotham, who said that judges did not have the right to proceed on leave without the permission of the Executive Council.

Barry went on leave in any case and a series of acrimonious letters passed between him, Higinbotham and the governor for over a year. Higinbotham's instruction to Barry, that 'No officer of my department should communicate directly with the governor on official business', was challenged and the issue then widened to the powers of the Executive Council to suspend judges. Finally a memorandum was sent to the governor by Higinbotham setting out the views of the ministers, and the Executive Council informed the judges of the Supreme Court that the questions of their rights, privileges and duties should be addressed to the attorney-general, as the minister responsible for the judiciary. Barry asked that the matter be referred to the Colonial Office but the secretary of state upheld Higinbotham's view. This, of course, did not please Higinbotham at all since he wished to have no dealings with the Colonial Office in domestic matters. He informed the judges that the London decision was not binding and there the matter was allowed to rest. Honour had been satisfied and the independence of the judges was preserved. Stawell was comfortable with Higinbotham as a judge for, although he considered him 'a dangerous politician', he thought that he would be a fearless and conscientious judge.

In 1886 Stawell resigned as chief justice and Higinbotham was appointed to replace him. As puisne judge he had indicated to the premier that he would not comply with the standing instruction from the governor that on any case involving a capital punishment the judge had to report to the Executive Council in writing and appear before it. He would only comply if he were asked to do so by the attorney-general, thus applying his own principle of accountability of the judges to the attorney-general.

As chief justice, Higinbotham would normally have been the automatic choice as acting-governor in the governor's absence. In the parlance of the day he 'stood out in the dormant commission', that is, if the governor died in office or took leave for a period, his place would be taken by the chief justice. Higinbotham had made it clear that if he received the commission he would not, as required by the code, inform the Colonial Office on matters of domestic policy. The governor asked Higinbotham to set out his objections to the Colonial Office's role and this he did. On being offered a knighthood, he refused it as a 'base contemptible distinction that merely gave a man a handle to his name'. When, in 1886, the governor wished to return to England on business, Higinbotham was asked if he would communicate with the Colonial Office by despatch on matters of domestic policy, if he were appointed as acting governor. He said he would not, and fellow Irishman Sir William Robinson of South Australia was appointed. Failure to swear in the chief justice as acting governor was unusual, but there was a precedent in 1875 when Sir Hercules Robinson, brother of Sir Willliam and governor of New South Wales, was absent in Fiji negotiating its annexation to Britain. Robinson refused to name the chief justice Sir James Martin as his acting governor. There was a record of tension between Robinson and Martin, which was seen by Martin as 'the equivocal condescension of the governor and his lady'. In 1892, the instructions issued to Victorian governors were redrafted to take into account Higinbotham's objections.

George Higinbotham was a man of compassion and high principle. He refused to join the Melbourne Club because he would not go where his wife Margaret was not welcome. He championed the cause of women's suffrage as early as 1873 and was ridiculed in the press for his efforts. His unremitting opposition to the power of the Colonial Office irritated some, but his position was vindicated towards the end of his life. He was a man of the people and disliked all forms of privilege. His financial support of the seamen in a maritime strike in 1890 earned him few friends amongst 'the wealthy lower orders', but he became a hero in the Trades Hall. He saw the maritime union as David in a struggle with the Goliath bosses. He left his mark on the law and in the statute books and was regarded by Sir William Shiels, a premier of Victoria, as Australia's noblest if not greatest man. Higinbotham disapproved of the additional £500 extra that he received as chief justice and with it he entertained his colleagues on festive occasions. His fees were less than half those of his peers, who objected to the class of people who constantly loitered around the corridors to his chambers seeking representation. A temperance advocate, Higinbotham also disapproved of gambling, believing that men should be protected from the evils of both. He earned for himself the sobriquet 'pompous prig' in the Melbourne *Punch*, for this moral dictatorship.

There were contradictions in this great man. He appointed Mitchie and Ireland as Victoria's first two Queen's Counsel, yet did not take silk himself. He refused to walk in the procession of chief judges of other colonies on the ceremonial occasion of the opening of the 1888 centennial exhibition in Melbourne because he believed that the speaker of the Legislative Assembly should walk behind the chief justices. His support of the maritime workers' strike was seen as inconsistent with the dignity of his office, which he called upon in his letter of support, which said: 'The chief justice presents his compliments to the president of Trades Hall Council and requests that he be so good as to place the enclosed cheque for £50 to the credit of the strike fund.'

He was shy and retiring privately, yet in public he would hurl invective at his opponents. His obsession with the Colonial Office was contrasted with his careful, considered and balanced judicial opinions. His compassion was contrasted with the obstinate refusal to attend at the Executive Council to discuss capital sentences when it was a matter of life or death to an individual.

Higinbotham diligently kept all his papers and diaries, yet ordered that these be burnt after his death and that his family should leave the colony. His son Edward was a student in Trinity in 1892, the year of the tercentenary of the College. Barry, Stawell and Irvine, all chief justices of Victoria were given honorary doctorates by Trinity, and so too was Darley, chief justice of New South Wales. Higinbotham received no honours from the University. A dignified statue near the former Treasury Building of the Victorian Government Offices commemorates a man about whom Sir Arthur Dean said, 'until Federation, the Bar produced no greater public figure than George Higinbotham'. He died on the last day of 1892.

Iceberg Irvine: Premier and Chief Justice

The tradition of appointing Irish chief justices continued after the death of Higinbotham. He was succeeded by Sir John Madden, born in Cork and educated in law at Melbourne University, and the first person to be awarded the LL.D degree of that university. The Trinity dominance was restored in 1918 when Sir William Hill Irvine (1858–1943) succeeded to the chief justiceship. Irvine was the son of Hill Irvine, a farmer and linen manufacturer from Newry County Down, and his wife Margaret Mitchel, sister of the 1848 rebel John Mitchel. Irvine entered Trinity in 1874 and after graduating in 1878, he read at King's Inns. Persuaded by his widowed mother to make a new start in Australia, they arrived in Melbourne in 1879. Irvine's first appointment was at Geelong College, but he was soon admitted to the Victorian Bar and practised successfully for ten years. He wrote occasionally, publishing a practice book on the *Justices Act* and a book based on the property rights of women.

In 1894 Irvine was elected to the Legislative Assembly on a free-trade democratic ticket and became successively attorney-general, leader of the opposition and then premier in 1902–03. He was known as 'Iceberg Irvine', which derived from his period as premier, which was notable for his unpopular suppression of a railway workers strike in 1903. In 1904 Irvine resigned from state politics and visited England and Ireland, and Trinity honoured him with the LL.D degree. On his return he declined a Supreme Court judgeship, taking silk instead and practising at the Bar. After only two years of this Irvine was elected as a member of the Federal House of Representatives, while maintaining his lucrative practice and appearing in major cases before the new High Court of Australia. In 1913–14 Irvine was the federal attorney-general and narrowly survived a motion of censure involving conflict of interest. A supporter of conscription, he lost this cause in the federal parliament and, at the end of the war, he accepted the position of chief justice of Victoria.

From 1857 until Irvine's retirement in 1935, Irishmen had served as chief justices of Victoria–a total of seventy-eight years. Apart from Madden's eighteen years, Trinity-educated lawyers held the post. Irvine administered the state as lieutenant-governor on a number of occasions and was acting governor from 1931–34. He was regarded as cold and detached, generally using precedence and not commenting on the state of the law. He carried the roles of premier, chief justice and lieutenant-governor with great dignity and authority – as is well captured in his portrait (see Fig. 28, p147), which hangs, with those of Stawell, Barry and Higinbotham, in the upper gallery of the library of the Supreme Court.

Figure 28. Sir William Hill Irvine, Chief Justice of Victoria, 1918–35.

The County Courts

The review of the legal system in Victoria carried out in 1852 provided not only for a Supreme Court but also for County Courts with powers and functions that were similar to those introduced in England. The courts were the successors to the Court of Requests and were limited to the recovery of amounts up to £50. Depending upon the amount, the case could be heard before a judge only, a judge with two assessors or, after 1869, a judge and jury. If the Supreme Court was dominated by Trinity-educated judges from its inception, so too were the County Courts. Of the twenty-five permanent judges appointed between 1852 and 1902, nine were educated at Trinity and two were closely connected to the College. These latter two were Hickman Molesworth and Arthur Wolfe Chomley, both of whom featured in the Kelly case.

The first of the Trinity-educated County Court judges and the second to be appointed to the court was Arthur N. Wrixon (1811–61). He came from Ballyclough, County Cork, the same district as Redmond Barry, and graduated in 1835. In 1850 the family arrived in Melbourne and Wrixon was appointed to the County Court, sitting mainly in the Western District of Victoria. His son Henry, who he sent back to Trinity, had an illustrious career and this will be described in the final chapter

Michael Macoboy, also born in County Cork, in 1809, graduated from Trinity in 1842 and migrated to Melbourne in 1850. After eight years at the Bar he was appointed judge of the County Court, initially at Castlemaine. He was so unpopular that he was soon transferred to neighbouring Maryborough. Serving as judge for twenty years, his main claim to fame is that he features in *The Wild Colonial Boy*:

> 'In sixty-one this daring youth commenced his wild career
> With a heart that knew no danger, no foe man did he fear
> He held the Beechworth mail coach up and robbed Judge Macoboy
> Who trembled and gave up his gold to the Wild Colonial Boy
> He bade the judge good morning and told him to beware
> For he'd never rob a decent judge who acted on the square.'

James Langton Clarke (1802–86), appointed as County Court judge in 1858, was educated at Sandhurst, Trinity, and Queens' College, Cambridge. He entered Trinity in 1824, aged 22, but 'incorporated' into Queens' two years later. Graduating in 1829, he was called to the Irish Bar and practised for twenty years. In 1855 Clarke went to Victoria and was appointed to the County Court three years later. According to J.L.Forde, Australia owes the name and fame of the famous Australian novelist, Marcus Clarke, to his uncle, Judge Clarke. Marcus Clarke was educated at Cholmley Grammar School, Highgate, where Gerard Manley Hopkins was a fellow pupil. After the death of his father in 1863, Marcus was sent to Victoria to live with his uncle James, who found him his first position in a bank. The job was not to Marcus's liking and James then found him work on a pastoral station in the Western District of Victoria. He took up journalism with the *Argus* and this set him on his writing career, which culminated with the publication in 1874 of his internationally successful novel *For the Term of His Natural Life*, issued originally in 1870 as a serial under the title of *His Natural Life*. This is one of the most durable works of Australian fiction, ranking with Boldrewood's *Robbery Under Arms* and Henry Handel Richardson's *The Fortunes of Richard Mahony*. Clarke's novel tells of the horrors of the convict system and, interestingly, Trinity-educated Thomas Rogers provided inspiration in the novel for the character Rev John North. Rogers had campaigned against the brutality of the convict system at Norfolk Island while he was chaplain there and the commandant had him transferred to Van Diemen's Land, where he continued his crusade.

Judge Clarke, who retired after thirteen years on the Bench, was a member of an extraordinary family. His brother Andrew became governor of Western Australia in 1846, and his nephew Sir Andrew Clarke became surveyor-general of Victoria before returning to England to become inspector-general of fortifications, responsible for the design and construction of the naval docks of Portsmouth, Chatham and Malta.

The fourth and fifth County Court judges educated in Trinity were Charles Prendergast Hackett and Samuel Henry Bindon. Hackett, son of Charles Hackett and Eliza Disney, graduated from Trinity in 1840, was called to the Irish Bar in 1842 and left for the Indian civil service shortly thereafter. Arriving in Melbourne in 1854 he served initially as police magistrate in Castlemaine and then in Melbourne. He became a County Court judge in 1868.

Samuel Henry Bindon (1812–79) graduated in 1838 and, although the family estates were lost in the Encumbered Estates Court in 1846, he joined the nationalist cause, writing for Gavan Duffy's *Nation* and serving as secretary to the Irish Tenant League. Bindon arrived in Melbourne in 1855 and practised in the County Courts. In 1864 he entered politics as an independent and was appointed as minister of justice in 1866. The appointment was short lived as he had shown too much independence and radicalism. He was a supporter of a tax on the wealthy to pay for their 'property rights' and was an advocate of a welfare state. At one time in parliament the Irish Catholic former premier, Sir John O'Shannassy, attacked him for being anti-British! Bindon's passion was to protect the underprivileged; he was a strong supporter of secular education and in 1868 successfully introduced a motion for religious equality in the taking of oaths. Bindon constantly promoted the need to develop the agricultural wealth of the country, a concern which not only reflected his constituents' needs in the agricultural district of Castlemaine but also his desire for economic independence from Britain. A great agricultural exhibition in 1866 was the result of special grants he obtained in parliament. Bindon's interests in economic development also found expression in the inspiration he gave to Australia's first official organisation for the advancement of technical education, the Technological Commission, which he chaired. This gifted man resigned from parliament in 1868 on his appointment to the County Court. He was one of the judges dismissed in the Black Wednesday political crisis in 1878, but he was quickly re-instated. His son, Henry, educated at Melbourne University, was counsel for Ned Kelly and is the man history has partly blamed for Ned's premature death.

During the 'Black Wednesday' crisis, as it came to be known, the attorney general was Richard Le Poer Trench, who later became a County Court judge. It is supposed in the local directories that Le Poer Trench attended Trinity but he does not appear in the alumni register. A grandson of the Earl of Clancarty, his father and his brother were Trinity graduates, so there was a family tradition of attendance at the College. The Black Wednesday crisis arose because of the rejection in December 1877 by the Legislative Council of a Bill that provided for the continued payment of salary to members of the Legislative Assembly. This undemocratic blocking device was designed to cause hardship to those who did not have the wealth of the Legislative Council members. While parliament was adjourned for the recess, the government, in retaliation against the Legislative Council, gazetted the dismissal of all judges of the County Courts and Courts of Mines, chairmen of general sessions, the police magistrates, coroners, wardens of the goldfields and a large number of public servants. George Higinbotham's brother, Thomas, was one of the victims, chosen for their supposed alliance with, or sympathy for, the Legislative Council.

Le Poer Trench was the attorney-general for most of this crisis and he, together with another Trinity man, his successor as attorney-general, Sir Bryan O'Loghlen, gave the government of the day the incredibly poor advice that warrants could be signed for the payment of money authorised by one chamber of parliament only, and that the dismissals were legal. Most, but not all, of those dismissed were subsequently reinstated, including Thomas Higinbotham. Le Poer Trench had been appointed as attorney-general in 1875, and again in 1877–78, without being an elected member of parliament, a most unusual circumstance. He was elevated to Queen's Counsel in 1880, and became a County Court judge in the same year, serving until 1885 when he made an unsuccessful bid in the Supreme Court to stay in office beyond the age of seventy.

Joseph Henry Dunne (1821–77) entered Trinity in 1841 but did not graduate. He was called to the Irish Bar in 1849 and practised until 1854 when he left for Melbourne. He was almost immediately involved in the trial of the Eureka Stockade rebels, assisting Richard Ireland in their defence. Thereafter, Dunne practised in Ballarat, until 1861, when he was appointed as crown prosecutor. Ten years later he was elevated to the Country Court Bench. In his authoritative *Pounds and Pedigrees*, de Serville records that Judge Dunne was linked romantically with Mrs Molesworth and 'took a room in a lodging house, ordered three bottles of brandy and a dozen of porter, locked the door and drank himself to death.'

Edward Blayney Hamilton (1845–1905) graduated from Trinity in 1864, and after ten years of successful practice in Dublin he migrated to Melbourne, where he practised again until his appointment as judge in 1887.

Finally, Richard Annesley Billing, one of the first two Queen's Counsel to be appointed in Victoria, was appointed to the County Court Bench in 1882. He died nine weeks later. Billing was a leader of the Bar, one of Victoria's first legal academics, and counsel in many important cases. He appears elsewhere in his role as Melbourne University's reader in law, and it is to the establishment of the university that we now turn.

CHAPTER 7

Halls of Learning

A costly toy, the very insanity of extravagance.

The Age (1853)

Foundation

On 3 July 1854, Governor Hotham laid the foundation stones of two monuments to Sir Redmond Barry. The first stone was laid at the site of the new university, on wasteland to the north of the town of Melbourne, and, as Sir Zelman Cowen tells it, 'then what Sutherland [the recorder of the event] was pleased to call the "cortege" wound its way to where land had been set aside for the Melbourne Public Library and Museum'. Barry had secured a government grant of £13,000 for a library that would be the envy of 'the large American universities', and it is now one of the finest libraries in Australia. In honour of its founder, a magnificent statue of Barry stands in its forecourt on one of Melbourne's most prominent city streets. Barry's influence on the architecture of the building is well recognised, and of special interest is the Queen's Hall, a reading room which is modelled on the Long Room of Trinity College's Library, before the alterations of 1862. The contemporary McManus prints (see pp.154–5) illustrate very well the dramatic effect of the Long Room's alterations.

There is no doubt about the identity of the founder of the Melbourne Public Library, but there is some argument about who founded Melbourne

Figure 29. Long Room of Trinity College Library before alteration.

Figure 30. Long Room of Trinity College Library after alterations in 1862.

Figure 31. Queen's Hall Reading Room, Melbourne Public Library.

University. The historian Geoffrey Blainey says that there is little profit in seeking the origins of Melbourne University in the activity or advocacy of one man. Rather, the university idea had its source in a body of opinion, expressed by a number of prominent people like Barry, La Trobe, Childers and William Stawell, that a university was the essential amenity of a civilised society. These influential people lent their enthusiastic support and capabilities to the development and implementation of the idea of a university. There was also the fact that Sydney had a university and this must have provided a powerful stimulus. According to Cowen, 'Barry's great contribution was his commitment to the task of breathing life into the institution which, in its earliest days, had to maintain itself in the face of a community which at times ridiculed it and questioned its worth'. On the day the university opened its doors the editor of the *Age*, whose proprietor, unlike the proprietor of the rival *Argus*, was not on the first council, called the new institution 'a costly toy, the very insanity of extravagance. It would be cheaper to send all the students of the new college to Oxford and Cambridge where each could live in luxury in term time and tour the continent on vacation for £300 per annum – half the money which the government would spend on educating each student in Melbourne.'

By the time Melbourne University was being established the climate of opinion was turning against universities, as bastions of privilege and purveyors of useless knowledge. The question being asked was whether the collegiate self-governing principles, so entrenched in the Anglican establishments of Oxford, Cambridge and Dublin, would be appropriate in the colonies where culture and the intellectual life would have to take second place to the immediate need for the training of doctors, lawyers, scientists, engineers and other professionals. Unlike Sydney, there was never any doubt about the unitary nature of Melbourne University. The strength of secular feeling was reflected in the limitation to four on the council who could be clergymen, the prohibition of appointing clergy to be professors, and a ban placed on professors lecturing on religious topics either inside or outside the university.

It is now widely thought that it was the intensive lobbying by Barry that stimulated the interest of Lieutenant-Governor Charles La Trobe and the auditor-general, Hugh Culling Eardley Childers, in the idea of establishing a university and, in 1852, Childers included the sum of £10,000 in the budget estimates for the purpose. Childers, an ambitious man known as 'Here Comes Everybody' Childers as a play upon his initials and his wide-ranging ambitions, arrived in Melbourne in 1850 aged twenty-three. A Cambridge graduate, he first became inspector of denominational schools and commissioner of national schools. In 1852 La Trobe appointed him auditor-general, and nominated him to the Legislative Council. He, La Trobe and Fitzgerald Foster were blamed for the budget deficit that contributed to the economic crisis of 1854 and Hotham, La Trobe's successor, tried to have Childers dismissed for incompetence. The auditor-general was able to call upon his friends in England for help, however, and Hotham was censured by the Colonial Office.

A small committee of the Legislative Council with three Irishmen, William Stawell, Francis Murphy and John O'Shanassy, together with Childers and John Pascoe Fawkner, was formed to consider the question of the establishment of a university. Stawell and Childers drafted the Bill for the *Melbourne University Act* and this received assent in January 1853. Redmond Barry was appointed as the first chancellor, with Childers as vice-chancellor. Childers returned to England in 1857, where he had a distinguished career in parliament, culminating in his appointment as Chancellor of the Exchequer. He took the credit for founding the university and remained its supporter for the rest of his life. He did say, however, that 'after its foundation by far the largest share of the university's work was done by Barry.' So, Barry is generally recognised as the founder of the university and, in its early years, it was nurtured by Irishmen and, particularly, by Trinity men. Unlike Sydney it was not an Oxford-Cambridge hybrid and its motto, chosen by Barry, *I shall grow in the esteem of future generations*, is more modest and more realistic than that of Sydney.

The first council of the university, chaired by Barry, had James Croke, William Stawell and Francis Murphy as members, and Fitzgerald Foster soon joined them when a vacancy arose. Trinity was, therefore, well represented. Indeed, reporting on the opening of the university, the *Age* commented acidly on the university's Irish origins: 'we are reminded', it said, 'of an Irish militia in which there were about twenty times as many officers as men'. Barry, with his appointment to the Bench and other activities, was already a well-known figure in Melbourne. Judges enjoyed high status and profile, but it was Barry's public contributions, for which he received his knighthood, rather than his work as a judge, that made him more prominent locally. Although, unlike Stawell, he has no town named for him, in the end he left a greater mark than Stawell did on the town of Melbourne, which was growing rich on the nearby gold, some of which he was able to divert into intellectual and cultural pursuits. Although he did not wish to create another Trinity College, Dublin, in Melbourne, Barry's devotion to the classics ensured that most of the initial educational focus would be on the liberal arts. Professional studies came later when factions arose to counter the commanding influence of the founding chancellor but, even at the beginning, a chair of political economy signalled a desire ultimately to serve the needs of the developing colony by the introduction of more practical areas of study.

The Professors

Council meetings were held initially in Barry's chambers and the chancellor would not hesitate to call a meeting at short notice, and to proceed no matter what the availability of the other members. Meetings of Council frequently took place with only the chancellor and his registrar present. Edward Graves Mayne, son of a Dublin lawyer, was the first registrar and first salaried officer to be appointed to the university staff. He was elected a scholar of Trinity in 1844 and graduated in 1845. Mayne was soon joined by others from Ireland and it is remarkable that the selection committee in London chose men from Irish universities to fill three out of the four foundation professorships.

Following the pattern of the Irish Queen's Colleges, chairs in mathematics, classics and ancient history, modern history and political economy were established. Unlike Sydney, the instructions to the selection committee in London did not stipulate that only Oxford or Cambridge graduates need apply but, rather, graduates of any university would be welcome. High salaries and good conditions were on offer and the first four professors were duly appointed. Three were from Irish universities, and William Hearn, the most distinguished of them all, was educated at Trinity College, Dublin.

William Edward Hearn (1826–88), from County Cavan, was educated at Portora Royal School and Trinity, graduating in 1847. In the same year Hearn married Rose Le Fanu, a member of a distinguished literary family of Huguenot origin whose forebears had settled in Dublin in the eighteenth century. The most illustrious was Joseph Sheridan Le Fanu, author of *Uncle Silas* and the short story collection *In a Glass Darkly*.

Hearn was admitted to the Irish Bar but did not practise because, at the age of twenty-three, he was appointed as professor of Greek at Queen's College, Galway. While there he developed his theories of political economy, and an essay on *The Condition of Ireland* won him the prestigious Cassell Prize. Following his appointment to the chair of law, modern history and literature, political economy and logic, at Melbourne in 1854, he produced his most notable work, *Plutology*, on the satisfaction of demand occasioned by human wants. This was an early treatise on the demand-pull theory of innovation and, in a break with Malthusian political economy, Hearn argued that there was sufficient under-utilised land in the world to negate the law of diminishing returns. The work received international acclaim for its originality and penetrating observations. His 1867 book *The Government of England: A Constitutional History*, which among other things explored the impact of the cabinet system on English constitutional arrangements, was prescribed reading in Trinity and at Oxford. Indeed, it is claimed that Herbert Spencer, the great English philosopher and sociologist, describing Hearn's work as 'a work of history and evolution grafted together', drew on it for his *Descriptive Sociology of England*.

In 1873, Redmond Barry, still the chancellor, proposed to Hearn that he might take on the deanship of the new faculty of law, without any additional remuneration, and in addition to his present duties. Though expressing reluctance, becoming dean of law suited Hearn very well, as it entailed losing the title professor, which meant, as far as he was concerned, that he would now be able to pursue his political aspirations. Barry had instructed the selection committee in London to inform candidates that the university was founded on 'a total abstraction from political and sectarian interference'. When Professor Hearn first offered himself for election to the Legislative Assembly in 1859 Barry was outraged, believing that Hearn had flouted an unwritten rule. Hearn was not elected and the university council then took the opportunity to adhere to Barry's injunction on political engagement among the professors and successfully introduced a statute that forbade professors from sitting in

Figure 32. Dr William Hearn, Dean of the Faculty of Law, Melbourne University.

parliament or becoming members of any political association. When Hearn relinquished the title of professor he was able to stand for parliament, which he did successfully in 1878, serving as a member of the Legislative Council until his death in 1888.

Hearn had previously served as adviser to the Legislative Council in its battle with the more democratic Legislative Assembly. As mentioned previously, his most notable piece of advice was to Charles Gavan Duffy on the proposed Land Bill of 1862. He and Richard Ireland worked on this Bill, which was intended to open up the land to smallholders by a process of 'selection' and it is suspected that they conspired to render the Bill ineffective. In the inimitable style of the day, Hearn was dubbed the 'professor of political dodgery' for this and his other activities in support of the squatters and the upper class.

During his time in parliament, Hearn's opinions on legal and constitutional matters were sought and respected, but his efforts to codify Victorian law, a task on which he was engaged during his last years in the Legislative Council, produced a code that was too abstract. It was left to George Higinbotham to revise the statutes later when he was chief justice.

Hearn was a member of the university council and took an active part in the debates that shaped the direction of the institution. He was elected as the third chancellor in 1886, in succession to Stawell, but his incumbency lasted only five months, for he was defeated in the following elections to council and was, therefore, ineligible to stand for the chancellorship.

(Sir) Frederick McCoy (1817–99), professor of geology and mineralogy, and curator of the museum at Queen's College, Belfast, was chosen to be the professor of natural science. Son of a physician and professor of materia medica at Queen's College, Galway, Frederick began medical studies in Dublin; it has often been claimed that this was at Trinity but there seems to be no evidence for this. Turning to paleontology and natural history, McCoy worked in Dublin for Sir Richard Griffith, half brother of Irish cousinage member, Charles Griffith. McCoy worked on classifying his collections in the Dublin Museum of Natural History and then left for Cambridge, where he worked with Adam Sedgewick as collaborator in the Woodwardian Museum. In 1849 he was appointed to the chair at Belfast and five years later, attracted by the salary offered in Melbourne, which was three times his salary at Belfast, and by other inducements like a house on 'Professors Row', McCoy arrived in Melbourne to take up his chair. An anti-Darwinist, he had a tumultuous career. He built up the museum, which subsequently passed into the hands of the state. He became associated with the Acclimatisation Society, which led to disruption of the Australian ecological balance by the introduction of exotic species, including the rabbit; and he wrongly advised the Legislative Council that mining deep reefs would produce no gold, only to be proved wrong by miners who paid little attention to academic geologists. Yet he had the satisfaction of being the first professor to be knighted for his services; he became a Fellow of The Royal Society and was admitted to the degree of doctor of science by Cambridge University in 1886, the only degree he ever possessed.

Englishman Henry Rowe, a fellow of Trinity College, Cambridge, was appointed to the chair of classics by the selection committee, but died five weeks after arrival as a result of illness during the voyage to Melbourne. He was replaced in 1856 by Martin Howy Irving, son of a declared heretic of the Church of Scotland. Irving, who had a brilliant academic career at Oxford, constantly tried to reform the curriculum in Melbourne. He succeeded in allowing students who were unable to attend lectures to sit for examinations;

but failed to have the university council approve a scheme for the introduction of an associate diploma in Arts for non-members of the university. In 1871 Irving left to become headmaster of Wesley College in Melbourne, but maintained his interest in the university by membership of the council from 1875 until 1900. As a member of the schoolmasters 'caucus' arguing for curriculum reform, Irving continually challenged the Barry dictatorship and once tried to have the chancellor replaced while he was overseas. When Barry died in 1880, new chairs in natural philosophy, engineering, pathology, chemistry and modern languages were created. Agitation by the schoolmasters caused Stawell, Barry's successor, to resign as chancellor in 1882, and the chancellorship was vacant until 1886.

When Irving moved to Wesley College in 1871 he succeeded James Corrigan, the foundation headmaster of this famous school. Born in County Donegal in 1823, Corrigan was the son of a teacher of mathematics in a Wesleyan Methodist school. He, too, took up teaching and was appointed as headmaster of the Wesleyan Training School in Dublin. He enrolled at Trinity at the same time and graduated MA and LL.B in 1861, and LL.D in 1864. A year later he accepted the headmastership of Wesley College. The new college was an enormous success under his leadership. He was a member of George Higinbotham's 1866 royal commission on education and supported Higinbotham's compromise view that there was a place for undogmatic instruction based upon common Christianity in the schools. Corrigan also served on the council of Melbourne University and on the Board of Education, which controlled primary schools.

The fourth professor to be appointed by the selection committee in London was William Parkinson Wilson. Educated at St John's College, Cambridge, he became professor of mathematics at Queen's College, Belfast, in 1849. He, too, was attracted to Melbourne by the salary and conditions, and arrived to give the university's first lecture in April 1855. Observing the relatively low numbers of students, he and Hearn issued a pamphlet that laid the blame for Sydney's 'want of success' on the Oxford model that it followed, and advocated a wider curriculum with classics as an option. This was rejected by the university council, or, more accurately, by Barry. Wilson next devised the first engineering course to be offered at any Australian university and in 1861 introduced a certificate course in civil engineering.

The First College

Deploring what he called the 'incomplete university, one without residential colleges to provide moral and religious education', Wilson became secretary to a committee, which included William Stawell, set up to found an Anglican College. In 1872, the first college, Trinity College, Melbourne, was opened with the Rev George Torrance as its acting Warden. Torrance (1835–1903) graduated from Trinity in 1864; he was ordained in the Church of England and held curacies in England and in Dublin before joining his brother in Melbourne in 1869. Torrance was an organist and composer and had studied piano and organ before entering Trinity. After he arrived in Melbourne, McCoy and Stawell supported him for an appointment as professor of music in the university, but Hearn opposed this, believing that music was a subject that ought not be taught at a university, and could not be taught efficiently. Torrance became the first person to be admitted to the doctor of music degree of Melbourne University in 1879 following the award of Mus.B and Mus.D by Dublin.

By 1875 it was clear that the fledgling Trinity College, Melbourne, was going to fail and Hussey Burgh Macartney and Edward Graves Mayne held a consultation on the little college's 'want of money and men'. The result was that Macartney found funds from church property rents and it was possible to appoint Alex Leeper, another Dublin man, as warden in 1876, replacing Torrance, who had been unable to attract sufficient students to make the college viable.

Alexander Leeper (1848–1934), son of a chaplain to Ireland's Lord-Lieutenant, entered Trinity in 1868 and had a brilliant undergraduate career there. Elected into a scholarship, he graduated in 1871 with first class honours, the Berkeley Gold Medal and the Vice-Chancellor's Prize. A near contemporary in Dublin, Oscar Wilde, who Leeper thought was a humbug, also won the Berkeley Gold Medal, which he pawned later in Oxford. Leeper, too, went to Oxford, but not before spending a year in Sydney as tutor to the children of politician Sir George Allen. While in Sydney he unsuccessfully applied for the chair in classical and comparative philology and logic at Melbourne. Returning to Oxford in 1872, he left without taking a degree from there and returned to Australia, attracted by Adeline, daughter of Sir George Allen, and by a position as a teacher in the prestigious Melbourne Grammar School. Shortly after his appointment as Warden of Trinity College, Melbourne, Leeper succeeded in affiliating the college with the university, despite the views of Redmond Barry, who vigorously opposed any kind of university-sanctioned denominational education. Leeper was also very successful in 'farming' students and obtained significant benefactions from local squatter families. The financial situation for Melbourne's Trinity College continued to be precarious for a time, however, and it was not until

Figure 33. Dr Alexander Leeper, Warden of Trinity College, Melbourne.

1881, with the establishment in the university of Ormond College, with Cambridge-educated Irishman Sir John McFarland as its principal, that the college system was secure.

Leeper was originally attracted to the Irish nationalist cause but he eventually became a committed supporter of the empire, the Orange Order and the Act of Union. He became the subject of a famous Norman Lindsay cartoon depicting him as the murderer of justice when he campaigned successfully against the reappointment of the 'immoral' Marshall Hall, the first professor of music in the university. Leeper's autocratic style prompted the students at one time to burn his effigy, with most of them departing from the college in ceremonial cortege; and during the First World War he attempted to have all university staff of German origin dismissed. But Leeper successfully introduced the college system into the university and his personality and contributions are of such magnitude that he is the subject of a major biography. He was fiercely loyal to Trinity College, Dublin, which honoured him in 1881 with the LL.D degree. The coat of arms that he chose for Trinity College, Melbourne, bears a remarkable resemblance to that of the family of Adam Loftus, even though he claimed that its inspiration was from Byron and Tennyson. He convinced Hussey Burgh Macartney of its appropriateness by comparing the green trefoils in the arms to Irish shamrocks. When Leeper set out for Australia he delayed his departure so that his Trinity friend John Winthrop Hackett could accompany him. Hackett was his deputy warden at Trinity College, Melbourne, for six years and then, as we shall see, Hackett went on to achieve fame and fortune in Western Australia.

The Teaching of Law and Medicine

Though Dublin men, Barry, Stawell, Hearn, Leeper and Hackett, made extraordinary contributions to the foundation of Melbourne University and its college system, the academic contributions of Billing and Atkins in law, Eades in medicine, Hearn over a wide range of subjects including law, and Thomas Rankin Lyle in natural sciences, were notable in the development of professional education and an international scholarly reputation for the university.

Despite his love of the classics, Redmond Barry recognised the importance of the university also meeting the needs of the colony for trained professionals. The historian of the Melbourne Law School, Ruth Campbell, regards Barry as unquestionably the 'father' of the law school. As early as 1856 he moved in the university council a motion on the desirability of having lectures on law and medicine and he, together with Dr Anthony Brownless, a medical doctor and member of council, were asked to draw up plans for each. Brownless concentrated on medicine and Barry on law. The first lectures in law took place in 1857.

The first part-time appointment to the law school was Oxford-educated Richard Clarke Sewell, who taught only for a short time. He was encouraged to resign after only a year because his attendance at lectures was erratic and he suffered considerable anxiety as to whether he could bear the burden of teaching. Sewell's successor was Henry Samuel Chapman, defence counsel at the Eureka trials. Chapman was sporadically reader in law for seven years before moving to New Zealand as a judge of the Supreme Court. When he took leave for the first time in 1858 he was replaced by John Wilberforce Stephen and Richard Annesley Billing. Stephen, a member of a well-connected family that was prominent in New South Wales, Van Diemen's Land and at the Colonial Office in London, lasted only two years. Billing, the Trinity man, was reader in law until the faculty of law was established in 1873, and lecturer in law from then until his elevation as judge of the County Court shortly before his death in 1892. Billing provided the continuity in teaching of the law that allowed the little school of law to survive its early years. He was a highly successful barrister and became Victoria's fifth Queen's Counsel. Campbell records him as a generous man, who gave a gold medal to the top student in his class from 1858 until 1873; a man who liked to dine with actors; and the owner of diamond buckles to a value of £200!

Billing was joined in 1862 by Irish barrister John Atkins, who graduated from Trinity in 1835. Atkins was appointed on the recommendation of Redmond Barry in unusual circumstances. The appointment as reader had been offered to, and accepted by, George Webb, a future Supreme Court judge. However, William Stawell and some other members of the council wanted the appointment reviewed even before the unfortunate Mr Webb gave a lecture. Though re-affirmed in his appointment, Webb resigned, leaving Atkins to take up the appointment. Whether or not there was pressure from the Trinity men, Barry and Stawell, to appoint a fellow Trinity man is not known, but Atkins was forced to resign a year later as a result of admissions he made in a case in which he was a defendant. The historian Ruth Campbell could find no record of that case or of Atkins's misdemeanour. He was re-appointed ten years later as lecturer in the faculty of law, and served until his death in 1878.

If Billing and Atkins served the fledgling school of law well, it was the first dean of the faculty of law, Dr William Hearn, who gave it its academic distinction. He was, as Campbell records, an 'academic supreme'. Though not his function, in the early days of his appointment he set the law examinations with Chapman and Billing, and helped to establish a law degree in 1861. Hearn was the first full time teacher in the law school, and chronicler of the Bar of Victoria, J.L Forde, suggests that it is impossible to conjecture the extent to which he must have influenced the law students who passed through his hands. He overcame the disadvantages of remote provincial publication, ranking second only to John Stuart Mill in political economy.

There is no doubt that Hearn's academic distinction brought great fame to the young university. In its early days he was equalled only by Thomas Rankin Lyle. Before turning to Lyle, however, it is important to mention one other Trinity man, Richard Eades, who promoted the development of medical education and science in general in Melbourne. The contributions of Trinity medical graduates to the Australian colonies have not been great; the reputation and output of the Scottish universities in the nineteenth century meant that they dominated the field. In New South Wales, Thomas Jamison and Henry Grattan Douglass were Trinity's most prominent medical graduates;

in Melbourne it was Sir Francis Murphy, who pursued a career in politics rather than medicine, and Richard Eades.

Richard Eades (1809–67) graduated from Trinity in 1836 with BA and MB and lectured on materia medica at some of the Dublin schools of medicine between 1838 and 1842. He then became physician at the Fever Hospital in Kilmainham until 1848, when he migrated to South Australia. The discovery of gold prompted a move to Victoria in 1852, and he not only practised medicine but engaged in a number of public activities. In 1853 Sir Andrew Clarke proposed to the Legislative Council that the government should set aside funds to establish a museum of modern history. Fitzgerald Foster, the colonial secretary, promised the money if Clarke and others who were interested in the subject would form themselves into a committee or initiate some society that would co-operate with the government in carrying out the objects in view. A committee was convened by Clarke, and Eades was elected chair. The result was the establishment of the Philosophical Society of Victoria, with Clarke as president and Eades as a member of the council. In parallel, a scientific society, the Victorian Institute for Advancement of Science was being formed, with Redmond Barry as its president, Clarke as vice-president and Higinbotham and Edward Mayne among the council members. This society was modelled on its British counterpart. It was soon clear, however, that the colony could not adequately support two societies with similar objects and, in 1855, the two joined forces as the Philosophical Institute of Victoria. In 1859 the institute received a royal charter, becoming The Royal Society of Victoria.

In the same year proposals for further exploration of Australia were considered, which led to the society's tragic Burke and Wills expedition, established to traverse Australia from south to north. As already noted, the exploration party set off with great ceremony, with Sir William Stawell leading the procession, and in the presence of Richard Eades, who was then mayor of Melbourne and vice-president of the Royal Society. Eades' most notable feat as mayor was his reading of the *Riot Act* in 1860 to a mob protesting against an inadequate land Bill. Although severe violence erupted he emerged unscathed.

In 1861, following his term as mayor, Eades began to lecture on materia medica in the Government Analytical Laboratory and, with Dr John Macadam, the city health officer, to provide an extramural course for medical students. There is no doubt that the activities of Eades and Macadam led to a swift opening of the university's medical school, and when this occurred in 1862 Eades was appointed as the first lecturer in materia medica and therapeutics. He held the position until he died in 1887. But the driving force behind the establishment of the medical school was undoubtedly Sir Anthony Brownless, vice-chancellor of the university at the time, who adopted Trinity's model of a five-year medical course. At that time only Dublin, of all the medical schools in the English-speaking world, had a five-year medical course, and it was not until 1892 that the British universities followed suit.

The Physics Laboratory

Writing in 1913, Sir Baldwin Spencer, professor of biology at Melbourne University said that Sir Thomas Rankin Lyle (1860–1944) was the greatest man, scientifically speaking, that Melbourne University ever had. Lyle entered Trinity in 1879 towards the end of a golden era in mathematics and physics in the College, which had its beginnings with the appointment in 1827 of (Sir) William Rowan Hamilton as professor of astronomy, while he was still an undergraduate. It is ironic that Sir George Airy, one of the selectors in London for the Sydney and Melbourne chairs, had been an unsuccessful candidate for the chair in Trinity that Hamilton filled with such distinction, for Hamilton would have been excluded from consideration for a chair in Sydney because he was not a graduate of Oxford or Cambridge. Hamilton is best known for his discovery of quaternions in mathematics and his name is commemorated by physicists every time the Hamiltonian operator is used in quantum mechanics.

Lyle became a student at Trinity as George Francis Fitzgerald was taking up the chair of natural and experimental philosophy there. Fitzgerald was one of Ireland's great scientists. He gave substance to the popular stereotype of the eccentric professor, uncaring of personal recognition, alternating between brilliant abstract theory and idiosyncratic experiment, such as his famous attempts to fly in the College Park using artificial wings. He predicted the contraction producing the null result of the Michelson-Morley experiment to determine the velocity of the earth through the ether. This Fitzgerald-Lorenz contraction, which predicts that a body becomes shorter as its velocity increases, was an important milestone in the development of the theory of relativity. Fitzgerald predicted the possibility of hertzian waves before Hertz produced them experimentally, and he collaborated with Hertz in the development of the concept. Had he carried his theories into experiment, the unit of electromagnetic measurement might now be Fz rather than Hz! John Joly, later to become professor of geology at Trinity, was Fitzgerald's assistant, and he achieved international eminence for his work on the age and surface history of the earth. He invented the Joly calorimeter and produced the first one-shot colour photographic system.

Lyle's career in Trinity was spectacular. He thrived in the pioneering atmosphere of one of the best physics departments in the world and graduated in 1883 with the highest honours and large gold medals in both mathematics and experimental science. Lyle's classmate (Sir) John Sealy Townsend joined Rutherford's laboratory in Cambridge and, with J.J.Thompson, discovered the charge on the electron, the sub-atomic particle named by Trinity-educated George Stoney in 1891.

Such was the competition for fellowships that Lyle narrowly missed being elected in 1888 and, instead of waiting for another year, he accepted the chair of physics in Melbourne. He joined (Sir) David Orme Masson and (Sir) Baldwin Spencer, and these three were responsible for establishing Melbourne's international scientific reputation. A gifted experimentalist and photography enthusiast, Lyle established the first physics laboratory in Australia and was able to put together the apparatus required to take Australia's first x-ray pictures within one month of publication of reports of x-rays in the journals. He served on the university council for fifteen years and was a member of the committee that recommended establishing a university in Canberra.

Lyle's scientific eminence led to his being called on to advise the government on scientific matters and to sit on a range of scientific committees. One of these was the Australian National Research Council (ANRC) of which he was president from 1929–32. In 1931 the ANRC recognised his outstanding contribution to science when it created the Thomas Rankin Lyle medal for distinguished Australian research in mathematics and physics. Establishment of the Australian Bureau of Meteorology was the result of advice tendered by a committee of which he was a member; and in 1915 he was one of a four-man delegation that advised Prime Minister Billy Hughes on the establishment of a National Scientific Laboratory. When the Advisory Council of Science and Industry, which became the Commonwealth Institute of Science and Industry (CSIR) was formed, Lyle was active in its affairs. Out of the CSIR came the powerful and successful Commonwealth Scientific and Industrial Research Organisation (CSIRO).

Trinity conferred upon Lyle the ScD degree in 1905; he was elected Fellow of the Royal Society of London in 1912; and, in 1922 he was knighted for his services. An enthusiastic sportsman, Lyle played rugby for Ireland on five occasions, followed Australian Rules football, and served on the tribunal of the Australian Football League.

Lyle brings to a conclusion the discourse on the university into which Sir Redmond Barry breathed life, and which, by the end of the nineteenth century, had drawn upon the talented people produced by Trinity College, Dublin, to launch it onto the international stage.

CHAPTER 8

The Province of South Australia

> A pauper has been placed on the Bench who will probably be sued in his own court by his English creditors.
>
> **Governor Hindmarsh (1836)**

Provincial Settlement

The principles upon which South Australia was established were fashioned by Edward Gibbon Wakefield while he was imprisoned in Newgate Prison for abducting an heiress in 1826. New South Wales and Van Diemen's Land had been established as penal colonies, and land had been granted to free settlers who were expected to put it to productive use. Victoria was initially settled by expansion from the nearby colonies of New South Wales and Van Diemen's Land and the squatters benefited from the initial lack of government policy with respect to the lands they settled.

Wakefield considered that when land is cheap or free it is impossible to obtain the labour to work it effectively. Even poor immigrants would want to rise to the rank of landowner and, in order to prevent this happening, Wakefield proposed that the price of land in the colonies should be sufficiently high to allow only those with capital to acquire it. An appropriate price would be that which would pay for the passages of sufficient labourers to work the land sold to the capitalists. These labourers would have no option but to stay on the land until such time as they had accumulated sufficient capital to acquire land of their own. Wakefield, despite his incarceration, won the support of influential figures like the Duke of Wellington, who used his influence to secure the passage of legislation to establish an Australian colony in which no portion of the land should become private property except upon the payment of some sufficient price.

The whole of the land fund thus accruing would be employed in conveying poor emigrants from Great Britain and Ireland to the new land. South Australia was to be a province, not a colony, and commissioners were appointed to carry through the provisions of the *South Australia Act*. The chief commissioner in London was Irishman Captain Robert Torrens, and a resident commissioner was appointed to act under the instructions of the commissioners in London and to liaise, in some unspecified way, with provincial officials such as the governor, the chief justice and the treasurer.

The Torrens family was descended from a Swedish Count who fought for William of Orange at the Battle of the Boyne and thereafter settled in Ireland. Robert Torrens' father and grandfather were Trinity-educated churchmen but Robert, born in 1780, was destined for the army, which he entered at the age of seventeen. His career was meteoric and by 1819 he was already a lieutenant-colonel. A brilliant political economist, Torrens published an *Essay on the Production of Wealth* in 1821 in which he became one of the first to recognise that the production of wealth was dependent upon 'the three instruments of production', namely land, labour and capital; and how the means of production is increased by the 'territorial division of labour'. In this remarkable work he also anticipated the law of diminishing returns. Some earlier work on the external corn trade led to his election in 1818 as a Fellow of the Royal Society.

Torrens entered parliament in 1831 and served as MP for Ashburton and Bolton until 1835. In that year he published a volume that fully supported Wakefield's theories of colonisation in the South Australian context. Attracting the attention of James Stephen, counsel to the Colonial Office, Torrens became chair of the commissioners appointed in 1835 to implement the colonisation. The Board of Commissioners, according to Stephen 'the most ill-managed an institution as could be imagined', was considered by Torrens, its chair, to be 'a lamentable waste of time, a debating club meeting in the Albany in London discussing objects'. The board's commission was revoked in 1839 and Torrens was appointed as one of the three commissioners who took over its work.

Torrens saw emigration as a means of alleviating poverty in Ireland and organised for one hundred families a month to be sent out. In this initial effort more than fifteen thousand people were moved to South Australia. By 1840, however, the commission was insolvent partly because of delays in surveying the land and partly because sales did not cover the cost of passages and administration. In a parliamentary inquiry into the affairs of the colony the first governor, George Gawler, was blamed and Torrens was forced to resign. The other two commissioners were exonerated, and it was claimed, probably with some justification, that this was because the secretary of state for the colonies, Lord Russell, was engaged to the sister of one of them.

Torrens maintained his interest in South Australia even after his loss of the commissionership, becoming a director of the Australian Mining Company in 1843 and a leader in the Society for the Promotion of Colonisation. The River Torrens, on which Adelaide is located, and Lake Torrens, are named after him. His son Robert Richard Torrens went to South Australia in 1840 and we shall deal with his notable contribution later.

The Duelling Chief Judge

The surveyor-general for South Australia, Colonel William Light, arrived in the province in August 1836, three weeks after the first emigrant ship, and it took him four months to decide upon the site for a principal town. The Act provided for a governor whose relationship with the chief commissioner, Robert Torrens, was unclear. There was also to be a resident commissioner, colonial secretary, chief judge and an advocate-general. The governorship was offered to Sir Charles Napier but, after first accepting it, he changed his mind because of the unspecified relationship between the governor and the commissioners. A similar fate befell the first judicial appointment when Henry Parker, appointed as judge of the Supreme Court, resigned before he left for the province because he believed that the undertaking promised to be 'attended with much unhappiness to all concerned in it'. The governorship was finally accepted by Captain John Hindmarsh, RN, and he arrived in 1836, closely followed by the first chief judge, Sir John Jeffcott.

John Jeffcott was born in Tralee in 1796, the older brother of William, who, as we have noted, was the second resident judge of Port Phillip District. The brothers were educated at Trinity and both were knighted for colonial service, but John was to have a tragically short life. He entered Trinity in 1815, described then by Hague, in his biography of Jeffcott, as 'a happy go lucky establishment immortalised in the novels of Charles Lever where Charley O'Malley and his cronies fought, drank, rioted and learned little under the guidance of faculty where eccentricity was as prevalent as scholarship'. Jeffcott graduated in 1821 and was called to the Bar at Middle Temple five years later. His practice at the Bar was not successful and he constantly applied to the

Figure 34. Sir John Jeffcott, Chief Judge of South Australia, 1835–37.

Colonial Office for an appointment. He was finally offered the chief justiceship in Sierra Leone and the Gambia, a very tough assignment. Only the first of the previous five chief justices had survived to return to England, but the salary was high and Jeffcott, a noted spendthrift, was in debt. The newspaper *John Bull*, on announcing his appointment, commiserated with him: 'we sincerely condole with the learned gentleman upon his affliction', wrote the editor.

Jeffcott was installed in Freetown in early 1830, the ceremony being described thus: 'His Honour, attended by a swarm of dusky constables, upheld the dignity of the judicial process, and diffused salutary awe over the proceedings by rolling in state to church to hear the assize sermon, the horses slowly pacing with becoming seriousness in order to prolong to the astonished multitude the phenomenon of a frothy and flowing wig and heavy scarlet robe.' Jeffcott conducted a relentless campaign against the slavers and during 1831 three men were hanged for kidnapping blacks.

In 1832 he returned on leave to England and while there he became engaged to the daughter of John Macdonald, a distinguished soldier and youngest son of the celebrated Jacobite heroine, Flora Macdonald. The engagement encouraged him to pursue with the Colonial Office an alternative to Sierra Leone, but the deteriorating situation there demanded that he return. The governor was being recalled because of incompetence, and it was important that the second most senior colonial officer, who was normally acting governor in the absence of the governor, should be there to encourage his departure and administer the colony. Jeffcott was knighted on 3 May 1832 to induce him to return to Sierra Leone, and he was ordered to sail on the *Britomart* on 11 May. In the interval between his being knighted by William IV and setting sail on the *Britomart*, disaster struck. As Hague records it, a newspaper in Exeter reported thus:

> 'Sir John had been introduced to a respectable family in the neighbourhood – the late Colonel Macdonald's – and paid his addresses to one of the daughters; and having been successful with the lady, and unobjectionable in the eyes of the family, preparations were making for the intended wedding. ... In this state of things Dr Hennis is said to have received a letter from a friend in town, containing some remarks on Sir John, and the doctor, placing some reliance on the statement of his friend, showed the letter to the family, and the judge was, it is reported, dismissed.'

We do not know what was in the letter that prompted Dr Hennis to show it to the Macdonalds. Nor do we know whether or not Dr Hennis knew Sir John during their undergraduate days at Trinity, for Hennis had graduated one year earlier than Jeffcott. Jeffcott saw Hennis after the letter had been shown to the Macdonalds, but the meeting only served to exacerbate the situation. Hennis demanded an apology from Jeffcott for calling him a 'traducer' and a 'calumniating scoundrel'; and Jeffcott refused to accept Hennis's explanation for his behaviour; thus the stage was set for a resolution on the 'field of honour'. On the afternoon of 10 May the two men fought a duel. Jeffcott fired prematurely and Hennis was severely wounded. Hennis did not fire and, according to his second, he had not intended to fire in any case. Though Jeffcott was distraught at the turn of events, the physician attending Hennis advised him that the wound was not immediately fatal, but, as to the prognosis, he was not very optimistic. Jeffcott left for Sierra Leone on the following day. He disembarked at Bathurst on the River Gambia in June because of ill-health, only to hear that Hennis had died. A warrant for Jeffcott's arrest was issued by the secretary of state and a despatch was sent to the Gambia ordering that he be taken into custody and returned to England. By the time the warrants arrived Jeffcott had already left British jurisdiction, going north from the Gambia to the French settlement of Goree for the milder climate there, which would help him to better health. The colonial surgeon in the Gambia had diagnosed 'complications of the tapeworm, hepatic infection and visceral derangement', and Jeffcott's move to the French territory was with the surgeon's approval. Meanwhile, his seconds had been arrested and tried for murder but, despite clear directions to the contrary by the judge, the jury acquitted them on the grounds that the seconds never touched the victim. Jeffcott was charged *in absentia* with 'having unlawfully, maliciously, and feloniously inflicted a wound upon Peter Hennis, MD, with a leaden bullet of which wound he subsequently died'. Certificates of ill-health written in French continued to allow Jeffcott to stay in Goree but eventually he returned to Normandy and sent a letter to the Colonial Office, through his brother William, to indicate his willingness to return to face trial.

Fortuitously, the Colonial Office looked upon Sir John with favour, possibly because of his service in Sierra Leone, and it was made known that if he returned to stand trial no evidence would be brought against him by Dr Hennis's relatives. Also, attitudes to duelling were still ambivalent. A judge of the old school reflected the lingering respect for a well fought duel when he remarked at the trial of a duellist, 'Gentlemen, the law says that the killing of a man in a duel is murder, and I am bound to tell you that it is murder; therefore, in the discharge of my duty, I tell you so; but I tell you, at the same time, that a fairer duel than this I have never heard in the whole course of my life.'

William Jeffcott, who had earlier attended the trial of the seconds and had argued that the verdict also exonerated his brother, accompanied Sir John when he took his place in the dock at Exeter Assizes in May 1834. Sir John is the only chief justice in British history to have stood trial for a murder committed while he was in office. He pleaded 'not guilty', the jury was chosen, and they were duly informed by the crown prosecutor that the friends of Dr Hennis did not intend to offer any evidence. A verdict of 'not guilty' was recorded and Sir John went free. He received back pay from the Colonial Office, which regarded the duel as an embarrassing misfortune, and, in April 1835, he was appointed as the first judge of the new province of South Australia.

When he left England on the *Isabella*, Jeffcott was deeply in debt and had to be rowed secretly on board to evade his creditors. Governor Hindmarsh, on learning of his appointment, complained that 'a pauper had been placed on the

Bench who will probably be sued in his court by his English creditors and will appear on the list of insolvent debtors'. Instead of proceeding directly to Adelaide, however, Jeffcott landed in Van Diemen's Land and stayed for three months at the home of his kinsman Francis Kermode, where he succeeded in becoming engaged to the daughter of the house, Anne Kermode.

When he eventually arrived in Adelaide he found a situation of dissension and chaos. On the one side of the warring factions was the resident commissioner, James Fisher, who, according to Governor Hindmarsh, 'had the folly to place himself at the head of the violent party who would oppose an angel were he only called governor'. On the other side was Hindmarsh, an old fashioned Tory authoritarian. Despite his forebodings about the judge, Hindmarsh had looked forward to Jeffcott's arrival. Governance was difficult in the absence of the second most senior colonial administrator, and the advocate-general, who was in the anti-governor camp, advised that no Acts could be passed until the chief judge had the opportunity to peruse them to ensure that they were not 'repugnant' to the laws of England. The advice Jeffcott gave was always accepted by Hindmarsh, who liked and respected the man who despite, or perhaps even because of, his past, he regarded as a gentleman.

As the two principal officers of the Crown, the governor and the judge were naturally drawn to each other and Jeffcott completely supported Hindmarsh. Writing to the secretary of state, Hindmarsh said, 'If I did not possess the cordial assistance of Sir John Jeffcott, whose upright and honourable behaviour I have every reason to admire, I should be alone in the Council'. Jeffcott's view of the resident commissioner, James Fisher, accorded with that of Hindmarsh. He was, Jeffcott said, 'a wily attorney, the very worst class of person that could have been selected for office, who by splitting hairs on every insignificant point wishes to put the governor into a false position'. One of the first tasks that Jeffcott and the governor undertook was the naming of streets and one of the principal streets of Adelaide is Jeffcott Street; there is a Kermode Street named after Sir John's fiancee; and O'Connell Street commemorates Jeffcott's patron, Maurice O'Connell, fellow student at Trinity and son of Daniel O'Connell.

On 13 May 1837 the first criminal sessions were held, at which Jeffcott delivered to a grand jury a most elegant, humanitarian and sensitive speech on behalf of the native population. The offence to be heard was theft by two white men of a jacket and warlike implements from a hut that the Aborigines had built. After giving due credit to the Aborigines for having constructed the hut in the first place, Jeffcott went on to say, 'they are entitled to the full protection of British law, and that protection ... shall be fully and effectually afforded them. I will go further and say that any aggression upon the natives, or any infringement of their rights shall be visited by greater severity of punishment than would be in similar offences committed upon white men. In our intercourse with them we should scrupulously avoid giving them offence; we should respect their property ... which is of importance to them; and, by setting them a good example in this respect reclaim them from any furtive tendencies which they are said to have, although I believe, in the quiet and inoffensive natives who have hitherto been induced to visit us, no such propensities have been found to exist'.

Jeffcott stayed only six weeks in his first visit to the province. All of his belongings and furniture were lost when the *Isabella* was wrecked on its way from Van Diemen's Land to Adelaide and he had to return to Van Diemen's Land to replenish his supplies. Back in Adelaide by October 1837, he set up the Supreme Court with rules and orders of proceedings that lasted until the 1850s. The historian L.A.Whitfield says of Jeffcott, 'Whenever he was actually available to perform his judicial duties they were well done'.

When Jeffcott first arrived in the province it was widely predicted that he would soon be seeking an appointment elsewhere. He disliked taking part in the quarrels between the two factions, and when, in November 1837, he asked the secretary of state to consider him for the judgeship in Van Diemen's Land the governor forwarded the application 'with considerable regret, not allowing any wish of my own to stand in the way of the promotion which, I believe, Sir John richly deserves'.

Jeffcott was impatient to visit Van Diemen's Land again, ostensibly to consult the judges there on difficult judicial issues that faced him in Adelaide. It was speculated, however, that the real purpose of his visit was, in an official's spiteful words, that 'being doubtful whether he can ensure the hand of his intended lady he has gone to make that affair sure'. At Encounter Bay, the departure point for Van Diemen's Land, he boarded a ship to take him there. It was blown from its moorings and wrecked. While waiting for another ship Jeffcott and Hindmarsh joined a small party engaged in exploring Lake Alexandrina to ascertain if there was a navigable outlet to the sea. In one of their forays, in a stretch of water now known as Jeffcote's Reach, Sir John's whale-boat sank and he was drowned. Thus ended the short and tragic life of the province of South Australia's first chief judge.

Sir John Jeffcott is remembered in the annals of South Australia not because he contributed greatly to development of the law in South Australia, but for the tragic and bizarre circumstances that brought him to the colony in the first place, and his premature death. He was succeeded by Charles Cooper in 1839, and a further eleven years elapsed before a second judge was appointed. This was George Crawford from County Longford, who graduated from Trinity in 1833. A universally popular and competent judge, he brought dignity to the court and was the first in the colony to wear a judicial wig. He died after only two years in office at the age of fifty three. Crawford in turn was replaced by William Boothby, implacable opponent of the revolutionary land title law, introduced by Robert Richard Torrens, son of Robert Torrens.

Torrens Title

Robert Richard Torrens (1814–84) grew up in County Kerry and entered Trinity in 1830. After graduation, he became a tidewaiter in the customs service in London and when Governor Gawler asked for an 'instructed officer of customs' to be sent to Adelaide, Torrens was nominated and set out for South Australia as collector of customs in late 1839. Described in the newspapers as 'bright as a rocket', the hotheaded Torrens was frequently the subject of scurrilous reporting. His violent response to a lampoon in the *South Australian Register* led to his arrest for assaulting the newspaper owner with his walking stick. Portrayed by his counsel as simply delivering a 'good old-fashioned Irish horsewhipping', Torrens was allowed to settle the matter out of court for a large sum.

In 1851 Torrens commenced his parliamentary career, being nominated for the Legislative Council first and six years later being elected to the Legislative Assembly. He served as registrar general and colonial treasurer, and, for a short time in 1857, was premier of the province. His greatest contribution to the province, and to Australia, was the introduction of *Torrens Title*, a system of land registration, which allowed for the investigation of title by a government official who would then issue a certificate that would be regarded as conclusive proof of title. The chaotic situation in South Australia with respect to land title, a consequence of survey inadequacies, meant that conveyancing costs were very high at the time.

In 1851 Torrens wrote to the governor, Sir Richard MacDonnell, to say that he wanted to reform the way in which land title was transferred. Torrens objected to the fact that land could be sold many times over with a conveyancing cost at each transaction. The practice of charging heavy fees by lawyers for retrospective investigations in every transfer of land, where the title

Figure 35. Sir Robert Torrens, Premier of South Australia.

had been investigated many times before, needed to be stopped. Opposition to Torrens's draft Act from the legal profession, including the chief justice, was inevitable. Torrens was advised to confine his attention to the duties of his office and not to meddle with land title law. Torrens persisted, however, and with the support of Governor MacDonnell his *Real Property Act* was passed in 1858. It provided for the abolition of retrospective title investigations; transfer of land by certificate of title alone; and simplified documentation to obviate the need for solicitors. Torrens promoted his system in other states and in New Zealand and, now known as *Torrens Title*, it is in force in all Australian states. In 1862 Torrens took leave of absence and sailed for England and, after a period of uncertainty as to whether or not he would return to Adelaide, he finally decided to stay in England and run for a parliamentary seat. He won the seat for Cambridge at the second attempt and continued thereafter to promote his land title system in Ireland and England.

The University

The University of Adelaide had its origins in a small institute of higher education, Union College, founded in 1872 by the Baptist, Congregational and Presbyterian churches for the training of young men for the Christian ministry. The province was less than forty years old and its total population was still only some two hundred thousand people, most of whom were pastoralists and farmers. It would not have seemed sensible at this time to contemplate the establishment of a university, but the success of Union College prompted the founders to think in terms of offering higher education generally and not just to those preparing for the ministry. Courses in classics, philosophy, English literature, mathematics and natural sciences were offered at a standard that would normally be expected of a university. Demand from the general public was clearly identified but there was no money for expansion. Fortunately, one of the founders, the Reverend James Lyall, had a wealthy pastoralist friend, Walter Watson Hughes, whom he approached about his possible support for the expansion of the College. When Hughes agreed to provide the then very large sum of £20,000, the ambitions of the College were immediately raised to the possibility of a university. Hughes presided over a university association formed to consider a set of proposals aimed at the establishment of the university, but it soon became clear to him that his donation would not be sufficient for the purpose and he left the association.

The impetus that had been given to the establishment of a university by Hughes's donation was sufficient to overcome his departure, and the association began to generate public support and to lobby the government. After many months of negotiation, the government agreed to provide a site in Adelaide; to recommend that up to £10,000 be allocated for buildings, provided that an equal amount was received from public subscription; to provide an annual grant of five percent on other private gifts; and to introduce a Bill into parliament to establish the university. The Bill was introduced late in the 1874 session of parliament and aroused so little interest that the bells had to be sounded to make up a quorum. There was no Hackett to speak to a vision for the university or to justify the need for such an institution to be founded in the province. The Bill for an Act 'to incorporate and endow the University of Adelaide' was modelled on the Acts that established the universities in Melbourne and Sydney, and it was passed on 6 November 1874. On the same day a second donation of £20,000 was made by another benefactor, Thomas Elder, a friend of Hughes, and this enabled the university council, chaired by the chief justice, Sir Richard Hanson, to commence planning. In December 1874, the first salaried appointment was made and Dr William Barlow, 'an accomplished legal man from Dublin', was chosen from thirty-one applicants to be the first registrar of the university.

The First Registrar

William Barlow (1834–1915) graduated from Trinity in 1855 and arrived in Adelaide in 1870 after practising at the Bar in Dublin. After twelve years as registrar, the most important administrative position in the university, he became the first dean of the Faculty of Law when it was established in 1883. In the previous year he was elected to the university council and served until his death in 1915. From 1896 until his death he was the vice-chancellor (now deputy chancellor) of the university. In 1884 Trinity admitted Barlow to the degree of LL.D.

Barlow's most enduring contribution was his success in persuading the Colonial Office to allow the University of Adelaide to admit women to degrees. Duncan has recorded that when the original *University of Adelaide Act* was enacted in 1874 no university in the colonies had the power to confer the degree of Bachelor of Science or Doctor of Science, or to confer degrees on women. Barlow himself said about this, 'Notwithstanding, it was determined here to attempt to obtain these coveted powers'. In 1878 a petition was made to the colonial secretary for 'letters patent' to be granted for the recognition of Adelaide's degrees including science degrees and for the admission of women to degrees. In response, the colonial secretary thought it preferable that Adelaide should conform to the practice at Oxford, Cambridge and the other universities in Australia, where there was no provision for the award of science degrees or the admission of women. In order not to delay the recognition of degrees by letters patent, the offending clauses were struck out of the petition, but by the time the amended version reached London the home government had changed its mind and the university was invited to re-submit its petition in the original form. This it did, and in March 1881 the University of Adelaide became the first university in Australia to award science degrees and to admit women to degrees. Barlow's *alma mater*, Trinity College, Dublin, did not admit women to degrees until 1904; Oxford followed suit in 1920; and Cambridge waited until 1948 before it implemented this reform. In 1885 the first woman to graduate from an Australian university, Edith Dornwell, received her Bachelor of Science degree from the chancellor, Augustus Short, the Archbishop of Adelaide.

In its formative years the University of Adelaide was served by two other Trinity-educated men, who occupied chairs in the humanities. Edward Boulger, born in Dublin in 1846, was appointed to the chair of English language and literature and mental and moral philosophy in 1883. He graduated from Trinity in 1869 with a gold medal in classics, and was appointed to a chair in Greek at Queen's College, Cork, in 1875. After eight years he accepted the chair in Adelaide and served also as the first staff member to be elected to the university council.

In 1894 he agreed to take on the duties of professor of classics when his Trinity-educated colleague, David Kelly, became ill. Kelly (1847–94) entered Trinity in 1869 on a classical scholarship from Dungannon School. He incorporated from Dublin to Clare College, Cambridge, and, three years after graduation in 1879, he was appointed as the Hughes professor of classics and comparative philology and literature in Adelaide. From 1886 his health began to deteriorate and he died in 1894. The additional duties given to Boulger as a result of Kelly's death caused him to resign at the end of 1894. No other Trinity-educated academics or administrators appear in the annals of the university during the rest of the colonial period.

CHAPTER 9

The Wild Western Shore

From the old Western world we have come to explore
The wilds of this Western Australian shore;
In search of a country we've ventured to roam,
And now that we've found it let's make it our home.

George Fletcher Moore (1830)

Administration of the Law

The British colony of Western Australia was proclaimed at Swan River settlement, now Perth, in June 1829 with naval Captain James Stirling as governor. William Mackie, educated at Cambridge, was appointed as the first chairman of Quarter Sessions, advocate-general and adviser to the government on legal matters. One year later the first Irish lawyer arrived on the *Cleopatra* with his four servants. George Fletcher Moore (1798–1886), from County Tyrone, entered Trinity in 1814, graduated in 1820 and was called to the Irish Bar a year later. He practised for six years on the north-west circuit and then applied for a position at the Swan River settlement. No position was forthcoming from the Colonial Office but, having private means, Moore decided to migrate to the settlement in any case. When a civil court was set up in 1832, Stirling appointed Moore as commissioner so that he and Mackie had

Figure 36. George Fletcher Moore, Advocate-General of Western Australia.

entire judicial responsibility for the new colony. The Colonial Office then decided to regularise the situation and Mackie was asked to take over the civil court from Moore and to relinquish to Moore the position of advocate-general. Stirling was anxious to emphasise that the change did not reflect on Moore's performance, which was entirely satisfactory to him and creditable to Moore. The governor, on his own authority, even increased the salary of the new advocate-general by one-third.

The duties of advocate-general were 'to advise on questions of law, to prosecute offenders and conduct all Crown cases'. In addition, Moore was required to serve as parliamentary draftsman, and he remarks in his diaries on some of the difficulties he faced: 'I have had several Acts to prepare for the [Executive] Council. One of them has been troublesome, not so much from the length of it as the finding out some mode of adapting the machinery of old countries to one infant state'. He also recorded the difficulties under which the law was practised: 'It is a most extraordinary thing', he said, 'that we are not furnished with the Acts or amendments in the laws which are taking place every day at home. How we are to know anything about them is open to conjecture'.

Immediately after his arrival in the colony, Moore obtained a grant of land on the upper Swan River, which he called *Millendon*, bought forty-four merinos and prospered. In only four years his flock numbered more than eight hundred and, by 1884, his holding amounted to twenty four thousand acres of land and some town allotments. Moore was a keen explorer and, in an expedition with a naval officer, he traced the course of the Swan River to its junction with the Avon, opened up the rich farming land of the York and Beverley Districts, and discovered the river that now bears his name. The coastal district around Point Moore, also named after him, and Champion Bay were settled as the result of a further expedition in 1839. On an expedition with the colonial secretary, Captain John Irwin, on a search for Aborigines suspected of being involved in a robbery, Moore began to learn their language, listened to their stories, and became very sympathetic towards them. In 1842 he published a descriptive vocabulary in London and, in 1837, *Evidence of an Inland Sea Collected from Natives of the Swan River Settlement* was published in Dublin. This extraordinary man was an accomplished diarist, and wrote informative, amusing letters to his family in Ireland, all of which were later published.

From 1834 until 1852 Moore held the substantive office of advocate-general. He returned to Ireland in 1841 to visit his father and, on his return in 1846, he became acting colonial secretary for six years. In 1852 Moore was again granted leave to visit his father, but distressed by the way in which the Colonial Office was treating him in respect of that leave, he resigned his position and lived in London for the rest of his life. Moore was one of those versatile, cultivated, optimistic men whose pioneering spirit kept them going when others were ready to give up. His diaries reveal the difficulties of establishing the machinery to introduce governance and the rule of law into the new colony. His public-mindedness led him into politics where he served in the Legislative and Executive Councils and represented the interests of the settlers well. When granting his first leave, Governor Hutt expressed the opinions of the legislators: 'His legal knowledge, local and practical experience, and the deep interest he has taken in the welfare of the country, combined with his conciliatory manner, will cause even his temporary absence to be greatly felt in our councils'.

When George Fletcher Moore went on leave in 1841, Richard West Nash (1808–50) took his place as advocate-general. The son of a Londonderry rector, Nash entered Trinity in 1824, graduated in 1829 and went to the Bar in 1839. He married the sister of fellow student John Schoales, and the couple migrated to Swan River where Schoales had already settled.

Nash was so successful as acting advocate-general that, on Moore's return, the Legislative Council minuted its appreciation. Nash brought traditional dignity to his court work, being the first to wear a gown and wig. When Moore returned and was appointed as acting colonial secretary in 1846, Nash was again installed as advocate-general. Like Moore, he had many other interests. A keen and successful vigneron and farmer, he wrote a manual for the cultivation of vine and olive in Western Australia, edited a newspaper, the *Inquirer*, and at one time was secretary of the agricultural and the vineyard societies. For a time Nash was also secretary of the General Board of Education from which came the Western Australian state school system.

Nash left the colony in 1849 on leave of absence and did not return. He became manager of the Colonization Assurance Corporation in London, founded to sponsor migration to Western Australia, and he died in London at the early age of forty-two. His brother-in-law, John Schoales, in addition to practising as a barrister in Fremantle, was also guardian of government juvenile immigrants, a post he held until his early death at the age of thirty-seven.

In 1849 the first crown solicitor of Swan River Settlement, William Lawrence, resigned and Bartholomew Urban Vigors (1817–54) was appointed to the position. Lawrence had carried on a private practice with Vigors in the latter part of his incumbency, and when Nash resigned as advocate-general Vigors became the third Trinity-educated incumbent of that position in a row. The governor, Sir Charles Fitzgerald, announced Vigors as 'a graduate of Trinity College, Dublin, who has practised in the courts of this colony with but one opinion as regards his high professional attainments and second to none in standing as a gentleman of unblemished reputation'. Vigors, the son of County Wexford clergyman Thomas Vigors, graduated in 1839 and arrived in Swan River settlement in 1844. He was in private practice until his appointment as crown-solicitor and then advocate-general. In delicate health for many years, Vigors died in office in 1854, ending twenty years of occupancy by Trinity-educated lawyers of the office of advocate-general of Western Australia. Their influence was critical to the development and administration of the law in the colony.

The Judiciary

The first judicial appointment in Western Australia, as the chairman of the Court of Quarter Sessions, was William Mackie, and he conducted the court until his retirement in 1857. In the following year Alfred McFarland, announced as a member of the Irish Bar and graduate of Trinity College, Dublin, was appointed judge and chairman of the Court of Quarter Sessions. McFarland took up his post in 1858 and immediately found that any necessary reforms to the legal system that he introduced were seen as criticism of Mackie, his predecessor. In historian Enid Russell's words, 'Mackie had attracted almost idolatrous worship'. The establishment of a Supreme Court was considered an urgent priority and McFarland prepared the necessary ordinance, which was sent to the secretary of state.

McFarland was seeking increases in his remuneration even before he took up his appointment, and he threatened not to undertake many of the duties that Mackie considered part of the position, given the circumstances peculiar to life in the new colony. McFarland informed the Executive Council that he had doubts about the extent of his jurisdiction in equity matters, anyway, and that he did not come to the colony to discharge the minutiae and multifarious duties of a master of the Court. He was prepared to carry out the duties on a temporary basis, but only on the condition that his salary was increased. The Executive Council ignored the salary request for a time and asked McFarland to prepare an ordinance that would relieve him of any anxiety with respect to his powers in equity. He responded that it was not part of his duties to prepare ordinances, even though he had prepared one for the establishment of a Supreme Court which, if passed, would increase his responsibilities and, therefore, his salary.

For the governor, Sir Arthur Kennedy, a fellow Trinity man, this was too much. He reported to the secretary of state that McFarland had agreed to carry out the duties performed by Mackie, pending a decision on his salary and other matters by the Colonial Office, and now was refusing to do so. In seeking his removal from office, Kennedy also noted: 'Mr McFarland has sought to force upon the government the necessity of increasing his salary by throwing impediments of his own devising in the way of performing the ordinary duties of his office!' Although the Colonial Office did not remove McFarland, neither did they accept his request for a pay increase, and, in order not to give McFarland any further cause for seeking one, the ordinance for the establishment of a Supreme Court was put aside. McFarland, in his first year or so in Western Australia had not only antagonised the governor, the Executive Council and the profession, he had also set back the development of the court system by his importuning at the Colonial Office. In 1859 he decided to leave the colony to go to New South Wales, but remained in office until his successor arrived in 1861.

In New South Wales McFarland did not make the same mistakes as he had in Western Australia, where it was said of him that his irony and sarcasm 'invariably worked his antagonists into a condition of fury, and it was only by the greatest self restraint that Governor Kennedy could maintain his dignity'. He was admitted to the New South Wales Bar, and practised for a time. He was then appointed to the District Court as judge, first for the metropolitan district of Sydney in 1865 and then in a southern country district.

When McFarland practised in Dublin he showed talent as an academic lawyer, and wrote *Treatise on Equity Pleading in Ireland* (1848) and *Observations on the Act to Regulate the Proceedings in the High Court of Chancery* in 1850. He continued his academic pursuits in Sydney when he became reader in jurisprudence at the university and member of the board of law examiners. He published several books, including *Mutiny in the Bounty* and *Story of the Pitcairn Islanders*, both in 1884. He died in 1891 heavily in debt, his possessions having been sold by the sheriff on behalf of creditors at a low figure.

The Carpetbag Judge

The second judge from Trinity to be appointed in Western Australia, and the second chief justice of the colony, was the colourful Sir Henry Wrenfordsley (1825–1908), who entered Trinity in 1841 but did not graduate. He is remarkable, and has a footnote in the history of the law in Australia, for the sheer number of judicial appointments that he held.

Wrenfordsley was articled to his father and practised as a solicitor in Dublin and London from 1849 until 1860, when he then he entered Middle Temple. It took him three years to go to the Bar, and he then received various deputy judicial appointments until 1877, when he joined the colonial legal service. His first post was in Mauritius as puisne judge and he was commended there for his work on a labour code and review of court procedure. He served, too, as advocate-general of the little colony. Disappointed at not being advanced to chief justice, Wrenfordsley applied for, and was offered, the position of advocate-general of Jamaica. He was also offered the chief justiceship of Western Australia in succession to Sir Archibald Burt, the first chief justice, who died in office in 1879, and he chose this option. Wrensfordsley stayed in Western Australia from 1880 until 1883 when, newly knighted, he moved to Fiji as chief justice. His stay in Fiji was short. He supported the planters in their opposition to the government's defence of native rights, criticised the

Figure 37. Sir Henry Wrenfordsley, Chief Justice of Western Australia, 1880–83.

government publicly and went heavily into debt. The Colonial Office considered his 'vanity' and his debts an embarrassment, and Wrenfordsley left Fiji on 'sick leave' in 1884.

We next hear of Wrenfordsley in Tasmania, where he was acting judge from 1885 until 1887. He then accepted a temporary judgeship in Melbourne where he was described as 'a journeyman judge who went about with robes in his carpet bag'. In 1891 he was back again in Western Australia as chief justice while the incumbent Onslow was on leave, and while in that post he oversaw the transition from the old legal procedures to the new when responsible government, at last, was granted to the colony in 1890. Finally, Wrenfordsley went to the Leeward Islands as chief justice and, as his entry in the *Australian Dictionary of Biography* says, 'he was as uniformly undistinguished in that post as he had been in all of the others'.

Sir John Winthrop Hackett

One of the Trinity-educated lawyers whose impact on Western Australia had nothing to do with the development of the law was Sir John Winthrop Hackett (1848–1916), newspaper baron, founder of the colony's university, philanthropist and politician. The Hacketts were of old English stock, settling in County Tipperary after the Norman invasion. Hackett's father, a Church of Ireland clergyman, sent him to Trinity in 1866 and he graduated with second-class honours some five years later. After going to the Bar, Hackett, like many lawyers before him, migrated to Australia, first to Sydney in 1875 and then, in the following year, on to Melbourne, where his close friend, Alexander Leeper, appointed him as deputy warden of Trinity College, Melbourne. The job offered board and lodging but no salary, so Hackett did some legal work and wrote for the newspapers to derive an income. He tried but failed to enter politics and then, in 1883, decided to try his luck in Western Australia.

Hackett's first job was at a country sheep station, but he soon moved to Perth to take up an appointment as business manager of the *West Australian* newspaper. Five years later he became editor of the paper and a proprietor. Recognising the power that the editor of a mainstream newspaper can have, Hackett made good use of the medium in his early days. Historian Geoffrey Bolton considers that his partisan zeal verged on the reckless. One of the celebrated debacles in which he became involved was the quarrel between Governor Broome and Chief Justice Onslow. This is of added interest to us because in 1878 Onslow married Madeline Emma Loftus, the second descendant of Provost Adam Loftus to reach Australian shores. Onslow, who was appointed as attorney-general of Western Australia in 1880, almost immediately engaged in activities that caused the governor, Sir William Robinson, to suspect him of conspiring against him. Because of Onslow's offensive behaviour, Robinson ceased all communication with him, except in the Legislative Council – a truly remarkable situation. Nonetheless, Onslow was appointed chief justice in 1883, by which time Robinson had moved to be governor of South Australia.

Onslow quarrelled with the new governor, Sir Frederick Broome, as well, and was suspended from office in 1887 for improprieties, including revealing the contents of confidential documents. Hackett and his newspaper sided with Broome and was forced into a position of opposition to all that Onslow stood for, including the granting of responsible government to Western Australia. An unrelated action for libel against the *West Australian*, presided over by Onslow after he had been reinstated as chief justice, went against the newspaper and Hackett petitioned the Legislative Council and the Colonial Office for

Onslow's removal for a second time. Even Broome considered the verdict reached in the trial a reasonable one, saying that 'more than once Mr Hackett has injured his case by indiscretion and hesitation'. Onslow was censured by the Legislative Council but the whole episode did not reflect well on either Hackett or Onslow. In 1890 Hackett became a member of the Legislative Council and his political career began. This will feature in the discussion on federation but for now we shall consider Hackett's most enduring achievement.

The University of Western Australia

Hackett's lasting contribution to the development of Western Australia was his crucial support for the establishment of a university in the colony. He had consistently used his newspaper to stress the importance of education, but his initial contributions were to campaign successfully for the abolition of government aid to the church schools. With the establishment of universities in New South Wales, Victoria and South Australia, and the achievement of responsible government and the growth of population in Western Australia, it was natural for the colonists to turn their attention to the idea of founding a university. In 1901, a motion in the parliament by Richard Septimus Haynes that, 'in the opinion of this House the time has arrived when a university should be established in Perth', was stood over. Hackett thought that the proposal was premature, and the colonial secretary annotated the proposal on its way to cabinet, that he could see no means of providing the funds. Hackett expressed his own educational principles in the debate, which would have given little comfort to Trinity, his *alma mater,* when he said that the university model to be adopted in Western Australia should not be sought in the older universities of England, Scotland or Ireland, which were being left far behind by Germany and the new establishments in the United Kingdom. 'I believe', he said, 'that the influence of Oxford, Cambridge and Dublin has been largely mischievous as far as the new countries of the Empire are concerned. Those universities devote themselves in a paramount measure to the study of the dead languages or to the pursuit of what is called the higher mathematics'. Despite his views about the older universities, Hackett accepted the honorary degree of LL.D from Trinity while he was visiting Ireland in 1902. It is thought that Hackett's experience at Trinity College, Melbourne, might have fashioned his opinions on the need for the university to be a part of, rather than remote from, the society that provided its prime support. For him, the university had to serve practical needs, and when the University of Western Australia was established in 1913 he endowed a chair in agriculture. In the 1901 debate he made his vision for the university clear. The university was to be 'the coping

Figure 38. Sir John Winthrop Hackett, Chancellor of the University of Western Australia.

stone not only of the grammar school system, but of a technical school system, of the school of mines system, and of the whole practical sciences'.

Despite the setback in 1901, the movement to establish a university gained momentum and visitors were brought to Perth, including the great Scottish scientist Sir Frederick Soddy, to raise the level of awareness in the population of the need to provide for higher learning in the colony. A graduates' union comprised of graduates of other universities was formed in 1906, to promote knowledge of science and arts, but it also acted to bring pressure on the government to make a grant of land for the purposes of creating a university and to establish a professorship to deliver extension studies. The Lands Department had already set aside more than four thousand acres for the endowment of a university and all that was needed was to gain parliamentary approval.

In 1907 the government was prevailed upon to set up a commission chaired by Hackett who, through his newspaper, was now actively promoting the idea of a university. The royal commission was to 'inquire and report as to the foundations upon which a university of Western Australia should be established'. The royal commission sought information from many universities in Britain, Ireland, North America and other Australian colonies. Hackett visited 'modern' universities in Britain and Ireland in 1909, and other commissioners visited the universities in London, Birmingham, Manchester and Liverpool.

The royal commission's report justified the establishment of a university in Western Australia in terms of need, population and national development. 'Who can say', they said, 'how much the community has lost by the shutting up of the avenue of higher education to receptive and ambitious spirits who suddenly find themselves before a closed door where they knock but will find no one to open'. It recommended that the university should find its inspiration not in the universities of the mother country but in those already in existence in the other Australian colonies. Hackett indicated that, although he had visited the 'modern' universities of Manchester, Sheffield and Belfast, and found much to commend them and others like them in the degree to which their teaching entered into the everyday needs of the working life of the community, he found great difficulties in proposing that their constitutional side, as he put it, should be emulated. Their governance was, for him and his fellow commissioners, too parochial, with excessive representation of local interests: '...the worst of the mistakes which could be made in the establishment of a Western Australian university would be to allow the voice of localism to be heard. In the case of our own state, the university must be in no sense provincial but national in the fullest meaning of the word'. He rejected, on the ground of incompatible constitutions, too, the models provided by the universities of the United States and Canada. The model proposed by the commission to the government was similar to that put into place in the University of Queensland, founded in 1903, 'a model of simplicity, effectiveness and closeness of touch to ourselves'. An Act establishing the University of Western Australia based on the royal commission's draft Bill was passed by parliament in 1911 and Hackett was appointed as the first chancellor, a position he held until his death in 1916.

Hackett's Contribution

In analysing the origins of the university, historian Fred Alexander attributes the successful outcome of the various moves to establish a university first of all to timing; and Hackett had unerring judgement in this. He did not propose the motion in 1901 because he thought that the timing was inopportune. The government simply did not have the funds to set aside at that time. Hackett took the opportunity, however, to lay the groundwork for the kind of university he thought Western Australia should have. Sir John Kirwan, fellow Irishman and member and president of the Legislative Council, wrote that from his first acquaintance with Hackett he talked and worked incessantly to establish a university; and Alfred Deakin, the Commonwealth of Australia's second prime minister, when commenting on the Western Australian representatives at the 1897 Federal Convention in Adelaide, referred to the rather overbearing premier of Western Australia and his university-conscious companion, Winthrop Hackett. Though Hackett was, indeed, university conscious, and had been long before Deakin made his remark, he did not let his enthusiasm lead him into an ill-timed attempt to gain parliamentary support. The result of Hackett's cautious policy was that he and his colleagues were able to command sufficient support, along the long road to the passing of the Act, to neutralise the negative elements that saw the proposed university as an enclave for the privileged. Hackett's support for a free higher education did much to alleviate this concern. A proposal not to charge fees was passed in the university council on Hackett's casting vote, making the university of Western Australia the only free university in the British Empire.

One of Hackett's strongest supporters was (Sir) Nobert Keenan (1864–1954), who entered Trinity in 1884 and went on to King's Inns and Middle Temple, qualifying as a barrister in England and Ireland. He migrated to Western Australia in 1895 and practised until 1905, when he entered the Legislative Assembly. He served as attorney-general for three years but lost his seat in 1911. He was a strong advocate for the establishment of a university and, when it was founded, he served on its senate from 1912–18. He returned to parliament again in 1930 as Nationalist leader and again served as a minister. By 1948, the year he was knighted, he had become Western Australia's oldest parliamentarian.

Hackett's influence on the university during the period of his chancellorship was profound. Not only did he endow a chair of agriculture, he also heavily influenced the decisions on the other disciplines that would be represented by the first chairs and those who would occupy them. In the report of the royal commission he had attempted to reconcile the old and the new disciplines, but he expressed the hope that the pride of place given to modern subjects and practical work would not be interpreted as iconoclasm, 'a desire to make little of the classical studies, which have made splendid the learning and teaching of the past. We want these also, but they will occupy a less lofty stage'.

One of the recommendations of the royal commission that can be immediately traced to Hackett was that a full-time vice-chancellor be appointed for the administration of the university. He had personally reported with great enthusiasm on the American system whereby a president exercised executive powers, 'working on his own initiative but loyally assisted by the confidence of his fellows'. When a full-time vice-chancellor was eventually appointed in 1927, the money to pay for the post was found in Hackett's bequest to the university.

A Bequest

With the death of his business partner Charles Harper in 1912, Hackett gained sole control of the *West Australian* and, when he himself died in 1916, responsibility as executor of his estate, editor and chairman of directors of the company devolved to Sir Alfred Langler. When probate was made on Hackett's estate there was a stipulation for a ten-year delay in winding it up. The value of the company at the time of his death stood at £93,000. The proportion going to the family was fixed at about ten percent, providing for Hackett's wife and the education of their five children. With respect to Lady Hackett, the will provided a sum of £1,000 to provide for her immediate wants, and for a sum of £20,000 to be set aside with the income only placed at her disposal. An additional annual sum of £2,000 was to be paid to Lady Hackett from the general income of the estate during her widowhood. This latter bequest was to cease if Lady Hackett re-married. The University of Western Australia and the Anglican Church were residual legatees and the sum of £2,000 was left to Trinity College, Dublin, the income from which was to be devoted to a prize for applied science.

Hackett had married Deborah Drake-Brockman against her family's wishes, when she was seventeen and he fifty-seven. They had one son and four daughters. Lady Hackett did marry again, two years after the death of Hackett, to Frank Moulden, lawyer and politician who was mayor of Adelaide for several years. Her new father-in-law, Arnold Moulden, was chairman of Broken Hill South Silver Mining Company and director of Electrolytic Line Co, and it may be due to his influence that she became interested in rare minerals, and tantalite in particular. Her success in developing the concentrates for the production of tantalum is legendary and, because of its strategic importance, her company, Tantalite Ltd, was resumed by the Commonwealth Government for the duration of World War II.

At the end of the ten-year moratorium on the winding up of the Hackett estate, the value of the company had increased under Langler's management to

£625,000. The University of Western Australia suddenly became wealthier, with an endowment of £425,000; the Anglican Church received £125,000 to construct a hall of residence for the university; and the family received the rest. At the opening of Winthrop Hall in 1932, built with the proceeds of Hackett's will, the university conferred upon Lady Moulden the honorary degree of LL.D.

Hackett's only son, Sir John Hackett, was born in 1910 and sent to Geelong Grammar School. Despite, or even because of, his father's strictures against the ancient universities, he was sent by his mother to New College, Oxford, graduating in 1930. The following year he joined the Royal Irish Hussars, the regiment of his great grandfather, and had a distinguished wartime career, which has been recounted in a number of autobiographical works. Sir John Hackett ended his military career in 1966 as Commander-in-Chief, British Army on the Rhine. On his retirement from the army this extraordinary military man and scholar became principal of King's College London. While on active service in Jordan during the Arab rebellion in 1937, he had found time to write a B.Litt thesis on *The Campaigns of Saladin during the Third Crusade*. On his death in 1997, the *Times* noted that Hackett Jnr is generally, if sometimes grudgingly, acknowledged as the cleverest soldier of his generation.

In my interviews with him in 1996, Sir John was philosophical about the way his father distributed his wealth. In his view, Sir Wintrop Hackett had benefited greatly from his life in Western Australia and wanted to put some of this back into the state by his benefaction to the university and the church. With respect to Lady Hackett, Sir John thought that his father wanted to protect her from 'gold diggers'. In earlier interviews, reported in the English *Sunday Times*, he observed, 'my father left us all enough to go to schools and universities and to have a little pocket money, but most – and the newspaper would be worth four or five million pounds today – went to the university and church in Western Australia. I was so grateful. I was a freebooter. I could do what I liked'.

CHAPTER 10

Governance, Politics and Federation

I hold that there is a tendency in these colonies to which we cannot close our eyes of advancing further and further in a democratic direction.

Nicholas Fitzgerald (1891 Federation Convention)

The First Irish Governor

In the period from the establishment of the penal settlement of New South Wales in 1788 to the achievement of responsible government for all colonies except Western Australia in 1856, the two principal administrators of the colonies were the governor and the chief justice. The governors, who were a part of the British colonial service, ruled with a greater or lesser degree of autocracy, depending upon their personalities and attitudes towards convicts and settlers. Initially, they took advice as they saw fit, and then formalised the advisory system by the establishment of an appointed Executive Council consisting of the principal administrators. In time, a partly elected Legislative Council emerged, and, finally, a full parliament, after the granting of responsible government. The chief justice ensured that any laws enacted were 'not repugnant' to the laws of England.

The first Irish governor to take up appointment in New South Wales, and the eighth governor to be installed, was Sir Richard Bourke, kinsman of Edmund Burke. Bourke arrived in the colony in 1831 and would have felt in familiar company, for three Irishmen, Roger Therry, John Kinchela and John Hubert Plunkett, held the most influential legal positions in the colony other than the chief justiceship. With Therry and Plunkett, Bourke was to form an Irish reforming triumvirate.

Richard Bourke (1777–1855) was born in Dublin and educated at Oriel College, Oxford, graduating in 1798. While he was at Oxford he spent his vacations at the home in Beaconsfield of Trinity's famous alumnus Edmund Burke, to whom he was related. He was present at Burke's death, witnessed his will and, in 1829, collaborated with Lord Fitzwilliam in editing the correspondence of his eminent relative. Sir Richard succeeded to his father's estate *Thornfields* in 1795, but instead of returning to Ireland after Oxford he joined the Grenadier Guards and, at the age of twenty-two, was wounded in the jaw during the Battle of Bergen. He felt later that the injury detracted from his ability to speak confidently in public and he did not enter parliament as he might well have done. He saw service in the Peninsular War and he came to the notice of Wellington, who placed him in posts of significant responsibility. In 1815 Bourke retired on half-pay to *Thornfields* with his wife Anne, two sons and three daughters. His concern for education of the very young was demonstrated at *Thornfields*, where he set up a little school for the children in the neighbourhood. Bourke's elder son, being blind, needed special attention, and the younger son had to be educated, so Bourke again sought a full-time appointment. Now a major-general on half-pay, he was offered the military command of Malta, and had accepted, when an emergency arose in Cape Colony and he was asked to take up the acting governorship. He remained there from 1826 until 1828, and was then offered the administration of New South Wales. In December 1831 he arrived in Sydney to be the first of six Irish colonial governors in Australia. His second son, Dick, did not travel with the family, as he had entered Trinity in 1829.

The Bourkes were typical of Norman families: more Irish than the Irish themselves, with an extraordinary record of colonial service. Sir Richard Southwell Bourke was governor-general of India and was assassinated there in 1872; and Richard's brother, Robert, Baron Connemara, was under-secretary of state for foreign affairs, and governor of Madras. Both brothers were educated in Trinity, and came from another branch of the Bourke family to which the governor of New South Wales belonged.

Sir Richard Bourke came to a colony that was undergoing change. His predecessor, Lachlan Macquarie, had entertained the claims of the emancipists – convicts who had served their terms – who generally suffered severe discrimination. Civil rights had not yet been granted and were being opposed

Figure 39. Sir Richard Bourke, Governor of New South Wales, 1831–38.

by the free settlers, the so-called 'pure merinos' who were not 'tainted' with convict blood. With Roger Therry and John Hubert Plunkett, Bourke set about reforming the law, introducing a system of primary education similar to his small-scale initiative at *Thornfields*, and proposing to the Colonial Office reforms to the Legislative Council, the governor's advisory body. The Council comprised seven officials and seven members appointed by the government in London. Bourke wanted a partly elected Council, but he did not succeed against the free settlers who were in the majority of appointed members. In 1836 Bourke had recommended to the home government that there should be a Legislative Council of thirty-six, twenty-four of whom would be elected by the people. This was rejected on the grounds that it was not appropriate to a convict colony. In 1842, following the ending of transportation, and long after Bourke's term of office, a Legislative Council of this kind was established.

Bourke, Plunkett and Therry first addressed the issue of trial by jury, extending jury membership for both civil and criminal cases to emancipists; and then a Bill was introduced that abolished the power of magistrates to punish assigned convicts. Whereas their masters could not legally punish them, convicts had to be taken to courts that were presided over by justices of the peace, who invariably were masters of convicts themselves. The potential for collusion between the convict masters to inflict punishments that were too harsh, in order to serve as examples to their own convicts, or simply unjust, was quite evident to Bourke and his supporters. The chief justice was asked to simplify the law that governed convicts: the sentences that could be passed were reduced, and the arbitrary power of the magistrates was removed by the establishment of Circuit Courts.

In 1833, Bourke and Plunkett promoted new policies for the support of the churches. As an Irish Protestant, Bourke was aware of the effects of sectarianism in Ireland and he set out to extend financial support to religions other than the Anglican Church. Estimating that one-fifth of the population was Catholic and Presbyterian and that other faiths had significant numbers of adherents in the colony, he proposed that government aid should be given in proportion to the numbers in the various congregations. In the face of opposition, Bourke's *Church Act* was passed in 1836. In 1842, after Bourke had left the colony, Plunkett successfully introduced a Bill designed to reduce even further sectarian tensions. This Bill prohibited party processions associated with religious or political differences that were designed to induce conflict. Bourke was less successful with the educational reforms he proposed. His educational model, which he developed with Plunkett, was based on the Irish National School System set up in 1831, but he could not overcome the opposition in the colony and the Bill failed.

In the inscription beneath the statue erected in Bourke's memory by the citizens of New South Wales, the foundation of the settlement of Port Phillip is attributed to him. As noted previously, when Bourke was informed in 1834 that settlers had sailed from Van Diemen's Land to Port Phillip, that they had brought sheep, seeds, plants and farm implements with them, and that they had purported to have bought some six hundred thousand acres of land from the local Doutta Galla tribe of Aborigines, he issued a proclamation declaring the agreement with the Aborigines void and recommended to the home government that official control be imposed. When permission was given to him by London to act as he saw fit, he sent Captain William Lonsdale on board HMS *Rattlesnake* to Port Phillip to take control. He visited the settlement himself in 1837 and named it Melbourne. One of Melbourne's principal streets now commemorates Bourke, widely regarded as the most popular governor in Australia's colonial history.

Bourke's resignation in 1838 was precipitated by an incident with the colonial treasurer C.D.Riddell, who sought the additional salaried post of chairman of Quarter Sessions, a judicial role. Riddell was not a lawyer and Bourke pointed out to him that his official position disqualified him from holding the additional office. Riddell agreed, but did not withdraw his nomination, which had been submitted by a group of disgruntled magistrates. Riddell was elected by one vote, afterwards found to result from 'an irregularity on the part of the returning officer', and, consequently, he declined the court position. Riddell was, by virtue of his office as colonial treasurer, a member of the Executive Council and, as a disciplinary measure, Bourke removed him from the Council but not from his substantive position of colonial treasurer. The secretary of state for the colonies, Lord Glenelg, was asked to approve his action. Glenelg, noting that in accordance with the governor's commission the colonial treasurer must be a member of the Executive Council, ordered Riddell's reinstatement on the Council. Bourke saw the instruction by Glenelg, a friend of Riddell's family, as compromising him and resigned the governorship.

The candidate Bourke had endorsed for the chairmanship of the Court of Quarter Sessions was Roger Therry, then a commissioner of the Court of Requests. Riddell was an exclusive, and friend of the magistrates who objected to the measures that Bourke, Therry and Plunkett had introduced to curb the power of the magistrates and to create a more just society. Bourke saw Glenelg's directive as a triumph for the exclusives; he resigned on principle, and left the colony in 1838. His son Dick, who had interrupted his legal studies at Trinity to join his father in Sydney, had already returned to Ireland to complete his studies, but his daughter Anne remained in New South Wales, as she had married the colonial secretary, Edward Deas Thompson. Bourke retired to *Thornfields* despite further offers of high official posts, and died there in 1853. Regarded as the most respected governor in the colonial period, such was his popularity that an appeal for subscriptions to erect a memorial to his honour was quickly filled and a fine statue now stands in front of the State Library of New South Wales.

From 1861 until 1872 three other Irish governors were appointed in New South Wales in succession. Sir John Young was chief secretary for Ireland before his appointment as governor in 1861. He was succeeded by Lord Belmore from Fermanagh, who is remembered only by the fact that a suburb and park in Sydney are named after him; and Belmore was replaced by Sir

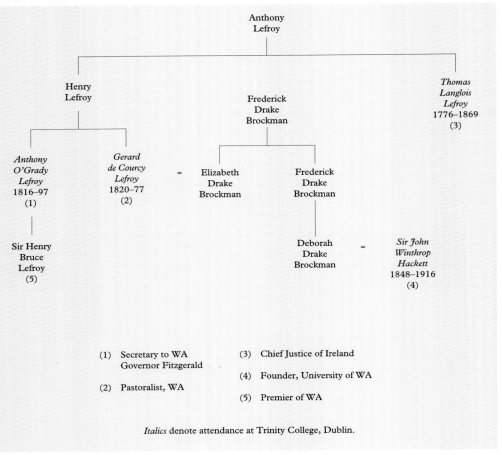

Anthony
Lefroy

Henry
Lefroy

*Frederick
Drake
Brockman*

*Thomas
Langlois
Lefroy
1776–1869*
(3)

*Anthony
O'Grady
Lefroy
1816–97*
(1)

*Gerard
de Courcy
Lefroy
1820–77*
(2)

=

Elizabeth
Drake
Brockman

Frederick
Drake
Brockman

Sir Henry
Bruce
Lefroy
(5)

Deborah
Drake
Brockman

=

*Sir John
Winthrop
Hackett
1848–1916*
(4)

(1)   Secretary to WA
        Governor Fitzgerald

(2)   Pastoralist, WA

(3)   Chief Justice of Ireland

(4)   Founder, University of WA

(5)   Premier of WA

Italics denote attendance at Trinity College, Dublin.

Chart 9. The Lefroys.

Hercules Robinson, from County Westmeath, who held a number of governorships before arriving in Sydney in 1872.

Western Australia and the Lefroys

In Western Australia the first Irish governor to be appointed was Andrew Clarke, son of a doctor from Belmont, County Donegal. Clarke served in the army until 1843 and then became governor of St Lucia. In 1845 he arrived in Western Australia and served as governor until 1848, when he was replaced by another Irishman, Sir Charles Fitzgerald. Fitzgerald is of interest because one of the Lefroys was his private secretary.

Anthony O'Grady Lefroy (1816–97) and his brother, Gerald de Courcy Lefroy, migrated to Western Australia in 1843. They were the sons of Henry Lefroy, Vicar of Santry, near Dublin, and were sent to Trinity in 1832 and 1839 respectively. A cousin, Henry Lefroy, had already migrated to Western Australia and the brothers decided to join him there. They took up a pastoral property, but Anthony, not being of a pastoral inclination, joined the civil service as private secretary to Fitzgerald, when he arrived as governor. After a short period Anthony became colonial treasurer and official nominee on the Legislative Council, a position he held until responsible government was granted in 1890. His son, Sir Henry Bruce Lefroy, a member of parliament for the electorate of Moore, became premier of Western Australia in 1917. Gerald de Courcy Lefroy continued to manage the family property and, showing the propensity of the Anglo-Irish to make good strategic alliances, he married Elizabeth Drake Brockman, aunt of Lady Winthrop Hackett. (see Chart 9, p.204)

The two pioneering Western Australian Lefroys, Anthony and Gerald, were the nephews of Thomas Langlois Lefroy, who entered Trinity in 1790 and enjoyed a brilliant academic career. Tom also enjoyed, albeit briefly, an association with Jane Austen, a story that is told in Constantia Maxwell's *History of Trinity College, Dublin*, and elsewhere. In the winter of 1795–96 Tom went to stay with his uncle, the Reverend Isaac Lefroy, at Ashe Rectory in Hampshire, not far from Steventon, where Jane Austen spent her youth. Jane was twenty at the time of Tom's visit and he was twenty-one. Many parties and balls were held in the neighbourhood and the note Jane wrote to her sister, Cassandra, regarding the rector's young nephew, tells us a great deal about the society of the time:

'I am almost afraid to tell you how my Irish friend and I behaved. Imagine to yourself everything most profligate and shocking in the way of dancing and sitting down together. I **can** expose myself, however, only **once more**, because he leaves the country soon after next Friday, on which day we **are** to have a dance at Ashe after all. He is a very gentlemanlike, good looking, pleasant young man, I assure you. But as to our having ever met, except at these three last balls, I cannot say much; for he is so excessively laughed at about me at Ashe, that he is ashamed of coming to Steventon, and ran away when we called on Mrs Lefroy a few days ago.'

The flirtation ended with Tom's return to Ireland. Tom went on to become chief justice of Ireland, and his bust adorns the Long Room of Trinity's Library.

Figure 40. Sir Arthur Kennedy, Governor of Western Australia, 1855–62; and Queensland, 1877–83.

The only Trinity-educated governor of Western Australia, and he served as governor of Queensland, too, was Sir Arthur Kennedy (1810–83), from County Down, who entered the College in 1823 but did not graduate. He joined the army in 1827 and after almost twenty years he retired and joined the colonial service, becoming governor of Gambia, Sierra Leone and, in 1855, Western Australia. He served there for seven years and was then successively governor of Vancouver Island (1863–67), West African settlements (1868–72) and Hong Kong (1872–77). In 1877 he became governor of Queensland, succeeding Sir William Wellington Cairns, who, as already noted, was the half brother of Lord Cairns, chancellor of Trinity from 1867–85. The city of Cairns is named after Sir William.

When Queensland achieved separation from New South Wales in 1859, Sir George Bowen, Oxford graduate and son of a rector in Donegal, became its first

Figure 41. Major Samuel Wensley Blackall, Governor of Queensland, 1868–71.

governor. After nine years Bowen was promoted to the governorship of New Zealand, and was succeeded in Queensland by Samuel Wensley Blackall. Blackall (1809–71), born in Dublin and the son of a major in the East India Company, and his brother Richard were sent to Trinity in 1824 and 1828 respectively, but neither of them graduated. Samuel joined the army in 1827, but sold his commission six years later and entered the House of Commons, representing Longford for four years from 1847–51. Entering the colonial service in 1851, he served as lieutenant-governor of Dominica until 1857, narrowly escaping recall on account of his high–handedness. Governorship of Sierra Leone and then the West African settlements followed and, finally, he went to Queensland, where he died in office in 1871. Blackall's governorship was plagued by constitutional crises in the colony, which were not finally resolved until the arrival of his successor. He is remembered in Queensland by the town of Blackall and a mountain range called the Blackall Ranges. He was the second of the Trinity-educated governors to have a mountain range named after him. The first was Richard Graves MacDonnell, governor of South Australia.

Sir Richard Graves MacDonnell

When responsible government came into effect in South Australia, Richard Graves MacDonnell (1814–81) was the first governor to be appointed under the new arrangements. MacDonnell was the eldest son of Provost MacDonnell. He entered Trinity in 1829, was elected scholar in 1833 and graduated in 1835. He was called to the Irish and English Bars and practised in London until 1843, when he applied for, and was appointed to, the chief justiceship of the Gambia. While in Gambia, he was involved in a dispute with Governor Fitzgerald, which resulted in the governor himself being replaced by MacDonnell. An intrepid explorer, MacDonnell organised a number of expeditions into the interior, and is said to have survived an assassination attempt during one of these. In 1852 he transferred to St Lucia and then to St Vincent as administrator. With a reputation for high-handedness and severity, he arrived in South Australia in 1855 and began immediately to set about devising a constitution Bill that would be acceptable to the Colonial Office. His view that only he knew best brought more conflict to what was already a fractious colony. After much debate, South Australia had a constitution with a democratically elected Legislative Assembly, and a Legislative Council with a property requirement for membership. In all of this, MacDonnell was keen to retain as much power to the governor as he could, and he was blamed for the passing of a constitution Bill that seemed to please no one except, perhaps, himself. His lack of diplomacy ensured that his relationship with the administration was strained. His support for fellow Trinity man, Richard Torrens, was crucial, however, to the passing of the *Real Property Act*.

MacDonnell's interest in exploration led him into the interior and he travelled extensively in the province. He supported John McDouall Stuart's efforts to cross the continent from south to north, and was duly rewarded when Stuart named a prominent mountain range in the very centre of Australia 'the MacDonnell Ranges'. It is thought that MacDonnell had little concern for the working people, believing that charity encouraged laziness and pauperism. This is borne out to some degree by his treatment of a particular group of unruly, unemployed women, who he 'reduced to obedience by the cooling effects of water from a fire engine'. This, according to A.N.Jeffares, may be the first recorded use of water cannon to quell disturbances! MacDonnell encouraged

Figure 42. Sir Richard Graves MacDonnell, Governor of South Australia, 1855–62.

the pastoral and agricultural industries, and was particularly optimistic about the prospects for the wine industry in South Australia under the management of German settlers. In 1862 he was posted as lieutenant-governor of Nova Scotia and retired as governor of Hong Kong in 1872. MacDonnell was succeeded in South Australia by Sir Dominick Daly, 'a courtly Irish gentleman from County Galway', whose urbanity was, apparently, a relief from the autocratic and high-handed style of his predecessor.

The Political Arena

When the legislatures were established in the 1850s in all colonies except Western Australia, two chambers were chosen to represent the people: the lower house, called the Legislative Assembly and the upper house of review, the Legislative Council. The presiding members of the two houses were the speaker and the president, respectively. John Hubert Plunkett was president of the Legislative Council of New South Wales for a time, as was Plunkett's great friend Sir Terence Aubrey Murray, both of whom we have noted in the chapter on New South Wales as having links with Trinity.

As with their influence in the law, it was in Victoria that the Trinity men had the greatest political impact. We have already noted the comments of the Melbourne *Argus*, where the number of Irishmen holding key positions in government and the bureaucracy immediately prior to the granting of responsible government was highlighted. But, as Cleary wryly notes in his *Irish Nation-Builders*, not one of these worthies 'kicked with the same foot' as the Catholic leader of the opposition, John O'Shanassy. In a contest between Trinity men in the first Victorian parliament, Francis Murphy defeated Charles Griffith for the speakership of the Legislative Assembly, and he chaired the Assembly for the first fifteen years of the parliament. Murphy was succeeded by (Sir) Charles MacMahon (1824–91), born in County Tyrone, the son of Sir William MacMahon, Master of the Rolls in Ireland. Charles's four brothers graduated from Trinity between 1830 and 1840, but he chose to join the army, retiring in 1851 with the rank of captain. He migrated to Melbourne in the following year, becoming assistant commissioner and then commissioner of police. In that role MacMahon opposed Governor Hotham's policy with respect to miners' licences. He disliked the behaviour of the police in enforcing it, and wrote to Hotham before the Eureka Stockade rebellion that the police 'are now more like a military barracks for coercion than a civil force for police protection'. He resigned from the police force in 1858, as a result of interference in the force by O'Shanassy, his departmental head. Ironically, he then served in the second O'Shanassy ministry (1858–59) and was minister without portfolio. Knighted in 1875, he lost the speakership in 1877 as the result of a campaign against him on the grounds of his being corrupt, namely, for favouring one of the parties. He was replaced by another Irishman, Charles Gavan Duffy, who in turn was succeeded by Peter Lalor, in 1880. Lalor was speaker for seven years and refused the customary knighthood.

In the Victorian Legislative Council only one Irish-born and Trinity-educated member became president. Sir Henry Wrixon (1839–1913) was born in Dublin, the son of Arthur Nicholas Wrixon and Maria Bace. In 1856 the family migrated to Melbourne, where Arthur was appointed as a County Court judge. Henry was one of the first students to enter Melbourne University but he left for Trinity in 1857, graduating in 1861. He was called to the Irish Bar, but soon found that there was little work in Dublin and returned to Melbourne in 1863.

Entering politics in 1868 on a radical reform ticket, he proclaimed that 'wealth is the only badge of our aristocracy, but it confers a nobility neither exclusive nor enduring'. His disdain for the wealthy may have been modified after he married a rich widow and purchased a great mansion, *Raheen*, which subsequently became the residence of the famous Daniel Mannix, Catholic Archbishop of Melbourne. Wrixon was solicitor-general in 1870–71, and did not contest the election in 1877, in order to tour in Europe. He returned to politics in 1880 and in 1886 became attorney-general, and had great pleasure in appointing George Higinbotham, whom he greatly admired as chief justice of Victoria. Wrixon moved to the Legislative Council in 1896 and was president from 1901–10. He served as vice-chancellor of the University of Melbourne from 1897–1910. Alfred Deakin, the second prime minister of Australia, who had dealings with him during the federation discussions, described Wrixon as 'loveable and entirely trustworthy [with] the sincerest and most unselfish desire to serve his country'.

Wrixon was a mixture of radical and conservative, advocating proportional representation, female suffrage, workers compensation and Saturday half-day on the one hand; and, on the other, opposing non-contributory old age pensions, maintaining a distinction between the deserving and the non-deserving poor, condemning the unemployed for holding meetings to demand public works, and introducing severe physical punishments for crimes against women and children. His sabbatarianism and conservatism earned him the nickname of 'righteous' Wrixon. He played an important role in the events leading up to federation.

Ministries in Victoria

If Trinity men and others associated with the College feature prominently amongst the presiding officers of the Victorian parliament, the ministries that were formed between 1856 and 1880 have an equally impressive representation from them. The first ministry (1855–57) included Stawell, Clarke and Molesworth as ministers in cabinet; the second (1857) contained Fitzgerald Foster as treasurer; and in the fourth (1858–59) Richard Ireland was attorney-general. In subsequent ministries Trinity men featured prominently until the end of the century.

In the fourth ministry, the minister of lands, Charles Gavan Duffy, as we have seen, was keen to unlock the lands, but his enthusiasm was not shared by many of his colleagues, who had a particular interest in maintaining the grip

Figure 43. Moses Wilson Gray, Victorian politician and Judge of the District Court, New Zealand.

that the 'wealthy lower orders' had on the land. Duffy's relationship with the radical Wilson Gray was of particular concern to the squatters. Moses Wilson Gray (1813–75) was born in Claremorris, County Mayo, and educated in England and at Trinity. He graduated in 1835 and was appointed an assistant commissioner to the Poor Law Inquiry in Ireland. Shortly after the end of the inquiry Gray spent some time at the University of Michigan and went to the Bar. He returned to Ireland to help his brother, (Sir) John Gray, in managing and editing the *Freeman's Journal*. Gray was a contemporary at Trinity of Thomas Davis and John Blake Dillon; and Charles Gavan Duffy, though a student at King's Inns, was also a part of this group. When the hopes of settlement of the Irish land question were not fulfilled, Duffy, accompanied by Gray, sailed for Melbourne in 1855 on the *Ocean Chief*.

Gray was admitted to the Victorian Bar on his arrival and worked as law reporter for the *Age* and the *Argus*. He became leader of the movement to unlock the lands and was a committee member of the Victorian Land League. Frustrated at the lack of progress in land reform he entered the parliament in 1860. His continuing concerns about the land question led him to declare that the Assembly should listen to the agitators outside parliament, and to wish that 'every man had a vote, a rifle and a farm'. He was especially disappointed with Duffy's defective 1862 *Land Bill*. Gray's efforts to effect easier purchase terms and other reforms failed, and he left for New Zealand in June 1862, refusing to have any banquet or testimonials on his departure. Instead, he attended a simple function at the Trades Union Hall. In New Zealand Gray served for thirteen years as a district judge, his indifference to wealth keeping him from accepting high office.

Wilson's brother, John Gray, whose statue is a prominent feature of O'Connell Street in Dublin, graduated MD from Glasgow University in 1839, and was proprietor of the *Freeman's Journal*. Also a radical, he was at one time sentenced to nine months imprisonment, later revoked, for conspiracy against the Queen. Gray was knighted in 1863 for his work as chairman of a committee set up to deliver a new water supply for Dublin. He was elected MP for Kilkenny and advocated abolition of the preference given to the Church of Ireland, reform of the land laws and free denominational education. Elected lord mayor of Dublin in 1868 he declined to take up office.

Edmund Dwyer Gray, Sir John's son, is famous for his rescue in 1865 of five people involved in a boating accident on Dublin Bay. His bravery in swimming out to the wreck and saving the drowning occupants was rewarded in two ways. First, he received the Tayleur Medal, the highest award of the Royal Humane Society; and, second, the rescue was witnessed by Caroline Agnes Chisholm, daughter of 'immigrants' friend' Caroline Chisholm. He was introduced to Miss Chisholm and they later married. Caroline Chisholm, an English social worker, settled in New South Wales in 1838. Concerned at the situation of impoverished and abandoned immigrant women she set up an office to assist and provide shelter for new arrivals. She assisted more than ten thousand women and children during the 1840s, persuaded the British government to give free passage to the families of convicts already transported, and set up the Family Colonization Loan Society, to which the New South Wales government voted £10,000 in 1852.

Premiers

The Victorian ministerial lists from November 1855 until August 1880 show many of the Trinity-educated men whom we have encountered in other contexts; of those on the lists, one, Bryan O'Loghlen, became premier. Bryan O'Loghlen was the third son of Sir Michael O'Loghlen, the first Catholic since the reign of James II to become a judge in either Ireland or England. Michael O'Loghlen (1789–1842) graduated from Trinity in 1809 and became Daniel O'Connell's junior, and when O'Connell entered politics Michael succeeded to a large part of the practice. In 1834 O'Loghlen was solicitor-general of Ireland and then became attorney-general. He was appointed a baron of the Court of Exchequer in 1836 and, in 1837, succeeded Sir William McMahon, father of the Victorian speaker, as Master of the Rolls.

Bryan O'Loghlen (1828–1905) entered Trinity in 1845 but left in 1847 to go to England to become a railway engineer. He worked on the family estate in 1850, and then, after a further period in London, decided to return to Trinity to complete his studies. Graduating in 1856, he was called to the Irish Bar and practised on the Munster Circuit for five years. He migrated to Victoria in 1862, practised for a while and was then appointed as crown prosecutor in Melbourne. On the death of his brother, Colman, in 1877, Bryan succeeded to the baronetcy and was nominated to the seat of Clare in the House of Commons. Elected despite his absence, he preferred to enter the Victorian parliament, becoming attorney-general in the government of Graham Berry in 1878. As a result, he lost his seat in the House of Commons.

O'Loghlen lost his seat in the Victorian elections of 1880 as well, but there was an election within six months and he was able to resume his parliamentary career. He declined a ministerial portfolio in the new Berry government, and moved a successful vote of no confidence in the government on a matter of reform of the Legislative Council. Asked to form a government himself, he became premier of what Alfred Deakin called 'a scratch team' from 1881–83, without a majority. In an attempt to improve his position, he dissolved the parliament but the election was a disaster and O'Loghlen lost his seat again. He regained it five years later and adopted a radical stance in the parliament. O'Loghlen spoke on behalf of the unemployed and, like Higinbotham, condemned the employers' refusal to hold a conference with the trade unions during a maritime strike. The Trades Hall Council's strike committee thanked him, as they also thanked Higinbotham.

O'Loghlen held his last ministerial portfolio in the government of Sir James Patterson in 1893. As attorney-general he became embroiled in a damaging dispute with Isaac Isaacs, his solicitor-general, over the proposed prosecution of the chairman and manager of a failed bank. It so happened that the chairman, Sir Matthew Davies, had been a member of the Legislative Assembly for ten years and, when he was committed for trial, O'Loghlen announced that the indictments would not proceed. Isaacs issued a challenge to this, proclaiming that he had the power to act independently of the attorney-general. The populace was on Isaacs's side but the law favoured O'Loghlen. Neither of them emerged with great credit from the affair, but Isaacs went on to become the first Australian-born governor-general of Australia. From the fall of the Patterson government in 1896 until 1900, O'Loghlen was in and out of parliament with no other ministerial appointments. A biographer observed that, 'but for his Irish Catholic background and a certain gentle and aristocratic indolence, he might have had more success in politics'.

O'Loghlen and Torrens were the only Trinity-educated men to serve as premiers of Australian colonies. Patrick Jennings, an honorary graduate, was premier of New South Wales, and William Hill Irvine, who we have already discussed in his role as chief justice of Victoria, was the only Trinity man to become the premier of a state. Jennings was a member of the New South Wales delegation to the 1891 Convention, which set Australia on the path to federation, and Irvine served in the federal parliament as attorney-general. It is to federation, and the role of Trinity men in that great political achievement, that we now turn.

Federation

William Charles Wentworth was an early advocate of a federal Australia and established the General Association for the Australian Colonies, which he thought of as a forerunner to a federal assembly, with power to legislate on internal matters. Even though the Crimean War was bringing home to the government and the colonies their vulnerability to naval attack, the British Government was not receptive to the notion when Wentworth presented it in London in 1854. However, the war did stimulate the formation of colonial armies and the construction of ships for what was to become the Royal Navy's Australian Squadron.

Even earlier than Wentworth, Governor Fitzroy of New South Wales had suggested to the colonial secretary, Lord Grey, that a single functionary should have responsibility to ensure that laws passed in one colony did not conflict with the laws in another. Grey agreed and named Fitzroy 'governor-general' with the power to call a general assembly of Australia if necessary. The idea was unpopular, because the independence of each colony from the others was, as always, of paramount importance. Fitzroy never used the power given to him

Figure 44. Delegates to the Australian Federal Convention, 1891.

and the title of governor-general was not used again until federation. The best that could be achieved was the formation of colonial committees in the late 1850s and inter-colonial conferences from 1863 until 1883.

At the 1881 inter-colonial conference, Sir Henry Parkes, premier of New South Wales, first suggested the establishment of a federal council, an organisation that would 'lead men to think in the direction of federation and accustom the public mind to federal ideas'. At the last of the inter-colonial conferences in 1883, Sir Samuel Griffith, premier of Queensland, repeated the call for a council of all Australia to enable the colonies to act together for their defence. Despite inter-colonial acrimony, distrust and insult following the conference, a federal council was set up in 1886, but though it represented a step towards federation, it achieved little, since New South Wales voted not to join it.

By the late 1880s concerns about defence were raised again and in 1889 Major-General J.B.Edwards, commander of the British forces in China, conducted a review of colonial defence preparedness, concluding that unless its defences were improved, Australia would be a rich prize for its northern neighbours. He recommended that the colonies commission a single army under a single commander. For Parkes, this also meant a single government, for, otherwise, which colonial government would control this single army? Parkes telegraphed the other premiers asking for a high level inter-colonial conference to discuss federation but he was referred to the ineffectual federal council. He decided to act, and at a famous speech made at a meeting held in the New South Wales town of Tenterfield he started the drive towards federation. As a result of his Tenterfield oration, Parkes became popularly known as the 'father of federation'; but he did not live to see his vision realised and it was others who could, in the event, lay claim to be the founders of federation.

Representatives from all the colonies met in Melbourne in 1890 to decide whether the time was right for the creation of an Australian government. The conference, attended by Edmund Barton and Alfred Deakin, the first and second prime ministers of Australia respectively, gave the answer – the time had come. The conference was a triumph for Parkes, who dominated it as much by his striking physical appearance as by his oratory. The conference paved the way for the crucial National Australasian Convention, held in Sydney over six weeks in 1891. Seven delegates from each colony, together with three from New Zealand, gathered to work out a means whereby the colonies could federate into a single nation while retaining a measure of identity and power. Parkes was elected president of the convention and proposals were put for a single army and navy, free trade between the states, and the right of each state to make laws except on matters of national importance. A draft constitution was drawn up by four lawyers on board the Queensland government's steamer *Lucinda*, in which Griffith had travelled to Sydney. The draft provided for two houses of parliament, the House of Representatives and the Senate, and the nation would be called the Commonwealth of Australia.

The delegates took the draft constitution back to their governments and the hard bargaining began. Parkes was defeated at the polls in New South Wales in 1891 and Barton, as president of the Australasian Federation League, which he founded in 1893, became the leading proponent of the 'one nation, one destiny' measure. Deakin, as leader of the strangely titled Australian Natives Association, joined him in the crusade. A key meeting of the Australasian Federation League, held in the small New South Wales town of Corowa, saw a breakthrough in which a further federal convention was proposed, with elected representatives from the colonies, and with the purpose of writing a new constitution. The convention took place over a period of one year commencing in March 1897, with elected representatives from each colony except Western Australia, which, instead, nominated John Winthrop

Hackett and Premier Forrest. The convention was held in three sessions – in Adelaide, Sydney and Melbourne – and its objectives were fulfilled. After a series of referenda, a Bill was passed in Westminster in 1900 that provided for the establishment of the Commonwealth of Australia, and approved its constitution.

Trinity and Federation

By the last quarter of the nineteenth century the number of Trinity graduates going to Australia was in decline, and this is generally reflected in the small number that were prominent in the federation movement. This is not to say that Irishmen or Irish-Australians were not well represented at the conventions, and Charles Kingston, of Irish parentage, who helped draft the constitution on board *Lucinda* is, according to Lahey in his *Faces of Federation*, 'one of the four or five figures who stand apart as giants of the federation story'. Charles was the son of Sir George Kingston from Bandon, County Cork, first speaker of the South Australian Legislative Assembly, whose only link to Trinity is that his brother William graduated from the College in 1822. Lahey lists at least ten Irish-born delegates to the conventions, of whom Henry Bournes Higgins was to achieve the greatest eminence as attorney-general in the federal parliament and judge of the federal High Court of Australia. While president of the Commonwealth Court of Conciliation and Arbitration, Higgins delivered a sensational judgement against H.V.McKay, manufacturer of the Sunshine combine harvester, in which he calculated the income a family of five would need to buy necessities, and then fixed that amount at seven shillings a day, to the outrage of employers. The Harvester judgement was a forerunner to the establishment of a basic wage for Australia.

Of the other Irish-born federationists listed by Lahey, four were educated at Trinity. Prominent in their contributions to the debates at the conventions were Sir Henry Wrixon, president of the Victorian Legislative Council; Sir John Winthrop Hackett, representing Western Australia; Patrick McMahon Glynn from South Australia; and Nicholas Fitzgerald, member of the Victorian Legislative Assembly and signatory, with his brother Edward, to the congratulatory address sent to Trinity by Victorian alumni on the occasion of the College's tercentenary.

Sir Henry Wrixon became something of a celebrity when he returned from London in 1888, where he had appealed to the Privy Council to reverse the Victorian Supreme Court's majority decision in the locally famous Toy v Musgrove case. A.H.Toy was a British subject from Hong Kong and the Victorian immigration authorities prevented his entry to the colony. However,

Figure 45. Sir Henry Wrixon, Attorney-General of Victoria.

the Imperial Government objected to discriminatory colonial legislation which restricted the number of Chinese immigrants to Victoria and which required them to pay a poll tax. Toy sued the Victorian government in the Supreme Court, with Musgrove, the collector of customs, as the defendant. Wrixon, then the attorney-general, led for the government and lost. The Supreme Court, mindful of the attitude of the Colonial Office, held that the colonial government did not have the authority to restrict numbers of immigrants from a particular race of people. Higinbotham, the chief justice, naturally dissented on principle. Wrixon, supporting Higinbotham, believed that the Supreme Court was simply adhering to the Colonial Office line, and went to London to persuade the Privy Council to reverse the Supreme Court's decision. He succeeded, and hence his popularity on his return.

Wrixon was chosen, with Nicholas Fitzgerald and five others including Deakin, to represent Victoria at the 1891 federal convention. His contribution was notable. He was, for a time, a part of the drafting group on board *Lucinda* and led the opposition to a provision that gave the proposed Senate power to alter money Bills. The debate produced what became known as the 'compromise of 1891', which was designed to prevent the federal Senate from amending money Bills submitted by the House of Representatives but allowing it to 'request' amendments. In taking the stance he did, Wrixon was drawing upon his experience in the Victorian parliament where the Legislative Council caused such havoc in its interference with money Bills. Wrixon failed to be elected to the 1897–98 convention, being narrowly defeated by Henry Bournes Higgins, who deeply regretted replacing him, so popular was Henry Wrixon.

John Winthrop Hackett was the only one of the seven-member Western Australian delegation to the 1891 Convention to vote for the 'compromise of 1891'. By 1895 he had formed the view that Western Australia's entry into the federation would have to be delayed until its industries were developed with the benefit of tariff protection. With his close relationship with the premier, John Forrest, and the power wielded through his newspaper, Hackett was central to the debate about Western Australia's entry into the a federated political structure. He supported federation but did not see any urgency in his own colony's entry. At the 1891 convention he uttered the famous phrase, that 'either responsible government will kill federation or federation in the form in which I hope we shall be prepared to accept it, will kill responsible government'.

Selected again for the 1897 convention Hackett prepared a manifesto, but on the constitutional sub-committee of which he was a member he changed his mind about the 'compromise of 1891'. At the crucial vote on the matter he was absent. Before the Western Australian referendum on federation, Hackett brought his paper around to supporting it, despite the continued opposition of his partner, Charles Harper. Hackett may have become fearful that the threat of secession by the goldfields districts, which were in favour of federation, would become a reality. Henry Augustus Ellis (1861–1939), a Trinity-educated physician, politician and inventor, who graduated MB, Ch.B in 1884, led the campaign to separate the goldfields from Western Australia with the motto 'separation for federation'. None of the Perth newspapers had previously supported federation and the change of direction of Hackett's *West Australian* was crucial. There was a resounding vote in favour of joining in a single nation in July 1900. Hackett and the premier, John Forrest, were disappointed at the lack of concessions to their colony, which had only recently achieved responsible government, but they pragmatically decided that the terms were as good as they would get, and that federation was inevitable.

Figure 46. Patrick McMahon Glynn, Federationist, Federal Attorney-General.

Patrick McMahon Glynn (1855–1931) is famous as the man who, despite much opposition, managed to have a reference to God inserted into the preamble to the constitution. The form in which this was eventually accepted was 'whereas the people of New South Wales, Victoria, South Australia, Queensland and Tasmania, humbly relying on the blessing of Almighty God, have agreed to unite ...'. Glynn, from County Galway, and the third son of merchant John McMahon Glynn, entered Trinity in 1875 even though the ban on attendance by Catholics at Trinity had just been imposed by the Maynooth Synod, held in the same year. Graduating in 1878, he studied at King's Inns and Middle Temple and went to the Bar. Finding insufficient work he set out for Melbourne in 1880 and there, too, he found that work was scarce, writing to his brother that 'trying to get business here is like attacking the devil with an icicle'. After a time as a 'traveller' for an insurance company and Singer sewing machines, he moved to South Australia in 1883 to open a law practice for an Adelaide firm of solicitors in a country town. He was able to buy the practice in 1886 and, while retaining it, moved to Adelaide, where he established a second practice and wrote for the newspapers.

In 1887 Glynn was elected to the Legislative Assembly and his political career commenced. He lost and gained seats several times during the first ten years of his political life and, for a short time in 1899, was attorney-general. In 1897 Glynn was elected as one of the ten South Australian delegates to the crucial federal convention, where he impressed the delegates greatly by his knowledge of constitutional law and use of the classic literature to illustrate his arguments. He caused a stir during the Sydney session of the convention when, as the result of his proposal of marriage, by letter, to Abigail Dynon, which she accepted by telegram, he rushed from the convention back to Adelaide to be married.

In 1901 Glynn was elected to the first federal House of Representatives, where he served until 1919. During that time he was attorney-general in Deakin's government of 1909–10, minister for external affairs from 1913–14, and minister for home and territories from 1917–19. His greatest contribution was in relation to the use and control of inland rivers, as he was able to draw on his South Australian parliamentary experience. There, he had been a member of the South Australian royal commission on the Murray waters for five years. Glynn retired from politics when he lost his seat in 1919.

The Fitzgeralds

In the congratulatory address sent to Trinity on the occasion of its tercentenary, the names of Nicholas and Edward Fitzgerald appear. Nicholas Fitzgerald (1829–1908) is the last Trinity-educated federationist with whom we shall deal. The Fitzgeralds were sons of a brewer of County Galway and they followed in their father's footsteps when they went to Victoria. Another brother, Sir Gerald Fitzgerald, was accountant-general of the British Navy from 1885–96. Nicholas entered Trinity in 1845, studied law at King's Inns and then moved to the new Queen's College in Galway in 1849. He lists no degree in the congratulatory address, whereas Edward has an LL.D from Trinity. Edward Fitzgerald migrated to Victoria in 1857 and applied for a licence to set up a brewery in the country Victorian town of Castlemaine. In 1859 Nicholas joined him and their brewery business 'expanded like no other in Australia', the Castlemaine Brewery becoming the foundation of the largest brewing empire in Australia. Two Irish brothers, Patrick and Thomas Perkins, became small shareholders of the Castlemaine Brewery, but after selling their interest they left in 1862 to

Figure 47. Nicholas Fitzgerald, Federationist and founder of Castlemaine Brewery.

set up their own brewery in Brisbane. They were to rejoin the Fitzgerald empire later.

In 1871, the Fitzgeralds, with James Perrin, established a brewery in Melbourne, which prospered until the early 1900s, when it was taken over by the larger Carlton and United Breweries. The original brewery in Castlemaine, operating as 'Fitzgeralds Brewing and Malting Company', was also taken over by Carlton and United Breweries in 1925 and closed. The name Castlemaine lived on, however. In 1877 a firm of general merchants in Brisbane, Quinlan Donnelly, seeking to expand their business into brewing, went into partnership with the Fitzgeralds to form the Fitzgerald, Quinlan Company. A distillery at Milton near Brisbane was bought and another 'Castlemaine Brewery' was built. In 1878 Castlemaine XXX beer, described by the *Brisbane Courier* as 'a delicious ale of the brightest amber, pleasant to the taste', was produced and the business was an enormous success. In 1916 another X was added to the label and

Figure 48. Fitzgerald Brewing and Malting Company label.

'Castlemaine XXXX' beer was born. This brand challenged the virtual monopoly then held by the 'Perkins City Brewery' and by 1928 the Perkins brothers were forced to merge. The resulting Castlemaine Perkins Brewery, with a distinctive label that has remained almost unchanged from the time of the merger, became Queensland's largest brewery. The brand is now internationally known, brought to the world by two intrepid Trinity men.

While pursuing his brewing interests, Nicholas also indulged his political ambitions. In 1864 he was elected to the Legislative Council and served for an extraordinary forty-two years. In all that time he declined ministerial office, preferring to do his duty as a private member. He was described as 'a warm, generous man, brilliantly gifted at flowery speech', who wore a distinctive pearl pin on his cravat. It was observed that he was at his best when speaking to his fellow countrymen on subjects appealing to their native sympathies. His commonest theme was Catholic education and his independence in parliament was aimed at allowing him to speak on issues like this without having to adhere to a party line. A prominent Catholic layman, Fitzgerald was awarded a papal knighthood by Pope Gregory XIII. In 1863 he married the daughter of Sir John O'Shanassy, the first Catholic premier of Victoria.

Figure 49. Sir Frederick Darley administers the Oath of Office to Lord Hopetoun, the first Governor-General of Australia.

Fitzgerald was one of the two conservative Legislative Councillors to be chosen to represent Victoria at the 1891 Federal Convention. The other was Sir Henry Cuthbert, from Boyle, County Roscommon, who was postmaster-general during the Black Wednesday crisis and who steadfastly refused to sack any postal workers for the entire period of this constitutional debacle. Fitzgerald's contribution to the convention was idiosyncratic and, of course, representative of the conservative interest. He saw no need for a federal High Court and was appalled at the notion that state governors might be elected. In his view, the Queen should appoint the governor-general, as 'I hold that there is a tendency in these colonies, to which we cannot close our eyes, of advancing further and further in a democratic direction'. This was no Henry Wrixon. He was an archetypal member of the old Irish gentry whose conservatism held such sway in the colony of Victoria for fifty years.

In New South Wales, Sir Frederick Darley, another of the conservative Trinity men, even as he was swearing in Lord Hopetoun as the first governor-general of Australia, was not convinced that Federation would work.

In 1902, Darley, the 'old Irish gentleman', privy counsellor, GCMC, and honorary LLD of Trinity, considered that 'Australian Federation is so far a pronounced failure'!

Tercentenary Address

THE ALUMNI OF THE UNIVERSITY OF DUBLIN RESIDENT IN VICTORIA, AUSTRALIA,
to THE PROVOST AND FELLOWS OF TRINITY COLLEGE, DUBLIN.

We desire to offer to you our hearty congratulations on the occasion of the Tercentenary of the University of Dublin, and to assure you that, although separated from you by many thousand miles of land and sea, we are one with you in love and reverence for our Alma Mater and in pride for the high place she has long held among the most distinguished seats of learning in Europe, which high place, as we cannot but know, has been made higher still by the achievements of those who are the leaders and teachers of the present generation of her students.

We have a lively recollection of the days we spent within the walls of our old college and a deep sense of gratitude for the opportunities afforded us there of making acquaintance with the wisdom and learning of ancient and modern times.

We beg to inform you that it is our purpose to perpetuate our sense of these benefits by founding in the University of Melbourne, with which many of us are incorporated, a gold medal or medals, to be identified by name with the University of Dublin, and to be annually bestowed as an encouragement here to the pursuit of some of the studies which are so successfully cultivated there. And thus we hope to establish among future generations a living link of sympathy with that great seat of learning where we have had the honour to be students.

As citizens of Victoria we remember with pride how large a share men who have been trained in Trinity College, Dublin, have had in the making of this Colony. The public careers of Sir William Foster Stawell, Sir Redmond Barry, Sir Robert Molesworth, Mr. Peter Lalor, and Dr. William Edward Hearn, to speak only of those who are no longer living, form no small part of the history of our adopted country ; and there is no university of the Old World with which the chief seat of learning in this Colony is more closely linked than our own. Of the five chancellors who have up to the present time presided over the University of Melbourne, three have been graduates of the University of Dublin.

We ask you to accept the assurance of our heartfelt and respectful regard, in token whereof we here affix our signatures.

GEO. HIGINBOTHAM, Chief Justice of Victoria.

BRYAN O'LOGHLEN, Bart., Q.C., late Premier of Victoria.

H. B. MACARTNEY, B.D., Dean of Melbourne.

H. J. WRIXON, Q.C., K.C.M.G., late Attorney-General of Victoria.

N. FITZGERALD, Member of the Legislative Council of Victoria.

E. B. HAMILTON, Judge of County Courts.

H. E. COOPER, M.A., Archdeacon of Hamilton.

P. TEULON BEAMISH, D.D., Archdeacon of Warrnambool.

ROBERT POTTER, B.A. Dubl.; Canon of St. Paul's, Melbourne; M.A., Melbourne; Theological Lecturer, T. C. M.

ROBERT WALSH, Q.C., Crown Prosecutor.

JOHN TREVOR FOX, M.A., T.C.D.

ALEXANDER LEEPER, LL.D., Warden of Trinity College, University of Melbourne.

THOMAS R. LYLE, M.A., T.C.D., Professor of Natural Philosophy in the University of Melbourne.

WM. BUTLER WALSH, M.D. (Dub. & Melb.); F.R.C.S.I.; late Examiner in Anatomy, University of Melbourne.

JOHN WILLIAM O'BRIEN, M.B., B.CH., Dip. St. Med.; F.R.C.S.I.; M.A., Melbourne.

H. B. MACARTNEY, Jun., M.A., Incumbent of Caulfield, Melbourne.

EVELYN G. HOGG., M.A., Mathematical Lecturer, Trin. Coll., Melbourne.

B. NEWPORT WHITE, M.A., St. Peter's Vicarage, Mornington.

EDWARD FITZGERALD, LL.D., T.C.D.

HOWARD COLE COGHLAN, Member of Institute of Journalists, Melbourne.

WILLIAM LEADER, Police Magistrate, Victoria.

ALEXANDER MACULLY, M.A., LL.B., Prof. of Elocution, Melbourne.

WADE SHENTON GARNETT, B.A., Barrister-at-Law.

P. P. LABERTOUCHE, Secretary for Victorian Railways.

PHILIP HOMAN, M.A., late Vicar of Ararat.

HERBERT B. FIGGIS, B.A., Melbourne.

W. R. MURRAY, late Clerk of Petty Sessions.

GEORGE WILLIAM TORRANCE, M.A., Mus. Doc.

JAMES ANTHONY LAWSON, Solicitor.

JOHN ERNEST FANNIN EVANS, B.A. (T.C.D.), E. Melbourne.

THOMAS B. HILL, Secretary, Melbourne Exhibition, 1880.

Dr. KELLY, Grosvenor, St. Mornee Ponds.

J. W. Y. FISHBOURNE, A.B., M.B., CH.M.

CHARLES P. M. BARDIN, Vicar of Christ Church, Brunswick.

PATRICK WHYTE, M.A., T.C.D.

THOMAS ELMES, J.P., F.R.C.S.I.

ALFRED MAC HUGH, M.A., T.C.D., Barrister.

ROBERT L. McADAM, B.A., M.D., CH.B., D.S.M., St. Kilda.

R. BEAUCHAMP CLAYTON, B.A., University Tutor.

RICHARD PHILP, M.A., LL.D., Inspector of State Schools.

HENRY LANGTREE, M.A., Barrister-at-Law.

CHARLES TUCKEY, B.A.

E. S. RADCLIFF, B.A., Canon, Registrar of Ballarat Diocese.

H. H. FLEMING, St. Arnaud, Victoria.

TOWNSEND MACDERMOTT, A.B., Barrister-at-Law, a former Solicitor-General of Victoria.

W. A. KIRKPATRICK, A.B., Ex-Sch., Barrister-at-Law.

G. R. MACMULLAN, M.A., LL.D., Barrister-at-Law.

Select Chronology of Arrivals

Year	Name	Colony	Position(s)
1788	*Thomas Jamison*	NSW	principal surgeon
1790	D'Arcy Wentworth	NSW	principal surgeon
1800	*Henry Fulton*	NSW	convict; chaplain
	Sir Henry Browne Hayes	NSW	convict
1814	Sir John Jamison	NSW	surgeon; landowner
1820	William Talbot	VDL	landowner
1822	*Samuel Bryan*	VDL	landowner
1824	William Bryan	VDL	landowner
	Henry Grattan Douglass	NSW	medical practitioner
1827	Sir Terence Murray	NSW	landowner; politician
1828	*James Murray*	NSW	medical practitioner; politician
1829	*Sir Roger Therry*	NSW	judge
	William H Browne	VDL	colonial chaplain; archdeacon
1830	Samuel Robdard Talbot	VDL	landowner
	George Fletcher Moore	WA	advocate-general
	'Rolf Boldrewood'	NSW	author
1831	*Dr John Kinchela*	NSW	attorney-general
1832	*John Hubert Plunkett*	NSW	attorney-general
1833	Samuel Pratt Winter	VDL	landowner
1834	*Bartholomew Vigors*	WA	advocate-general
1835	*Edward McDowell*	VDL	attorney-general
1836	*Sir John Jeffcott*	SA	chief judge
	William Hobson	PPD	governor, NZ
	Sir Francis Murphy	PPD	speaker, medical practitioner
1837	Trevor Winter	VDL	landowner
1838	*Benjamin Pratt Winter*	SA	dep. surveyor-general; landowner
	Edward Jones Brewster	PPD	chairman Quarter Sessions

1839	Sir Redmond Barry	PPD	Supreme Court judge
	James Croke	PPD	crown prosecutor; solicitor-general
	George Winter	VDL	barrister; landowner
	Richard West Nash	WA	advocate-general
	William Colburn Mayne	NSW	auditor-general
1840	Thomas Callaghan	NSW	Supreme Court judge
	Benjamin Darley	NSW	master mariner
	John L Forde	PPD	judge associate; historian
	Acheson French	PPD	landowner; police magistrate
	Charles Griffith	PPD	landowner; politician
	James Moore	PPD	landowner; politician
1841	Sir Robert Richard Torrens	SA	premier; land title pioneer
	Fitzgerald Foster	PPD	colonial secretary; politician
	Samuel Raymond	PPD	sheriff Supreme Court
	Sir Valentine Fleming	VDL	barrister; chief justice
1842	Sir William Foster Stawell	PPD	barrister; attorney-general; chief justice
	Anthony O'Grady Lefroy	WA	colonial treasurer
1843	Sir William Jeffcott	NSW	barrister; resident judge, PPD
	Gerald de Courcy Lefroy	WA	landowner;
	William Bailey	VDL	convict; teacher
1844	James Martley	PPD	solicitor-general; politician
1845	Rev Thomas Rogers	NSW	chaplain;
1846	Andrew Clarke	WA	governor
1848	Hussey Burgh Macartney	PPD	Anglican Dean of Melbourne;
	Richard Eades	PPD	clinical teacher; Lord mayor
	Frances Chomley	PPD	sister of Charles Griffith
1850	Travers Adamson	Vic	barrister; solicitor-general; politician
	John Tuthill Bagot	SA	chief secretary
	Arthur N Wrixon	Vic	County Court judge
	Michael Macoboy	Vic	County Court judge
	George Crawford	SA	Supreme Court judge
1852	William J Foster	NSW	District Court judge
	Sir Patrick Jennings	NSW	premier
	Richard Le Poer Trench	Vic	attorney-general, County Court judge
	Sir Robert Molesworth	Vic	Supreme Court judge

	Peter Faucett	NSW	Supreme Court judge
	Edward Graves Mayne	Vic	first registrar, Melbourne University
	Hugh Kennedy	NSW	registrar, Sydney University
	Sir Charles McMahon	Vic	police commissioner; speaker
	William Tully	Qld	surveyor-general of Qld
	John Moore	Vic	assistant colonial secretary
1853	Richard Davies Ireland	Vic	barrister; attorney-general; politician
	John Foster McCreight	Vic	barrister; politician; premier BC
	Robert Walsh	Vic	attorney-general
1854	Joseph Henry Dunne	Vic	barrister, County Court judge
	William E Hearn	Vic	foundation professor, University of Melbourne
	George Higinbotham	Vic	attorney-general; chief justice
	Townsend McDermott	Vic	solicitor-general;
	Charles P Hackett	Vic	County Court judge
	Peter Teulon Beamish	Vic	archdeacon of Warrnambool
	Hibbert Newton	Vic	barrister; politician; postmaster-general
	Sir Frederick McCoy	Vic	founding professor, University of Melbourne
1855	Sir Richard MacDonnell	SA	governor
	Sir Arthur Kennedy	WA	governor; brother Hugh Kennedy
	James Langton Clarke	Vic	County Court judge
	Samuel Henry Bindon	Vic	barrister; cabinet minister; County Court judge
1856	Richard Annesley Billing	Vic	barrister; reader in law; County Court judge
	Moses Wilson Gray	Vic	barrister; politician; judge, NZ
1857	Edward Fitzgerald	Vic	barrister, brewer
	Thomas Higinbotham	Vic	engineer-in-chief, Victorian Railways
1858	Alfred McFarland	WA	judge
1859	Nicholas Fitzgerald	Vic	brewer; politician
	Charles Blakeney	NSW	District Court judge, Qld
1860	Sir William Owen	NSW	Supreme Court judge

1861	Sir Bryan O'Loghlen	Vic	barrister; premier
1862	Sir Frederick Darley	NSW	barrister; chief justice
1863	Frederick L Smyth	Vic	crown prosecutor
	Marcus Clarke	Vic	author
1864	Sir Henry Wrixon	Vic	barrister; attorney-general; vice-chancellor, University of Melbourne
1866	James Corrigan	Vic	first headmaster, Wesley College, Melbourne
1868	Samuel Wensley Blackall	Qld	governor
1869	George Torrance	Vic	acting warden, Trinity College Melbourne
1870	William Barlow	SA	first registrar, Adelaide University
1874	Alexander Leeper	Vic	warden, Trinity College Melbourne
	William Henry Coffey	Vic	barrister; District Court judge, NSW
1875	William Cairns	Qld	governor
	Sir John Winthrop Hackett	WA	founding chancellor, University of WA
	Edward B Hamilton	Vic	County Court judge
1877	Henry Deane Walsh	NSW	engineer-in-chief, Sydney Harbour Trust
1879	Sir William Hill Irvine	Vic	barrister; premier; chief justice
	David Kelly	SA	professor of classics, University of Adelaide
1880	Sir Henry Wrenfordsley	WA	chief justice
	Patrick McMahon Glynn	SA	federal attorney-general
1883	Edward Boulger	SA	founding professor, University of Adelaide
1889	Sir Thomas Rankin Lyle	Vic	professor of physics, University of Melbourne
1895	Sir Norbert Keenan	WA	attorney-general

Code: NSW = New South Wales; VDL = Van Diemen's Land; PPD = Port Phillip District; SA = South Australia; WA = Western Australia; Vic = Victoria; Qld = Queensland; *Italics* denote attendance at Trinity College, Dublin.

Select List of Colonial Governors

New South Wales

1788	Arthur Phillip
1795	John Hunter
1800	Philip Gidley King
1806	William Bligh
1810	Lachlan Macquarie
1821	Sir Thomas Brisbane
1825	Sir Ralph Darling
1831	Sir Richard Bourke
1838	Sir George Gipps
1846	Sir Charles Fitzroy
1855	Sir William Denison
1861	Sir John Young
1868	Lord Belmore
1872	Sir Hercules Robinson
1879	Lord Augustus Loftus

Van Diemen's Land
(*Tasmania* from 1853)

1803	David Collins
1810	Joseph Foveaux
1813	Thomas Davey
1817	William Sorell
1824	Sir George Arthur
1837	Sir John Franklin

Port Phillip District
(*Victoria from 1851*)

1830	Charles Joseph La Trobe
1854	Sir Charles Hotham
1856	Sir Henry Barkly

1863	Sir Charles Darling
1866	Lord Canterbury
1873	Sir George Bowen

South Australia

1835	John Hindmarsh
1838	George Gawler
1841	Sir George Grey
1845	Frederick Robe
1848	Sir Henry Young
1855	*Sir Richard Graves MacDonnell*
1862	Sir Dominick Daly

Western Australia

1831	Sir James Stirling
1839	John Hutt
1846	Andrew Clarke
1847	Frederick Irwin
1848	Charles Fitzgerald
1855	*Sir Arthur Kennedy*
1862	John Hampton
1869	Frederick Weld
1875	Sir William Robinson

Queensland

1859	Sir George Bowen
1868	*Samuel Wensley Blackall*
1871	Lord Normanby
1875	William Wellington Cairns
1877	*Sir Arthur Kennedy*
1883	Sir Anthony Musgrave

Italics denote attendance at Trinity College, Dublin.

Select Bibliography

Alexander, F. *Campus at Crawley: A Narrative and Critical Appreciation of the First Fifty Years of the University of Western Australia.* Melbourne, 1963.

Auchmuty, J.J. 'The Anglo-Irish Influence on the Foundation of Australian Institutions', *University Gazette.* Melbourne, 1969.

Auchmuty, J.J. 'The Idea of the University in its Australian Setting: A Historical Survey', *The Australian University*, Number 1, 1963.

Barker, A. *What Happened When: A chronology of Australia from 1788.* St Leonards, 2000.

Bennett, J.M.(ed.) *A History of the New South Wales Bar.* Sydney, 1969.

Bennett, J.M. *Portraits of the Chief Justices of New South Wales 1824-1977.* St Ives, 1977.

Bennett, J.M. & Castles, A.C. *A Source Book of Australian Legal History.* Sydney. 1979

Blainey, G. *A Centenary History of the University of Melbourne.* Carlton, 1957.

Blake, L.J. *Peter Lalor: the Man from Eureka.* Belmont, 1979.

Bolton, G.C. 'A Trinity Man Abroad: Sir John Winthrop Hackett', in Reece, B. *The Irish in Western Australia.* Nedlands, 2000.

The Book of Trinity College Dublin 1591-1891. Belfast, 1892.

Brennan, G. 'The Irish and Law in Australia', *The Irish Jurist*, Number 21, 1986.

Brown, K.M. 'Doctor Douglass and Medical Sociology', *The Medical Journal of Australia*, 22 May 1943.

Bull, P. McConville, C. & McLachlan, N. *Irish Australian Studies.* Melbourne, 1991.

Burke, B. *A Genealogical and Heraldic Dictionary of the Peerage and Baronetage of the British Empire.* London, 1856.

Burke, B. *A Genealogical and Heraldic History of the Colonial Gentry.* London, 1891-1895.

Burtchaell, G.D. & Sadleir, T.U. (eds.) *Alumni Dublinenses: a Register of the Students, Graduates, Professors, and Provosts of Trinity College, in The University of Dublin.* London, 1924.

Campbell, R. *A History of the Melbourne Law School 1857-1973.* Parkville, 1977.

Campbell, R. 'Irish Lawyers in Victoria, 1838-1860', in Bull, P. et al. *op.cit.*,1991.

Cannon, M. *Old Melbourne Town Before the Gold Rush.* Main Ridge, 1991.

Carboni, R. *The Eureka Stockade*. Melbourne, 1855.

Castles, A.C. *An Australian Legal History*. Sydney, 1982.

Castles, A.C. *An Introduction to Australian Legal History*. Sydney, 1971.

Cleary, P.S. *Australia's Debt to Irish Nation-Builders*. Sydney, 1933.

Coffey, H.W. & Morgan, M.J. *Irish Families in Australia and New Zealand 1788-1979*. South Melbourne, 1978-1980.

Combe, G.D. *Responsible Government in South Australia*. Adelaide, 1957.

Coupe, R. *Achieving Nationhood: The Story of Federation*. Frenchs Forest, 2000.

Cowen, Z. *The Redmond Barry Centenary Oration*. Melbourne, 1980.

Dean, A. *A Multitude of Counsellors: A History of the Bar of Victoria*. Melbourne, 1968.

Deutsher, K.M. *The Breweries of Australia: a History*. Port Melbourne, 1999.

de Serville, P. *Port Phillip Gentlemen: and Good Society in Melbourne Before the Gold Rushes*, Melbourne, 1980.

de Serville, P. *Pounds and Pedigrees: the Upper Class in Victoria, 1850-80*. South Melbourne, 1991.

de Serville, P. *Rolf Boldrewood: a life*. Carlton, 2000.

Dixon, W.M. *Trinity College, Dublin*. London, 1902.

Dowling, J.A. 'The Judiciary', *Journal and Proceedings Australian Historical Society*, April 1907.

Duncan, W.G.K. & Leonard, R.A. *The University of Adelaide 1874-1974*. Adelaide, 1973.

Dunstan, K. *The Amber Nectar: a Celebration of Beer and Brewing in Australia*. Ringwood, 1987.

Finn, P.D. *Law and Government in Colonial Australia*. Melbourne, 1987.

Finn, E. *The Chronicles of Early Melbourne, 1835 to 1852*. Melbourne, 1888.

Fitzpatrick, D. 'Irish Emigration to Nineteenth-Century Australia', in Kiernan, C. (ed) *Australia and Ireland 1788-1988: Bicentenary Essays*. Dublin 1986.

Ford, E. 'Thomas Jamison and the Beginning of Medical Journalism in Australia', *The Medical Journal of Australia*, 14 October 1954.

Forde, J.L. *The Story of the Bar of Victoria from its Foundation to the Amalgamation of the Two Branches of the Legal Profession 1839-1891: Historical, Personal, Humourous*. Melbourne, 1913.

Forth, G.J. *A Biographical Register and Annotated Bibliography of Anglo-Irish Colonists in Australia*. Warrnambool, 1992.

Forth, G.J. 'Anglo-Irish', in Jupp, J. (ed.) *The Australian People*. North Ryde, 1988.

Forth, G.J. 'The Anglo-Irish in Australia: Old World Origins and Colonial Experiences', in Bull, P. et. al. *op.cit.* 1991.

Forth, G.J. *The Winters on the Wannon.* Warrnambool, 1991.

Foster, R.F. *Modern Ireland 1600-1972.* New York, 1988.

Fox, P. (ed.) *Treasures of the Library, Trinity College Dublin.* Dublin, 1986.

Galbally, A. *Redmond Barry: An Anglo-Irish Australian.* Carlton, 1995.

Hague, R.M. *Sir John Jeffcott: Portrait of a Colonial Judge.* Parkville, 1963.

Hague, R.M. *Mr. Justice Crawford: Judge of the Supreme Court of South Australia 1850-1852.* Adelaide, 1957.

Headon, D.J. & Perkins, E. (eds) *Our First Republicans: John Dunmore Lang, Charles Harpur, David Henry Deniehy: Selected Writings: 1840-1860,* Leichhardt, 1998.

Heron, D.C. *The Constitutional History of The University of Dublin.* Dublin, 1847.

Hewitt, E.E. *Judges Through the Years.* Melbourne, 1984.

Hocking, G. *To the Diggings!: A Celebration of the 150th Anniversary of the Discovery of Gold in Australia.* Port Melbourne, 2000.

Holland, C.H. (ed.) *Trinity College Dublin and the Idea of a University.* Dublin, 1991.

Houghton, R.W. *The World of George Berkeley.* Dublin, 1985.

Jacobs, P.A. *Judges of Yesterday.* Melbourne, 1924.

Jeffares, A.N. 'Torrens: An Irishman in South Australia', in Kiernan, C. (ed.) *Australia and Ireland 1798-1988: Bicentenary Essays.* Dublin, 1986.

Jones, C. *Presiding Officers of the Victorian Parliament 1856-1986.* Melbourne, 1986.

Jupp, J. (ed.) *The Australian People.* North Ryde, 1988.

Kavanagh, A.C. *John Fitzgibbon, Earl of Clare.* Dublin, 1997.

Kennelly, B. '*It's the weekend that gets them*', in Holland, C.H., *op.cit.,* 1991.

Kiernan, C. (ed.) *Australia and Ireland 1788-1988: Bicentenary Essays.* Dublin, 1986.

Kiernan, C. (ed.) *Ireland and Australia.* North Ryde, 1984.

Kiernan, C. 'Irish Protestants', in Jupp, J., (ed.) *op.cit.,* 1988.

Kiddle, M. *Men of Yesterday: A Social History of the Western District of Victoria, 1834-1890.* Melbourne, 1961.

King, H. *Richard Bourke.* Melbourne, 1971.

Lahey, J. *Faces of Federation: An Illustrated History.* Melbourne, 2000.

Lawlor, H.J. *The Registers of Provost Winter (Trinity College Dublin) 1650 to 1660, and of the Liberties of Cashel (Co. Tipperary), 1654 to 1657.* Dublin, 1907.

Lee, S. (ed.) *The Dictionary of National Biography.* London, 1930.

Luce, J.V. *Trinity College Dublin: the First 400 Years*. Dublin, 1992.

Macintyre, S. *A Colonial Liberalism: The Lost World of Three Victorian Visionaries*. South Melbourne, 1991.

Maxwell, C. *A History of Trinity College, Dublin 1592-1892*. Dublin, 1946.

Malcomson, A.P.W. *John Foster: The Politics of the Anglo-Irish Ascendancy*. Oxford, 1978.

McClaughlin, T. 'Protestant Irish Settlement', in Jupp, J., *op.cit*, 1988.

McConville, C. *Croppies, Celts & Catholics: The Irish in Australia*. Caulfield East, 1987.

McConville, C. 'The Irish Townspeople of Nineteenth Century Melbourne', in Bull, P. et. al. *op.cit*, 1991.

McDowell, R.B. & Webb, D.A. *Trinity College Dublin 1592-1952: An Academic History*. Cambridge, 1982.

McGurk, J. 'Trinity College, Dublin: 1592-1992', *History Today*, March 1992.

McKenzie, B. *Stained Glass and Stone: The Gothic Buildings of the University of Sydney*. Sydney, 1989.

Molony, J.N. *An Architect of Freedom: John Hubert Plunkett in New South Wales 1832-1869*. Canberra, 1973.

Montgomery-Massingberd, H. (ed.) *Burke's Irish Family Records*. London, 1976.

Morris, E.E. *A Memoir of George Higinbotham*. London, 1895.

Nairn, B. (ed.) *Australian Dictionary of Biography*, Vol. 6. Melbourne, 1976.

Nairn, B., & Serle, G. (eds) *Australian Dictionary of Biography*, Vols. 7-10. Melbourne, 1979-86.

O'Brien, C.C. *The Great Melody: A Thematic Biography and Commented Anthology of Edmund Burke*. Chicago, 1992.

O'Farrell, P. *The Irish in Australia*. Kensington, 1987.

Partington, G. *The Australian Nation: Its British and Irish Roots*. Melbourne, 1994.

Pearl, C. *The Three Lives of Gavan Duffy*. Kensington, 1979.

Pescott, R.T. 'The Royal Society of Victoria from then, 1854 to now, 1959', *Proceedings of the Royal Society of Victoria*, Number 73, 1961.

Perry, W. *The School of Mines and Industries Ballarat: A History of its First One Hundred and Twelve Years, 1870-1982*. Ballarat, 1984.

Phillips, J.H. *The Trial of Ned Kelly*. North Ryde, 1987.

Pike, D. (ed.) *Australian Dictionary of Biography*, Vols. 1-5, Melbourne, 1966-74.

Plomley, N.J. 'Some Notes of the Life of Doctor Henry Grattan Douglass', *The Medical Journal of Australia*, 3 June 1961.

Poynter, J.R. *Doubts and Certainties: A Life of Alexander Leeper*. Carlton, 1997.

'Quatercentenary Papers', *Hermathena: A Trinity College Dublin Review*. Dublin, 1992

Rankin, D.H. 'George Higinbotham', *The Victorian Historical Magazine*, Number 27, 1956.

Records of the Tercentenary Festival of Dublin University held 5th – 8th July 1892. Dublin, 1894.

Reece, B. (ed.) *The Irish in Western Australia*. Perth, 2000.

Rickard, J. *H.B Higgins: The Rebel as Judge*. Sydney, 1984.

Ritchie, J. *The Wentworths: Father and Son*. Carlton, 1997.

Russell, E. *A History of the Law in Western Australia and its Development from 1829 to 1979*. Nedlands, 1980.

Russell, E. 'Early Lawyers of Western Australia', *The Western Australian Historical Society Journal and Proceedings*, Number 4, 1951.

Ryan, P. *Redmond Barry*. Melbourne, 1972.

Scott, E. *A Short History of Australia*. London, 1928.

Serle, G. *The Golden Age: A History of the Colony of Victoria, 1851-1861*. Melbourne, 1963.

Smith, F.B. 'Sir Redmond Barry', *Journal of the Cork Historical and Archaeological Society*, Number 93, 1988.

Smith, F.B. 'Stalwarts of the Garrison: Some Irish Academics in Australia', *Australian Cultural History*, Number 6, 1987.

Smith, J. (ed.) *The Cyclopedia of Victoria*, Vols. 1-3. Melbourne, 1903.

Stawell, M. *My Recollections*. London, 1911.

Sydney Quarterly Magazine. 'Sir Frederick Darley', September 1887. Sydney.

Sydney Quarterly Magazine. 'Mr Justice Faucett', December 1887. Sydney.

Therry, R. *Reminiscences of Thirty Years' Residence in New South Wales and Victoria*, Sydney, 1863; Facsimile edition. Sydney, 1974.

Travers, R. *Henry Parkes: Father of Federation*. East Roseville, 2000

Turney, C. Bygott, U. & Chippendale, P. *Australia's First: A History of the University of Sydney*, Volume 1. Sydney, 1991.

Webb, D.A. & Bartlett, J.R. *Trinity College Dublin Record Volume 1991*. Dublin, 1992.

Wedgwood, C. V. *Thomas Wentworth: First Earl of Strafford 1593-1641*. London, 1961

Whitfield, L.A. *Founders of the Law in Australia*. Sydney, 1971.

White, M.A. *Richard West Nash in Western Australia, 1839-1849: A Biographical Sketch*. Bentley, 1999.

William, H. & Jean, M. *Irish Families in Australia and New Zealand*. South Melbourne, 1978 –1983.

Woodburn, S. *The Founding of a University: the first decade*. Adelaide, 1983.

Young, J.McI. *Sir William Foster Stawell*. Carlton, 1989.

Index